BUCKINGHAM
GLEBE TERR
1578–1640

Edited by
MICHAEL REED, F.S.A.

BUCKINGHAMSHIRE RECORD SOCIETY

No. 30

MCMXCVII

British Library Cataloguing in Publication.
A catalogue record for this book is available from the British Library

Typeset by
Denham House, Yapton, West Sussex
and printed in Great Britain by
Progressive Printing (UK) Limited, Leigh-on-Sea, Essex

CONTENTS

ACKNOWLEDGEMENTS

I owe a very real debt of gratitude to Mr Hugh Hanley, County Archivist at the Buckinghamshire Record Office, for having these documents micro-filmed for me and then to his staff for indefatigably producing the documents themselves in order that I might check the film against the originals. I have profited from the advice and guidance of Dr Scarff, the General Editor of the Society. Mrs Margaret Gelling read through the section on place-names and gave invaluable advice on indexing. The indexes were compiled by Mr Simon Neal, and the material relating to place-names was checked by Dr Arnold Baines. For their contributions to this volume I am very grateful. Mrs Shirley Horner, of the Department of Information and Library Studies at Loughborough University, guided me with inexhaustible patience through the mysteries of word-processing and saved me from total disaster on at least two occasions. Mr Ralph Weedon, of the Centre for Urban History in the University of Leicester, gave me invaluable assistance in the last stages of the preparation of this volume for the printer. Without the encouragement and support of my wife and the generosity of my son this volume would never have been completed.

The Council of the Buckinghamshire Record Society wishes to express its gratitude to the Council of Management of the Marc Fitch Fund for its generous grant in aid of printing costs.

The publication of this book has also been assisted by a grant from the Scouloudi Foundation in association with the Institute of Historical Research.

EDITORIAL PRACTICE

The documents are transcribed in full save for that preamble to the 1607 terriers for the reasons outlined in the Introduction. [...] indicates illegible material. Very occasionally acre and rood have been added in order to clarify the measures being employed, but this has only been done where the actual measure is clear from the document itself. Some terriers consist of one long paragraph. This has been sub-divided at convenient breaks in order to assist legibility. Attempts to standardize and to introduce modern punctuation were abandoned when it became clear that there was a real danger of imposing a modern interpretation upon seventeenth century documents. They have been allowed to speak for themselves. The Buckinghamshire County Record Office reference number is given at the end of each document.

INTRODUCTION

The documents printed here comprise all the surviving and legible glebe terriers from 1578 to 1640 which were once in the archives of the archdeaconry of Buckingham, formerly housed in the Bodleian Library in Oxford and now in the Buckinghamshire County Record Office in Aylesbury. There is one exception. The terrier for Ludgershall of 1637 is now in a family archive, that of the Martyns, also in the Buckinghamshire County Record Office. It looks very like a copy of the 1607 terrier. These terriers form a discrete collection and have not been compared with those of the diocese of Lincoln now in the Lincoln County Record Office, although there would in fact appear to be little overlap between the two series.[1]

Glebe terriers were first called for in the canons issued by Archbishop Parker in 1571.[2] This canon must lie behind the earliest document printed here, a terrier for Addington of 1578. The canons were reissued, extended and amplified, in 1604, when Canon 87 stated:

> 'We ordain that the Archbishops and all the bishops within their several dioceses shall procure that a true note and terrier of all the glebes, lands, meadows, gardens, orchards, houses, stocks, implements, tenements and portions of tythes lying out of their parishes (which belong to any Parsonage or Vicarage or rural Prebend) be taken by the view of honest men in every parish, by the appointment of the Bishop (whereof the Minister to be one) and be laid up in the Bishop's registry there to be for a perpetual memory thereof.'[3]

1 There are over 50 more glebe terriers here in this volume, principally for 1639, than are listed in M. W. Beresford, 'Glebe Terriers and Open Field Buckinghamshire, Part 1', *Records of Bucks.*, XV, pt. 5, 1951-52, pp.283-98, and Part 2, *Records of Bucks.*, XVI, pt. 5, 1953-54, pp.14-23. There are additionally some 260 glebe terriers held at the Lincolnshire Archives for the period *c.*1571 to 1640. Almost all relate either to other parishes in Buckinghamshire or are of different dates to the terriers printed in this volume. A preliminary list (which omits some parishes) and card index are available at Lincolnshire Archives and Buckinghamshire Record Office.

2 D. M. Barrett, ed., *Ecclesiastical Terriers of Warwickshire Parishes,* vol. 1, Dugdale Society, 22, 1955, p.xiii.

3 M. E. C. Walcott, *The Constitutions and Canons Ecclesiastical of the Church of England,* 1874, p.126.

Following upon this Canon the bishop of Lincoln, William Chaderton, appointed William Folkingham, gent., as general surveyor of the church possessions throughout the diocese of Lincoln. He was almost certainly the same William Folkingham, of Helpringham, Lincolnshire, who published *Feudographia: The Synopsis and Epitome of Surveying Methodised* in 1610.[4] His appointment by a decree of the bishop under the Canon is almost always mentioned in the rubric to the 1607 terriers and in a formula which varies so little from one document to the next that it has every appearance of having been determined by Folkingham himself. It is given in full at the head of the first of these terriers, that for Amersham, but is thereafter abbreviated, save in that handful of cases in which the formula is not used, at Stoke Goldington, for example, and Grove and Dinton, when the rubric is given in full. The comparatively systematic arrangement of the terriers for 1605–1607, proceeding from homestall to edifices to meadow, pasture and arable and the concluding paragraph disclaiming knowledge of any further endowments may well also be due to his influence, echoing as it does the very words of the Canon.

The appointment of Folkingham would appear to have been very unusual, if not unique,[5] although the rubric to the terrier of 1625 for Hitcham indicates renewal in 1611 and again in 1625 by John Williams, then bishop of Lincoln and Lord Keeper.

Archbishop Laud carried out a thorough and vigorous metropolitan visitation in 1633–1636, although the Canons were not reissued.[6] One consequence was the terriers of the 1630s published here. There is no fixed preamble to these documents and so their headings are given in full.

The Canon of 1604 laid particular emphasis upon the parsonage house itself, the glebe lands, meadows, gardens and orchards, together with tithes lying outside the parish. It also required an account of stocks, implements and tenements, but in the surviving Buckinghamshire terriers there is invariably nothing to return under these headings. The matters to be enquired into would appear to have been added to over time, more especially in the years after the Restoration.[7]

---

4 See P. Eden, ed., *Dictionary of Land Surveyors and Local Cartographers of Great Britain and Ireland, 1550–1850, Supplement,* 1979.

5 D. M. Barrett, *op. cit.,* p.xxii.

6 For an account of this visitation see I. Mortimer, ed., *Berkshire Glebe Terriers,* Berkshire Record Society, vol. 2, 1995, pp.x–xii.

7 R. Potts, ed., *A Calendar of Cornish Glebe Terriers, 1673–1735,* Devon and Cornwall Record Society, New Series, 19, 1974, p.xii.

The terriers themselves were compiled by the incumbent, with the assistance of the churchwardens, sidesmen and other inhabitants. In practice this means that anything from three or four up to eight or nine parishioners, invariably men and by no means always literate, were responsible for the surveying of the parsonage and its glebe, drafting and then copying out the document. There is a chance reference in one, that for Water Stratford for 1639, to the existence of ancient terriers. Although this may mean nothing more than a terrier of 1607, the possibility of surveys before 1571 is very real, the 1639 terrier for East Claydon referring to one of 1545. Nevertheless, even if they are based upon earlier documents, the terriers themselves must stand as monuments to the detailed topographical knowledge of those who compiled them.

The Parsonage.

The terriers here printed reveal the Buckinghamshire clergyman of the early seventeenth century at home. It is clear that they enjoyed, or endured, a very wide range of circumstances, from the 30 rooms at Burnham to the three small ones at Padbury, whilst the clergymen at Barton Hartshorne, Chetwode, Dorton and Hedsor had no parsonage house at all. The largest parsonage seems to have been that at Horton, with 21 bays of building. At Hardwick there were 19 bays. At Burnham and Amersham there were 16 bays, and at Ludgershall there were 14. These appear to have been the largest, with the great majority of between four and six bays of building, with perhaps six to ten rooms. In other words, the domestic life style of the Buckinghamshire clergyman approximated to that of a yeoman farmer, with a handful enjoying that of a minor country gentleman whilst a small minority had to exist on the same level as the poorest agricultural labourer.

The great majority of parsonages are built of timber.[8] That at Broughton is said to be 'framed and builded all of timber crossways'. Only a handful are built of other materials: stone at Bow Brickhill, Maids Moreton, Wolverton, Drayton Beauchamp (which was built of ragstone), Radclive, Stowe and Newton Blossomville. Those at Shalstone and Great Linford were of timber and stone, whilst parts of Swanbourne were of tile and thatch, wood and earth. The parsonage at Burnham was built of loam, and those at Ludgershall and West

8 The distribution of building materials in later Buckinghamshire glebe terriers is plotted on Figure 37 in M. W. Barley, *The English Farmhouse and Cottage*, 1961, p.257.

Wycombe were of roughcast. At Medmenham the walls were of mud and roughcast, whilst at Hughenden the walls were of timber plastered with earth mortar. The two bays of the parsonage at Upper Winchendon were built partly of rough stone and partly of earthen matter, whilst at Wendover the walls were of stud. Brick is nowhere mentioned. The use of this building material is a post-Restoration phenomenon as far as the Buckinghamshire clergy are concerned.

Roofs are either of thatch or tile, sometimes, as at Aston Sandford, of both. The dormer windows at Hartwell were tiled in the midst of an otherwise thatched roof, and at Wingrave in 1607 the roof was covered with tile and straw and ridged with turves.

Most parsonages were of two storeys. That at Bow Brickhill in 1607 was said to be of three, and at Cublington in the same year there were said to be five storeys to accommodate ten rooms. At Wingrave, also in the same year, the parsonage was described as partly in one storey, partly in two. It is clear that many rooms were lofted and boarded over, to create upstairs rooms, but it is equally clear that in many parsonages this process was by no means complete. Thus of the 19 bays at Hartwell ten were said to be lofted over, but two were not, whilst at Aston Sandford of the four bays one was unlofted. At Chalfont St. Giles in 1607 only the hall remained unlofted, but by 1639 all the rooms were lofted over. At Pitchcott the hall had been recently ceiled over as had the chamber over it.

In a number of parsonages the kitchen is still a detached building, at Hartwell, Swanbourne, Shalstone, Westbury and Newton Blossomville, for example. At Burnham the kitchen, together with larder and wash-house, stood separately. At Swanbourne it was a detached building of three bays, thatched, in spite of the fire risk, with a stable adjoining. There is an Outkitchen at Radclive, and at Great Brickhill an Old Kitchen. The parsonage at Chesham Leicester had seven rooms, including a kitchen with a chimney, but there was also an 'outward' kitchen, with a chimney, oven and well in it.

Most parsonages seem to have had a hall, parlour and a number of chambers as their basic living accommodation. It is clear that not all rooms are invariably listed, making generalizations difficult. It would appear that all are listed at Chenies, but this is unusual. A number of parsonages have a study, as perhaps is to be expected. This must have been the only room which would have distinguished a parsonage from the other houses in the village. They were to be found in a dozen parsonages in all, including Chenies, Burnham and Saunderton. At Wavendon it is called the little with-drawing room or study, a hint at changes in domestic living styles which were yet to come. Five parsonages, Denham, Little Marlow, Tingewick, Farnham Royal and Chalfont St. Giles, had a gatehouse, and three, Horton, Wexham and

Little Missenden, were partly or completely moated. Burnham had two lodging chambers for servants, but they could not have been unique. Wavendon also had a tiled coal house.

At Aston Clinton all the rooms were said to have chimneys. Glass was by this time usual in farmhouses and cottages up and down the county, so that only two terriers, those for Chesham and Wraysbury, found it necessary to mention it. The terriers do not, however, describe the interiors of the parsonages in any detail or provide any information about furnishings. For this it is necessary to turn to probate inventories.[9]

A parsonage, like any other household in the early seventeenth century, had to be much more self-contained than any household in the late twentieth century, with baking and brewing, using home grown produce, taking place on the premises as a matter of course. Thus there is a bakehouse at Burnham, brewhouses at Amersham and Farnham Royal, where there was also a boulting house. But the parsonage was not only the residence of a clergyman, it was also very often the centre of a working farm, and this is reflected in the wide range of farm buildings to be found, and the larger the parsonage the greater the number of specialized rooms, both domestic and agricultural. At Bow Brickhill there were four bays in the house itself, but 18 bays of stables and barns. Barns are very common, and that at Medmenham was said to be aisled. Cheddington had separate barns for wheat, barley, beans and hay, a clear indication of the nature of the crop rotation practised in that village. The hay barn at Foxcote was set upon posts, as was the milk house at East Claydon. There were hen houses at Amersham, Denham and Hawridge, milkhouses at Drayton Beauchamp, Dunton, Gayhurst and Denham, where there was also a kine house and an applehouse. There was a chaff house at Wavendon, a cart house at Farnham Royal, and dairy houses at Cublington and Lavendon. There were dove houses at Burnham, Tingewick and Farnham Royal, and pig sties at Hawridge, Dunton and elsewhere.

Most parsonages had a garden and an orchard. There were apple and plum trees in the orchard at Broughton, but that at Burnham contained very few trees, whilst at Medmenham the orchard was said to be well replenished. The orchard at West Wycombe contained ten young fruit trees and that at Bow Brickhill was described in 1633 as being recently planted. The orchard was new at Chalfont St. Giles, whilst the garden at Pitchcott was said to be newly made. At Upton, however, the trees in the orchard were said to be old, and at Water

---

9 The probate inventories of nine clergymen are to be found in M. Reed, ed., *Buckinghamshire Probate Inventories, 1661–1714*, Buckinghamshire Record Society, 24, 1988.

Stratford there was both an old orchard and a new one. At Stoke Hammond there were two little orchards, and at Taplow there were great and little orchards and two gardens. The garden and orchard at Wexham were said to be well-fenced and ditched, whilst the garden at Stowe was walled and the orchard was surrounded with a hedge. That at Little Marlow was surrounded with a ditch. The garden and orchard at Great Linford in 1607 were fenced about with quicksets, and at Wing in 1607 the orchard was impaled and hedged.

The upkeep of the parsonage was the responsibility of the incumbent,[10] and there is some evidence in these terriers of improvements carried out by the clergyman. The parsonage was said to be newly repaired at Stoke Poges, and there was a new built study with a buttery under it at Turweston. At Chalfont St. Giles in 1607 the incumbent had recently added two bays to the parsonage, including a brewhouse, planted a new orchard and built the cow house. At Pitchcott the incumbent had newly ceiled over the hall and a chamber over it, made a new garden and built a new barn and cock loft, which he could take away if he wished. The parsonage at Turweston in 1639 had a newly-built study with a buttery underneath and a wool-loft over it. The parsonage at Wraysbury was said to be in good repair, and at Radclive there was a cullis lately built of timber.

The principal improvements to parsonages in the early seventeenth century seem to have been the lofting over of rooms to provide accommodation upstairs — the staircases at Burnham, Bledlow and Aston Clinton are actually mentioned — and the incorporation of the kitchen into the main part of the house. Further improvements in the interests of privacy and comfort, and particularly building and rebuilding in brick, would have to wait until after the Restoration. The parsonage of early seventeenth-century Buckinghamshire was firmly rooted in the vernacular tradition and could have had little to distinguish it from the great majority of the dwellings of the parishioners amongst whom the clergyman lived.

The Glebe.

'Every church of common right is intitled to house and glebe, and the assigning of these, at the first, was of such absolute necessity, that without them no church could be regularly consecrated'.[11] If this was a general statement of the law, then there were several examples of its

---

10 J. F. Williams, ed., *Bishop Redman's Visitation, 1597*, Norfolk Record Society, 18, 1946, p.20.

11 R. Burn, *Ecclesiastical Law*, vol. 1, 1763, p.585.

breach in early seventeenth-century Buckinghamshire. Neither Barton Hartshorne nor Chetwode, Dorton nor Hedsor nor Boarstall, had a parsonage house, whilst Chilton, Datchet, Dorton, Hughenden and Lillingstone Dayrell were without glebe. It is further stated that although the freehold was with the parson he might not alienate it. This was modified by constitutions of Archbishop Langton, which provided that no alienation could take place without observing the form of the canon, that is to say that the bishop required the consent of the chapter and other ecclesiastics the consent of the bishop. These measures were further re-inforced by statute, 1 Elizabeth I, c.19 and 13 Elizabeth I c.10, which provided that property of the church could only be leased, either for 21 years or else for three lives, and that no exchanges could be made. In practice, of course, these provisions were widely ignored, and certainly by the end of the seventeenth century bishops were openly recognising that exchanges were taking place. Articles for the enclosure of Great Linford by agreement were drawn up in September of 1658. In July of 1662 the bishop of Lincoln issued his decree assenting to the terms of the enclosure and exchange. Sir Richard Napier, lord of the manor, and the other freeholders had expressed their great care of the church and had specially agreed that it should have a very beneficial recompense. The incumbent, Theodoricus Graves, had received 28 acres near to the parsonage, and both he and the bishop 'are assured that the rectory was bettered and had gained by the said allotment as the said 28 acres were not only much better in value but being laid out together so near to the said parsonage were much more convenient, commodious and profitable'.[12] In 1709 the bishop of Lincoln granted a licence for the exchange of glebe lands in Tyringham.[13]

Exchange often took place as part of the enclosure movement which swept across northern Buckinghamshire during the course of the sixteenth and seventeenth centuries, much of it carried out by agreement among the inhabitants, who would have included the incumbent. Closes of Mr Chibnall are mentioned at Astwood, whilst at Chearsley the glebe was largely enclosed meadow and ley ground, with only half an acre of arable. A hybrid state would appear to have prevailed at Aston Sandford, where there is mention of arable closes with lands dispersed within them. Such agreements were then frequently enrolled in the court of Chancery in order to give them legal effect. Again, however, in practice, they could be questioned, sometimes many years after the date of the first agreement. In March

---

12 Buckinghamshire Record Office, DU/1/48/1,5.

13 Lincolnshire Archives, Bishop's Register 36, f.125.

of 1625 an agreement was made to confirm enclosures already made in Leckhampstead and Foxcote. The rector of Leckhampstead was to have three parcels of land, amounting in all to 67 acres, and the rector of Foxcote was to have a mansion house, with barn, stable, malthouse, orchard and garden, together with eight acres of pasture, 14 acres in Garrell Field and two and a half acres in Bowbridge meadow. The rector of Leckhampstead then died, and his successor contested the agreement. The court of Chancery ruled in 1630 that he must accept the three parcels of land allotted.[14] The Leckhampstead terrier does not survive, but that for Foxcote shows the glebe corresponding almost exactly with the terms of the award. At Milton Keynes it was stated in 1683 that exchange and enclosure had taken place, some 20 years ago and more about 90 years ago. The enclosure and exchange were generally beneficial, arable in the common fields before enclosure letting for anything up to 6s. 8d. the acre, and after enclosure up to 20s. the acre. The rector did not complain until after he ploughed up his lands and got poor crops.[15]

The glebe was composed first of all of the original endowment of the church and secondly of later gifts. It could be lost by impropriation, as at Barton Hartshorne, for example, neglect or fraud, and the compilation of a terrier would certainly help to prevent further loss. The parson of Wavendon added a note to his terrier 'with protestation of addinge more if more be to be found belonginge to the parsonage'. One of the most interesting endowments is to be found at Wooburn in 1639, where a rent charge of £20 from the Glory Mills and seven cottages had been given to the church by Sir Francis Goodwin in 1631. The Glory mills were paper mills.[16]

The terriers printed here contain a number of examples revealing that in practice the glebe could be, and was, exchanged, and occasionally lost. Thus at Chenies the incumbent received four nobles a year and his diet at the steward's table as a composition for land which had recently been taken into the park. At East Claydon and at Little Marlow there are sad notes referring to land which had been lost, although at the latter 'full satisfaction is promised to bee made'. Some exchange had taken place at Radclive and at Middle Claydon where, it was noted, it was considered 'no good exchange'. On the other hand the glebe at Brill had been augmented by allotment of seven acres of land upon the disafforestation of the Forest of Bernwood in the 1630s. At Boarstall, however, enquiry revealed no evidence of any glebe of

14 Public Record Office, C78, 640/6.
15 Public Record Office, E134, 35 Charles II Easter 21.
16 *Victoria County History of Buckinghamshire*, vol. 3, 1925, pp.106, 112.

any kind, whilst that at Datchet was a pension of £11 per annum paid by the Dean and Prebends of Windsor.

It is clear from these terriers that open field agriculture was widely practised in Buckinghamshire north of the Chilterns, and that some open fields were to be found in the Chilterns themselves and in the parishes along the Thames.[17] Some clergymen must in practice have been substantial farmers. Thus at Amersham the glebe extended to 56 acres of arable and 16 acres of wood ground, whilst there were 40 acres of arable at Chalfont St. Giles and 18 acres of arable at Broughton. The glebe was sometimes extensive, but it was also minutely subdivided, as the terriers for Pitchcott and Tingewick make abundantly clear. Who actually did the work? Did the parson himself labour in the fields of a week day, or did he employ agricultural labourers, or was the glebe let out? There are no clear answers to these questions in the terriers printed here, although at Burnham there were two chambers for servants in the parsonage itself, and at Datchet in 1639 the parsonage, garden and about an acre of ground were said to be let out at a rent of £5 a year. Canon 76 provided that ministers were at no time to forsake their calling or 'to use themselves as laymen'. At Semer, in Norfolk, the rector was presented in 1597 because he 'worketh in harvest tyme in bynding of oats without anie hatt on his head, or dublett on his back, but onelie in his hose and shirte'.[18] He could not have been the only one.

The strips of arable, often called acres or lands, and both would have been traditional measures bearing little relationship to the statute acre, were arranged first of all into furlongs and then into fields. This is the classical Midland open field system. Sometimes there were three fields, as at Aston Sandford, occasionally more, as at Maids Moreton and Aston Clinton. The bounds of the individual strips are sometimes minutely described, as at Tingewick, for example, and sometimes the individual strips are said to be marked with balks, as at Aston Sandford. A careful reading of the description of the location of these strips reveals again and again a regular pattern of neighbours. The frequency with which Randall at Bow Brickhill, Mr Duncombe at Broughton and John Olliffe at Pitchcott are mentioned cannot be entirely fortuitous. This may of course be a consequence of the consolidation of holdings into the hands of substantial farmers, but it may also represent the last remnants of the systematic way in which the land was laid out when the open field system was itself first

---

17 See M. W. Beresford, *op. cit.* For a more general account of Buckinghamshire see M. Reed, *The Buckinghamshire Landscape*, 1979, *passim*.

18 J. F. Williams, *op. cit.*, p.20.

introduced into the individual parish at some date well before the
Norman Conquest.[19]

The barns at Cheddington, for wheat, beans, barley and hay, indicate
clearly the nature of the system of crop rotation in the open fields.
There are also occasional references to hemp and flax.

In the Chilterns the pattern appears to have been one of largely
enclosed land. At Great Hampden the incumbent himself had sub-
divided some closes with hedges. But there are exceptions. The arable
at Chalfont St. Giles lay in five closes, but there was also an open field
called Oute Feyld, whilst at Chalfont St. Peter some glebe land lay in
Dewlande, a common field, but a further 47 acres lay in eight closes.
At Farnham Royal there were 20 acres divided up into closes and 20
acres in the common fields, lying in four several pieces. The parson
here also had an acre of land in Hedgerley.

In practice the glebe often made up a farm, with little to distinguish
it from any other farm in the village, so that the parson often also had
meadow, pasture and wood. The meadow was sometimes lot mead,
that is to say, it was allotted again each year, so that neither the clergyman
nor his fellow parishioners knew from one year to the next exactly
where their season's meadow would lie. As the terrier of 1605 for
Broughton puts it 'the particular places wherein the sayd 10 roodes
and dimidium do lye are not alwayes constant in one and the same
place but do alter and shift *pro aequalitate et inaequalitate annorum Domini*
according as doth the meadowe of the Lord and all the freeholders of
the mannor of Broughton'. At Beachampton two roods of meadow in
Sydmead were laid out by lot and another rood lay certain. There are
references in two terriers, those for Broughton and Maids Moreton, to
meadow books. These would have contained a written statement of
the method of allocating lot mead, and at Broughton there would
appear to have been two of these books, one for odd number years
and another for even number years. Unfortunately neither of these
books seems to have survived, although a copy of the mead book of
1569 for Newton Blossomville has survived.[20] The meadow is sometimes
staked out, as at Aston Sandford, for example, and that at Foxcote is
said to be enclosed with rails.

At Bow Brickhill there were Lammas Ground meadow and leys
which were held by the parson in severalty from the Annunciation of
the Blessed Virgin Mary, 25 March, to Lammas Day, 1 August, and
then were held in common.

Pasture for grazing livestock was an essential element of the open

---

19 See M. Reed, *The Buckinghamshire Landscape*, 1979, p.89 *et seq.*

20 Buckinghamshire Record Office, PR/154/28/1.

field system. In some parishes the parson had pieces of pasture ground, a close at Bow Brickhill for example, a piece of about three roods at Chalfont St. Giles, whilst at Hoggeston the entire glebe was almost completely down to pasture, one pasture ground of 56 acres and another of 11 acres. There was no pasture at all at Little Kimble. Sometimes, however, the parson had the right to common his livestock in the same manner as his parishioners over the open fields once the harvest was home as at Wingrave, where it is stated that there is no pasture but commons for four beasts and 10 sheep in the fields of the parish. At Emberton the incumbent had four beast commons, and at Grove he had rights of common in the three fields for 10 sheep, one cow, a weaner and horse and hogs, whilst at Gayhurst he had commons for nine great cattle and 30 sheep. At Water Stratford he had common and meadow ground belonging to two yard lands 'as other yarde lands in the toune have'. At Shalstone the parson had common of pasture in the woods of Shalstone, Westbury and Biddlesden without stint. At Pitchcott the incumbent had common of pasture for 40 sheep and six horses at Lammas, 'and by an olde custome cowes may be put for horses'.

Wood was more common in the Chilterns than in the north of the county. At Little Kimble the glebe included a plot of ground with wood and box growing upon it. Amersham had 16 acres of wood ground, Bradenham a parcel of wood ground lying in common.

There are a number of references to tithes and church dues, although the Canon of 1604 did not require specific details of these. At Astwood it is noted in 1639 that the whole of the tithes of the parish belong to the parson, as they did at Little Kimble, whilst at Caversfield the tithes of three and a half yard lands lying in the common fields of Stratton Audley were said to belong to the parsonage. At Grove the house of Sir Robert Dormer at Broughton in the parish paid a rate tithe of 116s. 8d. a year together with the small tithes, and a little close in Little Hampden paid all manner of tithes to the incumbent of Great Hampden. At Long Crendon, however, the parson had only the small tithes, amounting to forty shillings a year. At Middle Claydon the new enclosures in the Lawne woods paid corn and hay tithes in kind. At Brill in 1639 the parson had tithe of milk, the 'Ods' of calf wool and lamb and of feeding cattle, of wood, flax, hemp, bees, fruit and garden produce. At Taplow in 1639 the parishioners paid milk tithe from the second of May until Lammas Day every tenth day, morning and evening. They also paid tithe calf, being the 10th when it falls or the tenth part if it be sold and the shoulder if it is killed. There is also mention of tithe fish and tithe osiers and tithes of wood and rabbits. At Radclive the parson had certain pieces of land in lieu of tithes, the apple slade in lieu of tithe apples and the Parsons sideling in lieu of the tithe of hades, meadows and balks, and at Shalstone the parson had four platts of meadow instead of the tithe of the fallow meadows of the lord's ground, and at Beachampton the parson held a plot of meadow ground in lieu of the tithes of the bridge meadows. At Cublington out tithes were paid from properties in the parish of Cheddington, and other out tithes are mentioned in Wingrave, Ivinghoe and Wendover.

The church dues are listed at Hedsor, where they included 6d. for churching, 6d. for a burial without a coffin and a shilling for burial with one, all of which amounted to about £20 a year. At Brill the incumbent enjoyed the dues paid at churchings, weddings and burials as well as the accustomed offerings of the communicants at Easter. The church dues are listed in some detail at Taplow, and at Ashendon the curate was said to receive the church dues and the Easter book.

Place-names

The documents here printed contain large numbers of field, furlong and strip names, as well as names of streets, brooks and other topographical features. Their interpretation is particularly hazardous since they are so late in their surviving forms. Nevertheless they repay some study, not least because so many were swept away by enclosure, parliamentary or otherwise, in the following centuries, and are often recorded nowhere else. They form an important part of that traditional, pre-industrial world which we have lost.[21]

Many field names are either directional or topographical — South, Middle, Foxhill, Clay — and may be comparatively late, perhaps reflecting a reorganization of the open fields such as took place at Thornborough in the early fourteenth century.[22] Such reorganization was a matter of regrouping existing furlongs, with little real need to change their names, so that it is very likely that furlong names survive from an older place-name stratum, although neither Windmill Hill furlong in Pitchcott nor that in Dunton could have been so named until after the introduction of the windmill at some time from the twelfth century onwards.

Furlong names themselves can point to topographical features which have long disappeared, even by the early seventeenth century. Perhaps the most interesting names are Wickcombe, or Wycomb, in

---

21 On field names generally see J. Field, *English Field Names,* 1972, 1989 reprint. Glebe terriers were used extensively in A. Mawer and F. M. Stenton, eds., *The Place-names of Buckinghamshire,* English Place-name Society, vol. 2, 1925.

22 M. Reed, *The Buckinghamshire Landscape,* pp.90–1.

Wingrave, and Wickhammon in Thornton. Whether these are hitherto unrecorded examples of *wicham* place-names, ultimately derived from the Latin word *vicus*, is an exciting possibility which at present, in the absence of older spellings, can only be suggested.[23]

Grimlow furlong in Water Stratford may contain either the Old Norse *grimr*, or else Old English *grima*, meaning a ghost, perhaps reflecting the same supernatural experience as is recorded in Ghost Hill, in Cheddington.

Lamp Acre in Bow Brickhill refers to land whose rent was used to maintain a lamp in the parish church, and Berry field, ultimately from Old English *burh*, hints at some long disappeared earthwork in Chearsley. Brache in Weston Turville probably refers to newly broken-in land, although this is something which would have taken place long before the terrier itself was compiled. Linch in Great Kimble and Lints in Pitchcott would seem to refer to hillside terraces, and Hatch furlong in Hartwell probably refers to land by a wicket gate. Stubb furlong in Marsworth would originally have referred to land covered with tree stumps, and hence recently cleared, although by the early seventeenth century the tree stumps themselves would also long have gone. Similarly, Eldernstubb in the same terrier would have referred to stumps of elder trees.

Both Aston Clinton and Marsworth contain references to Icknield Way, as Ecknill furlong and Ecknell way. Gorbroad in Pitchcott refers to the broad strips in the gore, or wedge-shaped piece of ground in the common arable field, whilst Bangore in Chedington may point to a gore of land upon which beans were grown. Delves furlong in Stoke Goldington refers to land by a quarry, and Mawme in Ellesborough and Malmefield in Wendover would seem to indicate light, loamy soil, whilst Catsbrain in Wingrave points to soil composed of rough clay and pebbles. Clayfield in Wendover speaks for itself. Street furlong in Wingrave and Overstreet in Cheddington would refer to Roman roads, and Meereway in Cheddington and Marewell in Walton probably refer to boundaries.

The glebe terriers here printed were created early in the seventeenth century and then preserved down to the present by the administrative machinery of the Church of England, and in this it was but continuing an ancient tradition by which the authorities of the church could demand the compilation of documents and its institutional longevity would then preserve them for future reference. Our knowledge of Anglo-Saxon England would be infinitely poorer if it were not for the

23 M. Gelling, *Signposts to the Past*, 1978, p.67 *et seq*.

stability of the Church in this manner. Ostensibly glebe terriers were created in order to record church property. In so doing they throw a shaft of light into the society and economy of early seventeenth-century Buckinghamshire. From Monday to Saturday there could have been little to distinguish a clergyman from his parishioners. His house was no larger than theirs and the manner in which he lived was bound into the same inexorable agricultural year. At the same time the record of field and furlong names hints at centuries of continuity in that cultivation of the soil upon which civilization depends.

LIST OF GLEBE TERRIERS TRANSCRIBED

GLOSSARY

acre	a strip of ploughed land, by no means always corresponding to the statute acre of 4840 square yards.
balk	an unploughed strip of land in the open fields, used either for access or as a boundary mark.
cullis, killis	a hipped roof.
furlong	a statutory measure of 200 yards in length, but also a group of strips in the open field.
hades	perhaps synonymous with balk.
hide	a very ancient measure of land, containing perhaps 120 acres or four yardlands.
hook	a projecting piece of land.
holme	a piece of flat, low lying, ground by a stream or brook.
homer	a piece of land nearer to home, the opposite to farther.
knappe	a small hill or knole.
lammas ground	meadow ground used for grazing after Lammas.
land	a strip of arable land in the open field, synonymous with selion, strip, ridge and acre.
ley, lea, lay	meadow land.
moor	waste or marshy ground.
pightle, pickle	a small piece of enclosed ground.
plash	a piece of wet or water-logged ground.
quabb	boggy land.
quillet	a small plot or narrow strip of land.
rood, rode	a piece of land 40 square perches in size, and a quarter of an acre, but often bearing little relationship to the statutory measure.
shott	a block of land divided into strips, synonymous with furlong.
sideling	a small strip of ground lying beside a larger piece.
slade	a piece of ground in a low lying, marshy situation.

swathe   a piece of meadow ground measured by the sweep of
                      the mower's scythe.

through,
thorough acre   a piece of land running the length of the furlong.

yardland   a measure of ground, perhaps a quarter of a hide, in
                      itself perhaps 120 acres.

BUCKINGHAMSHIRE GLEBE TERRIERS

ADDINGTON 1578

A terrier of all such glebe land as well Leyes medow as arable ground belonging to the parsonage of Addington in the Countie of Bucks now in the tenure of Thomas Andrewes Clerk parson there made the 12 day of February in the 20th yeare of the Reinge of our Soverange Ladie Queene Elizabeth *Anno Domini* 1577.

South Field.

Imprimis one hafle acre of Medow towards Claydon brook lyinge betweene Henry Ward on the South and Richard Sheffield on the north.

Item one halfe acre of ley ground betweene the land of Mistriss Winsor on the south and Robert Chappell on the North.

Item one halfe acre ley ground lyinge betweene George Gebbs on the south and Edward Palmer on the north buttinge upon Mistriss Winsores hedge west, and upon Thomas Smithes head ley east.

Item One halfe acre ley ground lyinge betweene the land of Mistress Winsor on the East and William Miller on the west, buttinge upon Mistress Winsors hedge.

Item one halfe acre ley ground lyinge betweene Edward Prest in the North and the same Edward on the South, buttinge upon Mistress Winsors hedge west and the gutter East.

Item One halfe acre in the gosses, lyinge betweene the land of Mistress Winsor in the east and John Chinhold on the West buttinge on the hedge called Mistress Winsors hedge and upon a head ley of Robert Chappells North.

Item one halfe acre in the slowe betweene the land of Mistress Winsor on the south and Edward Prest on the North.

Item two yeards of ley ground lyinge betweene the land of Mistress Winsor on the west and Robert Chappell on the East butting on the land of Mistress Winsor on the North and the land of Edward Prest on the south.

Item one halfe acre of ley ground lyinge between the land of Mistress Winsor on the west and the land of William Miller on the east buttinge upon the land of Edward Prest on the south and the high way on the North.

1

Item one yeard of ley ground lyinge betweene the land of Henry Brampton on the west and the land of Edward Prest on the east, buttinge on the land of Thomas Smith south and upon the furlonge called Arwell hole north.

Item one halfe acre of lea ground lyinge betweene the land of Mistress Winsor on the East and Edmund Holden west and butteth upon the arable land of Mistress Winsor North and upon the highway south.

Item one halfe acre of ley ground lyinge betweene the land of Edward Prest on the east and Thomas Smith on the west, buttinge on the land of Mistress Winsor north and on the highway south.

Arwell Hole.

Item one halfe acre of ley ground lyinge betweene the land of William Miller on the East and the land of Edward Palmer on the west and butteth upon the hedge south upon the headland of Mrs Winsor north.

Item one halfe acre ley ground lyinge betweene the land of Mrs Winsor on the East and the land of William Norington on the west, buttinge on the hedge south and west and upon the headland of John Croxton North and west.

Water Farrowes.

Item one halfe acre of ley ground lyinge betweene the land of Mrs Winsor on the south and the land of John Eversley on the north, buttinge on the land of Edward Prest eastward, and upon Edwards way westwards.

Item one gore of ley ground betweene the land of Mrs Winsor on the northwest and Edwards Way on the south east, buttinge upon the land of John Eversley northwards.

Stome land.

Item one halfe acre of arable betweene the land of Mrs Winsor on the east and the land of Edward Palmer on the West buttinge on the headland of George Gibs north and the land of Mrs Winsor south.

Item One halfe acre arable betweene the land of Mrs Winsor on the east and the land of Thomas Smith on the west buttinge on the lands of George Gibs northwards and upon a land of Edward Palmer south.

Arwell hole.

Item one halfe acre arable betweene the land of Mrs Winsor on the North and the land of George Gibs on the south buttinge on the land of Henry Brampton west and upon the head land of Mrs Winsor East.

Item One half acre of arable betweene the land of Mrs Winsor on the south and the land of Edward Prest on the North buttinge upon the headland of Edward Palmer East and on the gutter West.

Item One halfe acre arable betweene the land of Mrs Winsor on the south, and the land of Thomas Smith on the north, and buttinge upon the gutter west and upon John Deverills headland east.

Harlat.

Item One halfe acre arable betweene the land of Mrs Winsor on the South and the land of John Croxton on the north, buttinge upon the gutter Eastward, and upon the land of William Miller westward.

Item one halfe acre arable betweene the land of Henry Ward on the south, and the land of Thomas Smith on the north buttinge on the gutter eastward and the land of Edward Palmer West.

Ridgway.

Item One land lyinge for an halfe acre betweene the land of Mrs Winsor on the South and the land of Thomas Smith on the north, buttinge on the land of George Gibs east and Edwards Way West.

Edwards Way.

Item One halfe acre arable betweene the land of Mrs Winsor on the West and Edwards Way on the East, buttinge upon the same Edwards Way South, and upon the parsonage land north.

Middle furlonge.

Item One halfe acre arable betweene the land of Mrs Winsor on the east and the land of William Miller on the West, buttinge on the land of Robert Chappell north and the land of John Eversley southward.

Item one halfe acre arable betweene the land of Mrs Winsor on the east, and the land of the sayd Mrs Winsor on the west, buttinge on the land of Henry Brampton north and the land of Edward Palmer south.

Item One halfe-acre arable betweene the land of Mrs Winsor on the east, and the land of Thomas Smith on the west, buttinge on the land of George Gibs northwards and the land of Thomas Smith Southward.

Middle furlonge.

Item One halfe acre called capons halfeacre betweene Mrs Winsor on the west, and John Eversley on the east, buttinge on the land of Edward Palmer north and upon the said Edwards land south.

Item Two yeards arable betweene the lands of Edmond Halden on both sides east and west, buttinge on the land of Edward Palmer north and upon the highway by the hedge south.

Flexmore path.

Item Two yeards arable betweene the lands of Edmond Holden on west and the land of Thomas Smith on the east buttinge on the land of Mrs Winsor south and upon Mrs Winsors hempe land northward.

Item one halfe acre arable betweene the land of Edward Prest on the west, and the land of George Gibs east, buttinge on the highway north and upon the land of John Eversley south.

Mill field.

Item one halfe acre betweene the land of Mrs Winsor on the west and the land of Robert Chappell on the east, buttinge on the land of Mrs Winsor westward and upon the parsons land south.

Windmill hurst.

Item one halfe acre of ley ground betweene the land of Mrs Winsor on the south and the land of John Eversley on the north buttinge on the highway on both ends.

Highway furlonge.

Item ij yeards betweene the land of George Gibs on the east, and the highway on the west, buttinge on the highway northwards and upon the land of William Dorington South.

Item one halfe acre betweene the land of Mrs Winsor on the west and the land of Thomas Smith on the east, buttinge on the land of John Croxton southward and on the highway northward.

Item One halfe acre arable betweene the land of Mrs Winsor on the West, and the land of George Gibs on the east buttinge on the land of George Gibs southward and upon the highway north ward.

Item one halfe acre arable betweene the land of Mrs Winsor westward and upon the land of William Miller on the east, buttinge on ledwell head on the south and upon the highway north.

Fox furlonge.

Item one halfe acre arable betweene the land of Mrs Winsor on the west and the land of Edward Prest on the east buttinge on the land of George Gibs on the south, and upon the land of John Croxton on the north.

Item one halfe acre arable betweene the land of Mrs Winsor on the west and the land of William Dorington on the east, buttinge upon the land of Edward Palmer on the north and on the land of George Gibs south.

Item One throughout acre betweene the land of Mrs Winsor on the south and the land of Edward Palmer on the west buttinge upon Edwards Way on the west, and upon the gutter on the east.

Item One yeard betweene the aforesayde longe acre on the north and the path way on the south, buttinge on the land of Mrs Winsor on the East, and Edwards Way on the west, from the highway northward.

Item One halfe acre arable betweene the land of Mrs Winsor on the east, and the land of George Gibs on the west, buttinge upon Newndip northward and the highway on the south.

Item one halfe acre arable betweene the land of John Deverell on the west, and the land of Henry Ward on the east, buttinge upon Newndip on the north and the highway on the south.

Item one halfe acre arable lyinge betweene the land of Edward Prest on the West, and the land of Mrs Winsor on the east, buttinge upon the cow leyes north and upon the highway on the south.

Item One halfe acre arable betweene the land of Mrs Winsor on the east and Thomas Smith on the West, buttinge on the headland of John Deverell on the north, and upon the highway on the south.

Falwell Crosse.

Item one halfe acre arable betweene the land of Henry Ward on the south and the land of Edmond Holden on the north, buttinge upon the land of Thomas Smith on the West, and the land of William Miller on the east.

North field.

Item one halfe acre arable betweene the land of Mrs Winsor on the south and the land of Robert Chappell on the north, buttinge on the land of Edward Palmer on the west, and upon the highway on the east.

Item One yeard arable betweene the land of Mrs Winsor on both sides, buttinge upon the land of Edward Prest on the west, and upon the highway on the east.

Item One yeard arable betweene the land of Mrs Winsor on the south and the land of John Eversley on the north, buttinge on the land of Mrs Winsor on the west and upon the land of Henry Brampton on the east.

Little Mores.

Item one yeard betweene the land of George Gibs on the west, and the land of Mrs Winsor on the east, buttinge on the land of Edward Palmer on the south and upon the gutter on the north.

Item a yeard under the mare betweene the land of Mrs Winsor on the east, and the land of William Miller on the west, buttinge on the moore on the south and upon the gutter on the north.

Item One halfe acre arable betweene the land of Robert Chappell on the West and the land of George Gibs on the east, buttinge upon the land of Edward Palmer on the north and upon the hedge on the south.

Latt Furlonge.

Item One halfe acre arable betweene the land of John Eversley on the west and the land of George Gibs on the east, buttinge upon the land of Mrs Winsor south and upon the gutter on the north.

Item one halfe acre arable betweene the land of Mrs Winsor on the east, and the land of Edward Palmer on the west, buttinge on the hedge on the south, and upon the gutter on the north.

Hill Furlonge.

Item One halfe acre arable betweene the land of William Miller on the north, and the land of Mrs Winsor on the south, buttinge on the highway on the east, and upon the hedge on the west.

Item one halfe acre arable betweene the land of William Miller on the south and the land of Robert Chappell on the north, buttinge upon the high way east and upon the gutter west.

Item One halfe acre arable betweene the land of Mrs Winsor on the south and the land of William Miller on the north, buttinge upon the land of Edward Palmer on the east and upon the gutter west.

At the end of Hill-furlonge.

Item One halfe acre arable betweene the land of Mrs Winsor on both sides, buttinge upon the land of Thomas Smith west, and upon the land of Edward Palmer on the east.

Dunway Hill.

Item one halfe acre arable betweene the land of Mrs Winsor on the south, and the land of Henry Brampton on the north, buttinge upon the parsonage land on the west and upon a ley of Edward Palmer on the east.

Item two yeards arable betweene the land of Mrs Winsor on the south and the land of William Miller on the north, buttinge on the land of John Deverell on the west and upon the cow pasture on the east.

Thistle furlonge.

Item One halfe acre arable betweene the land of Henry Ward on the south and Thomas Smith on the north, buttinge upon the land of George Gibs on the west and upon Edward Palmers headland east.

Item one halfe acre arable betweene the land of Mrs Winsor on the south and the land of George Gibs on the north, buttinge upon the high way on the west, and upon the parsonage land east.

Wips furlonge.

Item One halfe acre arable betweene the land of Henry Ward on the south and the land of William Miller on the north, buttinge on the land of Edward Palmer on the west and the head land of John Croxton on the east.

Moreley ground.

Item one halfe acre of ley ground at Little furrs betweene the land of Mrs Winsor on the south and the land of George Gibs on the north, buttinge upon the land of Edward Palmer west and upon the land of John Croxton east.

Item one halfe acre of ley ground betweene the land of Mrs Winsor on the south and the land of William Miller on the north buttinge upon the hedge on the west, and upon [...] east.

Item one halfe acre called medow ground betweene the land of Mrs Winsor on the east and the land of Edward Palmer on the west buttinge on the land of George Gibs on the south and upon the brooke on the north.

Lange Land.

Item one halfe acre ley ground upon Lange land betweene the land of Mrs Winsor on the south and the land of William Dorington on the north buttinge upon the land of George Gibs on the west and the land of Edward Palmer east.

Parsons bush.

Item One halfe acre ley ground betweene the land of Robert Chappell on the west and the land of Mrs Winsor on the east, buttinge on Henry Brampton south and upon the brooke on the north.

Black abbe slade.

Item One halfe acre ley ground betweene the land of William Miller on the north and the land of Mrs Winsor on the south buttinge upon the land of Mrs Winsor on the west and upon the common east.

Black abbe.

Item One halfe acre betweene the land of Mrs Winsor on both sides buttinge on the land of Thomas Smith south, and upon the brooke north.

Item Two yeards betweene the land of Mrs Winsor on the east, and the land of William Dorington on the west, buttinge upon the land of Mrs Winsor south and on the brooke north.

The meade.

Item Two poole betweene the lot of Mrs Winsor on the east and the lot of Edward Palmer on the West, buttinge upon the land of Mrs Winsor south and the brooke north.

Item Two poole betweene the land of Mrs Winsor east and the lot of Edmund Holden on the West, buttinge upon the brooke on both ends.

Item one halfe acre of ley ground on the south side of black abba slade betweene the leyes of Mrs Winsor on both sides, buttinge upon the common in black abba slade west and upon the common in the cow pasture east.

[...]way Hill.

Item One halfe acre of ley ground by [...]way hill [...] land of Mrs Winsor on the south and the land of Thomas Smith on the north, buttinge upon the land of Edward Palmer on the east and Bucks way on the west.

Vewed and perused by us

Thomas Andrew   parson there
Edward Palmer
William Dorington
Edward Prest
and others.
Concordat cum Registro Examt.   John Pregion *Registrarius*

November 9 1639   we certifie that this is a true copie and terrier of the glebe land.

Robert Whitehall   parson there
Edward Brampton   mark   Churchwardens
Anthony Godwin
(D/A/Gt/1/1/1)

2. AKELEY 1639

A Seedule or Terrar of the parsonage lands in Akeley in the county of Bucks made the first day of November *Anno Domini* 1639.

In the feild.

Imprimis One messuage or tenement and out howseing thereunto belonging contayneing by estimacon Nyne bayes of building with a home close thereunto belonging contayneing by estimacon Two acres.

One acre of Arable land the land of Robert Smyth gent lying on the West side therof and the land of Thomas Hobbs on the East.

One acre lying on Norton on the hill the land of the sayd Mr Smyth lying on the South side therof and the land of Richard Ingram on the North.

One acre lying on Loomsway furlong the land of Roger Knight lying on the West side therof and the land of Thomas Ingram on the East.

One acre lying on Galloway Baulke the land of the said Mr Smyth lying on the North side therof and the land of John Jellard gent on the South.

One acre and a half acre lying at the Parsons pill The land of the sayd Mr Smyth lying on the North side therof and the land of Thomas Clarke on the South.

In Churchill feild.

Two Acres lying in Churchill furlong the land of the sayd Mr Smyth lying on the South side therof and the land of John Kemp on the North.

Six lands contayneing by estimacon two acres lying on Galloway the land of the said Mr Smyth lying on both sides therof.

One acre lying in Chadwell the land of the sayd Mr Smyth lying on both sides therof.

In Stockwell feild.

Fower Acres of land lying on Crabtree Greene, neere unto Pillox hill the land of the sayd Mr Smyth lying partly and the Common wood partly and the land of Thomas Henns on the South.

One Acre of land lying on Neales hill the land of the sayd Mr Smyth lying on both sides therof.

One Acre lying on Sammins Townsend The land of John Kemp lying on both sides therof.

One peece of land contayneing by estimacon Two Acres The land of the sayd Mr Smyth lying on both sides therof.

One Acre more lying on the same furlong the land of the sayd Mr Smyth lying on both sides therof.

One Acre of Ley grownd lying at Berry lane end The land of the sayd Mr Smyth lying on both sides therof.

One Acre lying on Nether furlong the land of the sayd Mr Smyth lying on the North side therof and the land of Thomas Clarke on the South.

Two acres of meadow grownd called the Hookes the land of the sayd Mr Smyth lying on the South side therof and the land of William Corby on the North.

Thomas Phillpott   Rector

Thomas Kemp
The Marke of Willime Grinsley   Churchwardens
(D/A/Gt/1/3/1)

3. AMERSHAM 1607

September 29 Anno Domini 1607 Anno Regni Domini Regis Jacobi Dei gratia quinto et quadrigesimo primo S.

A survey or Terrour of all the possessions belongeing to the Rectry of Agmondesham made and taken by the view perambulation and estimate of the mynister, Churche-wardens, Sidemen and other inhabitants ther (whose names are subscribed) beinge therunto nominated and apppoynted by William Folkingham Gentl. generall surveiour of Churche gleabes and possessions within the diocesse of Lyncolne, by vertue of a Commission decreed by the Reverend Father in god William Lord Bishop of Lincolne in execution of the Canon in that behalf established.

Homestall.

Imprimis The Homestall or Scite of the parsonage scituate and lyinge betwene the lande of Sir Frauncis Cheney knyght on the west, and on the North East and South upon thother lands belongeinge to the Rectorie and within the sayd bounds are conteyned one garden, one orcharde, with two Court yards contayneinge by estimacon 2 acres.

Edifices.

Item the dwellinge house of the parsonage consists of 16 bayes, built with tymber and covered with tyles beinge chambred and boarded and disposed into necessarie roomes and two stories.

Item 2 barnes consistinge of bayes 10 built with tymber and covered with tyles and stables with other out houses bayes 12 built with tymber and covered with tyles.

Item one Acre of Pasture abuttinge upon the land of Sir Frauncis Cheney knight upon the west and the rest upon the lande belonginge to the Rectorie.

Item one Meadow called Ponde Wicks 2 Acres and di. abuttinge upon the river on the South and upon the backe lane upon the North and upon the grounde of Francis Newman on the west.

Item one other Meadowe contayneinge by estimacon one Acre and 20 Poole called Churche-meadow buttinge upon the Church yarde on the west, upon the town on the South or the whole river compasseinge yt.

Item three feelds of Arable ground, one called witche feild, the seconde tenter feild, thother woode grene feild and one litle pightle contayneinge by estimacon 56 Acres and woode grounde lyeinge within tharable contayninge 16 Acres, all which abutt them selves upon the lande of Sir Frauncis Cheney Knight west and parte upon the backe lane and the river South and parte upon the landes of the Earle of Bedforde and Roberte Bachelar Easte and Northe.

Item the quite Rents within the franchises of the sayd parsonage yearely 40s.

Item 3 Cottages with their bakesides one in the tenor of Richard Gregory ioyneinge upon the foresayd pond wicks west upon the lane North and upon the ground of John Gregory East and South. The Seconde is in the tenor of Thomas Whittington ioyneinge to ponde wicks west and upon the lane East and upon the lande of Hughe Huggins North and the land of Gyles Watkins on the South. The thirde and last is in the tenor of Henoch Wyer ioyneinge on the highe way South and on the river North and on William Bauldwins tenement East and on widdowe Bennets lande wherein Aaron Baker dwells west.

A roialty to kepe Court Leete and Barron with Constable and Tithing men for the Frenches belonginge to the parsonage out of which the quitt rents arise, which Frenches is a great part of the northe side of the towne, devided from the borrowe by a gutter or ditche.

Robert Chaloner   pastor

William Garrit   Churche Wardens
Thomas Wilkinson

Henry Leues
Thomas Fynche   thelder
Hugh Huggins
Christopher Clark

(D/A/Gt/1/4/1)

4. AMERSHAM 1639

A Terrier of the house and glebe Land of the Parsonage of Agmondesham Comit. Bucks. June 24 1639.

Inprimis A hall with a loft over it.

Item a Parlor with a chamber over it within the parlour a chamber below, and another over the same.

Item a Buttery and a little seller and a room over them.

Item a Kitchen with a Roome over and a chimney at the East end of it.

Item a dry Larder with a chamber over it and chimneys in them.

Item a lower Roome with a chamber over it and chimneys in both.

Item at the East end of the hall a boultinge house next to that a wet Larder and a chimney in it and Roomes over both.

Item a Brewhouse with a chimney.

Item adioyning thereto on the Southside a henhouse and a water carthouse.

Item at the East end of those Roomes is a saddle house and a Row of Stables with a chaffe house standing betweene the saddle house and the Brewhouse.

Item one great Barne contayning six bayes.

Item one other Barne and a porch contayning five bayes.

Item a Row of low buildings called the pease barne and heybarne adioyning to the Northend of the lesser barne standing East and West conteyning six small bayes.

Item at the Southend of the little barne a Carthouse contayning two small bayes.

The Land.

Item on the Southside of the parsonage house two gardens and a little orchard.

Item one feild called Witchfeild lying on the Southside of the house contayning foure and Twenty acres or thereabouts.

Item two little plots of ground lying on the Northside of the house containing three acres or thereabouts.

Item on the Southeast side of the Churchyard one little Meadow called Churchmead contayning two acres or thereabouts.

Item on the Northside of the said Mead one feild called Teinterfeild conteyning eighteene acres or thereabouts.

Item one copse of wood called Marly grove of three acres or thereabouts lately made arable ground and Laid to Teinterfeild.

Item at the Northend of Teinterfeild one wood containing sixteene acres or thereabouts.

Item on the Northside of the said wood one feild called Woodgreene feild conteyning two and twenty Acres or there abouts.

Item one Meadow lying on the Northside of the middle of the Towne called Pondwicke conteyning by estimacon three acres or thereabouts.

All these feilds and Meadows are enclosed and well mounded.

Item a Franchise of the yearly Rent of five and forty shillings or thereabouts.

The Chancell and Parsonage house with the edifices thereto longing are well repayred.

The marke of John Martlew   Church wardens
John Moreton
[...]
(D/A/Gt/1/4/2)

5. ASHENDON AND POLLICOT 1639

October the 8th 1639.

The Curat theare hath and dwelleth in one little tyled howse which belongeth to the Rectory of Ashendun impropriate which howse conteyneth twoe bayes of buildeinge whearein are twoe lowe roomes, and twoe high roomes: the grownd wheareon the howse standeth is by estimation one roode of grownd; the house abutteth east and west the Church yard on the South side and the highe street on the North: And the saide Curat receaveth one yearely stipendiary pension of tenn powndes, paide from Christs Church in Oxford, which saide Christs Church is patron of that Rectory: he hath allso the Easter booke, and the dues theare ofChristnings, Marriages and Burialls.

Thomas Tailor   *Curat ibidem*

Robert Cherry
William Rice   Churchwardens
(D/A/Gt/1/5/1)

6. ASTON CLINTON 1639

A Terrier of the Rectory or Parsonage of Aston Clinton [...] Sixteenth day of June *Anno Domini* 1639 by these parties whose names are here under [...]

Imprimis the dwelling house contayninge nyne bayes a hall an entrie with a little chamber adioyninge and a chamber over the entrie All the roomes upon the West side of the hall two Parlors and three Chambers over them a stare case with a studie and a laynetoe adioyninge All the romes on the East side of the Entrie, A Kitchin Celler, with three chambers over them a brewhouse seaven Chimneyes in all the forenamed romes.

Item Barnes Stables and Cowhouses Contayninge Fifteen bayes.

Item one orchard one garden contayninge one acre the dwelling house one the north side.

Item one Close adioyninge to the dwelling house Contayninge by estimacon thirteene acres with a Tennement standing upon parte of it Contayninge three bayes the highe way leading from Aylesburie to Tringe one the North side and a brooke called Wannell head runninge alonge one the south side adioyninge the Feilde called Wannell Downe feild one the East, and one Close in the tenure of Thomas Cooke one the west.

Item a little pightell Called Preistwicke Contayninge one rode with a Tennement standinge upon parte of it contayninge two bayes with hell lane one the North, a streete Called greene end leading out of the Nether feild into the towne on the East, The dwellinge house with the appurtenances of Thomas Wells the elder one the South and West sides.

Item one pightell lyinge in St. Leonards Contayninge by estimacon one rode, the land of Henry Westside, abuttinge the Chappell of the East side, and the Chappell grounde lyinge one the South and North sides.

Arrable land and layes.

In a feild Called Wannell Downe feild seaven acres   iij rodes.

In a furlonge One the west side of Deane Croft two rodes the land of Henry Sandwell south east and the land of Hellen Russell North west ij rodes.

In a furlonge under Aston hill shotinge East and West next Deane Croft, one halfe acer the land of William Well junior south East, and the land of William Cooke North West   di.

In a furlong at the North East end of Mouse hill, two rodes, the land of William Wells senior south West and the land of William Brigginshaw North East   ij rodes.

In a furlonge one the North parte of Clottne Deane abuttinge upon Ecknell way two rodes, Hellen Russell one Southwest side, and the land of Thomas Woster North East   ij rodes.

In a furlonge lyinge betweene Ecknell way and Clotten Deane shotinge North and South ij rodes, Hellen Russell South West and the land of William Wells senior North East   ij rodes.

In a furlong above Ecknell way shotinge North west and South East, one halfe acre the land of Henry Sandwell North West and the land of Hellen Russell South West   j d.

Bradnedge furlonge one halfe acre Hellen Russell one the North East, and Henry Waterhouse South West   j d.

In the same furlonge one rode the land of Thomas Woster North East, one rode of William Brigginshaw south west   d.

One the West side of Bradnedge furlonge one halfe acre the land of Agnes Worster North West and Ecknell way lyinge one the South East side   d.

In Bradnedge Frulonge next Ecknell way one halfe acre Agnis Worster North West and the land of Triamore Harvey one the South East   d.

In a furlonge under Bradnedge shotinge into Tickles hedge one half acre, the land of Silvester Baldwyn south East, and the land of Hellen Russell North West.

In More end furlonge one halfe acre John Cost, North East, William Well senior south west   d.

In Crosse Furlonge one halfe acre beinge a headland the land of Richard Babham one the south West side one other halfe acre the land of William Brigginshaw North East, and Thomasin White South West ij d.

In a furlonge at the North West end of Gosse furlonge two rodes Thomasin White North West   ij d.

In a furlonge shotinge South and North into the More, one halfe acree, the lands of Richard Fulkes North East and the land of Hellen Russell South West   d.

Middle Downe Feilde 2 acers.

In a furlonge shotinge into Bryer bush furlonge one halfe acre the land of Hellen Russell one the North East, and the land of Agnis Worster south west   d.

In a furlonge shotinge into Humphries Hole two rodes Richard Babham south East and Thomas Worster North   ij.

In a furlonge shotinge into sorehamway towards the East, one halfe acre, the land of Thomas Bampton North east, and the land of Richard Illinge south west   d.

One other halfe acre Dele Vach one the south East side   d.

Sandwell Downe feild   3 acres 2 rodes.

In a furlonge beneath Ecknell way two rodes the land of Thomas Worster South East and the land of De la Vach North west   d.

In a furlong Called longe hill furlonge one halfe acre, the land of Richard Fulkes south West and the land of William Wells senior North East   d.

In a furlonge upon the North West side of Ecknell way abuttinge upon longe hill, one half acre the land of Hellen Russell one the South west side   d.

In Marrwell furlonge two rodes, Triamore Harvey South East, and Richard Fulkes North West   ij r.

In a furlonge upon the East side of Whiteway shotinge into Hare land one halfe acree the land of Thomasin White South West, and the land of John Waterhouse North East   d.

In a furlonge next the last towards the South East, shotinge as the last one rode the land of William Brigginshaw North East, and Richard Fulkes south west   ir.

In Ragg Pitt furlonge on halfe acre, John Gost North West, and Triamore Harvey south East   d.

In a furlong at the North West end of Catts braine two rodes the land of Richard Illinge South East and the land of Richard Smyth North West   ij r.

Nether Street feild   i acre.

In a furlonge shotinge unto Goodson bridge two rodes the land of Thomasin White North West, and Hellen Russell South East ij rodes.

In a furlonge shootinge in Wickens one halfe the land of William Cooke Northe and Hellen Russell South West   d.

West Feild.

In a furlonge Called longe Ridge way one half acre the land of Henry Sandwell South East, and Hellen Russell North West   d.

Overstreete Feild.

In a furlong shotinge into Aylesburie way one half acre the land of Richard Smyth North West, and William Briggeshaw South East   d.

One other halfe acre, John Gost North West, and Richard Illinge South East   d.

One rode William Cocke North West, the land of William Wells senior South East   j r.

Three rodes more Triamore Harvey North west, Richard Illinge South East   iij r.

One halfe acre the land of John Cowden North West and William Cocke South East   j d.

One other halfe acre Richard Illinge North West and Henry Grange South East   d.

In a furlonge at the east side of the last, one halfe acre the land of John Durrant Southwest, and the land of John Waterhouse North West   d.

In a furlonge shotinge North West and South East next the upper parte of Buckland hedge One halfe acre the land of Richard Illinge South East and Hellen Russell North west   d.

Benhill Feild   2 acres 3 rodes.

In Stone bridge furlonge one halfe acre beinge a head land William Wells senior South East   d.

In a furlonge Called Studd furlonge one halfe acre Margaret Gammond North East and John Gost South west   d.

In a furlonge abuttinge upon Cuttle brooke one halfe acre, the land of Hellen Russell South West, and De Le Vach North East   d.

In Middle Benhill furlonge two rodes, the land of William Brigginshaw North East and John Durrant South West   ij r.

One other rode beinge a head yard the yard of John Gost one the North West side   i r.

In a furlonge Called the Vachgarden One halfe acre the land of William Wells senior North West, and Hellen Russell South East   d.

North Feild   3 acres 1 roode.

In a furlonge Called Balls herne at the end of Phipps lane one halfe acre Richard Fulkes South East, and William Wells junior North West   d.

In a furlong betweene Hillway and Hareway one halfe acre the land of Richard Fulkes South east and William Brigginshaw North West   d.

One other halfe acre being a head ley Hellen Russell one the south east side   d.

In Honnyum lease one halfe acre, Agnis Worster south west and Hellen Russell North East   d.

In Bann furlonge one rode John Waterhouse North North West, Richard Fulkes southest   r.

One halfe acre, William Wells junior North West, and Richard Fulkes South East   d.

In Buckham Meare Furlonge one halfe acre Richard Fulkes Southwest and Thomas Bampton North East   d.

Middle Feilde 4 acres.

In a furlonge abuttinge upon Balsherne one halfe acre Hellen Russell North East and de le Vach South West d.

In a furlong Called Flaxlands one halfe acre, Richard Fulkes South west, and Richard Smyth North East d.

In Great Maustest one halfe acre, Hellen Russell South West and John Mountayne North West d.

One other halfe acre Hellen Russell South East and de le Vach North West d.

In a furlonge called North langs one halfe acre, de la Vach North west Hellen Russell South East d.

In West furlonge one halfe acre Richard Illinge North West, and Hellen Russell south East d.

One halfe acre the land of Silvester Baldwyn North West and de le Vach South East d.

In a furlonge at the South end of the last one halfe acre, the land of Richard Fulkes North east, and John Gost South west.

Nynnings Feilde 3 acres 3 rodes.

In Nether Banlands one rode William Wells senior North east, Thomasin White South West 1 r.

In Middle Furlonge one halfe acre de le Vach South West and Richard Fulkes North East d.

In a furlonge at the south east end of the last two rodes, the land of Richard Smyth North West and Triamore Harvey South east ij r.

In Middle way furlonge one halfe acre De le Vach North West and Hellen Russell South East d.

Two rodes the land of De la Vach North West and William Cocke Southeast d.

One halfe acre the land of William Cooke North West and William Cocke Southeast d.

In Westlonge furlonge one halfe acre William Brigginshaw North West and Robert Fulkes South East d.

One other halfe acre, the land of De la Vach North West and Richard Fulkes South east d.

Meadow ground.

One Meadow Called the parsonage meade contayninge six acers and one rode Middle Northfeild one the West, a furlonge Called horse shoe north west, Monnes Meade North east, and the North Feild at the south end vj acres jr.

In a meadow Called Merrimeade two mens worke as it ariseth by lott Contayninge ij acres et d.

In a meadow Called Chickens Meade two mens worke as it ariseth by lott Contayninge   ij acres and d.

William Gerard   Rector of the foresaid parish.
Christopher Wells
Thomas Dancer
William Brigginshaw
John Dancer
(D/A/Gt/1/7/2)

7. ASTON SANDFORD 1639

A terrier of the Parsonage of Aston Stanford *alias* colde Aston in the County of Bucks and of the gleebe land apperteining there unto, written *Anno Domini* 1639.

First the Parsonage house consisteth of foure bayes of building, of which the one is tyled and the other bayes are thatched, one bay hath bin and is unloafted the other are loafted ouer.

The barne of the same Parsonage consisteth of three bayes of building and a cut end.

The stable and sties belonging to the same Parsonage consist of one bay of building and a cut ende.

There is adjoyning and belonging to the saide Parsonage house (beside the Churche yarde) one close, of ley grounde which is by estimation two acres or there about, and it lyeth on the back side of the house.

This parsonage house, barne, stable and close above mentioned are situate betweene the houses and closes of Richard Blacket on the one side, and of Edward Big on the other side.

Also there belongeth to the said Parsonage a plat of meadow ground esteemed to be one acre which lieth in a meadowe called the West meade, about the middle of the same meade, it is staked out and lieth betweene the grounde of one Mr Brightwell at the one end and of Mr Beake of Haddenham on the other ende.

Also there belongeth another plot of meadow ground esteemed at one acre which lieth in the meade called towne meade, which is staked out and lieth betweene the parishe of Dinton and the residue of the same towne meade.

Also there belonge to the said Parsonage two lots of meadowe ground in the said towne meade counted at two acres, which cannot be bounded as the rest above written because they fall out by lot and are changeable every year as also are the parts of all the parishioners which have parts or lots in that towne meade.

Also there belongeth to the saide Parsonage one half acre of lea
grounde in a place called olde berrye Lease in the parts of Aston
abovenamed, which halfe acre lieth betweene the lea groundes of
Richard Whitesed and of Iohn Chapman.

Also there belong to the saide Parsonage these parcels of arable
land: in little burrowe feild, one land marked with a little baulke on
the ridge at both ends, lying betweene the lands of Richard Whitesed
and of Nicholas Carter And another land there, marked after the same
maner, lying betweene the lands of Mr Fletwood and of Iohn Chapman:
another land so marked lying betweene the lands of Richard
Whitesed; and another land so marked lying betweene the lands of
Richard Whitesed: and another land so marked lying betweene the
lands of Richard Whitesed and John Brightwell.

In long ridge feilde are these landes all marked with little balks
at both ends on the ridge, one betweene the lands of Iohn Chapman
and Richard Whitesed: another betweene the lands of Iohn Chapman
and Christofer Brookes another betweene the lands of Iohn Chapman
and Richard Blacket: another betweene the lands of Nicholas Carter
and Christofer Brookes: another betweene two lands of Iohn
Chapman: another betweene two lands of Edward Big: another
betweene the land of Mr Fletewood and of Nicholas Carter: another
betweene the land of Mr Fletewood and of Mr Brightwell another betweene
the land of Nicholas Carter and of Richard Whitesed: another betweene
the land of Iohn Chapman and of Richard Whitesed: another between the
lands of Iames Saunders and of Nicholas Carter: another betweene
the lands of Edward Big and of Richard Blacket and lastly one lying
betweene longridge feilde and the middle fielde.

In the arable closes of William Welled lying at the ende of longridge
field are seaven lands of the gleebe land belonging to the parsonage of
Aston Stanford, lying in severall places, but all of them aunciently
marked with little balkes at both ends on the ridge, and every of them
lying betweene some lands of the said William Welled.

In the middle feild of Aston Stanforde are these landes herefollowing,
belonging to the Parsonage above named and they are all marked at
both the ends of the lands with little balkes on the ridge. one land lying
betweene the land of Mr Fletewood and the land of Richard Whitesed:
and another land lying betweene the land of Mr Fletewood and the
land of Richard Whitesed: and another land lying betweene the land
of Mr Fletewood and the land of Iames Saunders and another land
lying betweene the land of Nicholas Carter and the land of Christofer
Brookes: and another land lying betweene the land of Mr Fletewood
and of Richard Whitesed: and another land lying betweene the land of
Rafe Whitesed and the land of Richard Whitesed: and another land

lying betweene the land of Iohn Chapman and of Edward Big: and another land betweene the land of Iohn Horton and of Iohn Chapman: and another land lying betweene two lands of Iohn Horton : and another land lying betweene the land of Nicholas Carter and of Richard Whitesed and another land lying betweene the land of Rafe Whitesed and the land of Iames Saunders Also at the ende of the middle feilde above mentioned betweene it and the parish of Ouleswicke A close conteining by estimation eighte acres of land belonging to the sayd Parsonage of Aston Stanford which lies betweene the land of William Welled on both sides.

Also in the feilde of Aston Stanford called dead hill feilde are belonging to the saide Parsonage those [...] all of them marked with little balks at both endes on the ridge; one lande lyinge betweene a land of Christopher Brookes and a land of Nicholas Carter and another land lying betweene the land of Richard Whitesed and of Edward Hance: and another land lyinge betweene the land of Mr Fletewood and the land of Edward Big and another land lying betweene a land of Edward Big and a land of John Chapman and another land lying betweene the lande of John Chapman and a land of Richard Blacket; and another land lying betweene the landes of John Chapman and of Richard Whitesed: and another land lying betweene the lands of James Saunders and of Christofer Brookes and lastly another land lying betweene the lands of John Chapman and of Richard Whitesed.

Ralphe Whitesed his mark   Richard Blackett

(D/A/Gt/1/8/1)

8. ASTWOOD 1607

October 3 Anno Domini 1607 Annoque Regni Domini Regis Jacobi Dei Gratia Anglie Francie et Hibernie quinto et Scotie quadragesimo primo.

A surveye or terror of all the possessions...

Imprimis the homestall or Scite of the Vicardige scituate and lyinge betweene the close of Godfraye Chibnall gent on the West, and a pightle belonging to Lincolne Colledge in Oxford on the easte, and betweene the Churchyard on the North, and a close of the same Mr Chibnall on the South and conteyneth by estimacon halfe an acre.

Item within the sayde boundes ys contayned an orchard by estimacon one Roode.

Item the Vicaridge howse consistinge of fowre bayes built of tymber and covered with strawe 2 bayes chambered over and boarded and the whole buildinge contrived into 2 stories and disposed into sixe roomes.

Item one Barne consistinge of 3 bayes builte of tymber and covered with strawe.

Item one pightle and halfe an acre lyinge betweene a close of the sayde Mr Chibnall on the west, and a messuage of Tyringham Norwood gent' on the easte, abbuttinge on the Kings highwaye on the North and a close of the sayde Mr Chibnall on the Sowth.

For such Implements, Tenements or anye other thinge Inquirable by the Canon (and not herein before intimated and expressed) there ys nothing belonginge to this Vicaridge as farre as wee knowe or can learne.

Tyringham Norwood   George Richardson Vicar

Jo. Long
William Harryson
Jo Buckley
Richard Pate
Henry Coate
(D/A/Gt/1/9/1)

9. ASTWOOD 1639

Terrier of such things as belong unto the Vicariage of Astwood 1639.

Inprimis the Vicariage howse Consisting of 4 bayes of building Covered with strawe.

Item one barne Consisting of 3 bayes of buylding Covered likewyse with strawe.

Item one Roode of Grownde wherein the sayed buyldings stand.

Item one pightle bounded South and West with Mr Thomas Chybnales Grownd East with Mr James Chybnales North with the high way and Consisting of one halfe acre of grownd.

Item 6 pole of meddow in broade meade bounded with the Common field North and South and with broade mead East and West, being about a Roode of Grownd.

Item to the Vicariage belongs the whole tyths of the parish.

Roger Barker   Vicar

The mark of Thomas Marshall   Churchwarden
(D/A/Gt/1/9/2)

10. BARTON HARTSHORNE 1639

November 23 1639.

We the minister and Churchwardens of Barton doe certifie under our handes that Mr Thomas Kisley Gentleman is the Impropriator of Barton and the Impropriation is worth three Score powndes a yeare. Mr Philip Stokes serveth the Cures of Barton and Chitwood And hath twentie powndes per Annum of Mr Kisley for serueing them he being the Impropriator of both the townes and there is noe house for the Curate to dwell in neither at Barton nor Chitwood.

Philip Stokes   Curat of Barton

Martin Tomes   Churchwardens
William Warr
(D/A/Gt/1/10/1)

11. BEACHAMPTON 1639

A true terrior of the houses and landes belongin to the Rectory or Parsonage of Beachampton in the county of Buck' And now in the possession of the present Incumbent or of his Assignes made made [sic] Anno Domini 1639.

Imprimis one Mansion or dwelling house consisting of fowre baies of buylding lofted and tyled.
Item one Barne consisting of fowre bayes of buylding of tymber and thatched.
Item one long howse consisting of fyve lesser baies of buylding of timber and thatched.
Item the yard orchyards, garden and homeclose lying next to the house, conteyning by estimacon Two acres and an half or thereabouts.
Item Nyne Roods of gleab medow ground lying in a medow calld Dawes mead at the upper end of the saied Mead next to Mr Edward Tyrrells ground.
Item three Roods of gleab meadow lying in a medow called Sydmead of which two roods are laied out by Lott and one Rood lyes certaine.
Item two Roods of gleab medow lying in a medow called Sowmead or South-mead layd out by lott.
Item one half Acre of gleabe medow at the lower end of the meadow called the Burge mead.
Item one plott of medow ground belonging to the said Parsonage

lying next unto the Mill called by the name of the Parsons Midsomer medowe or Millhome conteying one Acre by estimacon be it more or lesse, which plott is and hath bene alwaies reputed in leiw of the tithes of the Bridge medowes excepting some certaine plotts of medow ground, And also such tithes and dues as formerly have bene paied and are payable out of the same medowes.

Item one ground inclosed called or Knownen by the name of Hanging Land conteyning by estimacon Twenty Acres or thereabouts, A certaine ground called Corne feild lying on the southwest parte or side thereof and the parsons homeclose on the north east parte or side thereof.

Item one other ground inclosed called the Parsons furzeny Close conteyning by estimacon six Acres or thereabouts, the ground of Sir William Andrews lying on the west side or parte thereof the ground of (*blank*) Head lying on the east side or parte thereof.

Thomas Byrchmore   Rector

William Elmer
Mathew Ellis
(D/A/Gt/1/11/1)

12. BLEDLOW 1639

July 25 1639.

A Terrier of lands belongeinge to the church and vicaridge.

Imprimis the Vicaridge house and a parcell of ground wherein itt standeth valued to bee on acre or thereabouts.

Item in the house five lower roomes.

Item above the staires some sixe roomes.

Item one outward Roome parted to severall uses.

Gulielmus Sharpe   Vic' *ibid'*
signum Arthuri Francklin   Churchwardens
signum Johannis Humphrey
(D/A/Gt/1/14/1)

13. BOARSTALL 1639

We know noe Glibe, land nor any other land belonging to our Church in our towne neither cann we heare of any that Ever was. We have Enquiered of our Antient Inhabitants And they Cannot Enforme us of Any that Ever they knew or hard of.

November the 17th 1639.

John Smyth   Churchwardens
George Harris
Robert New   Sidesman

(D/A/Gt/1/16/1)

14. BRADENHAM 1607

Septembris nono Anno Domini 1607 Annoque Domini Regis Jacobi dei gratia, Quinto et quadragesimo primo.

A survey or terror of all the possessions...

Homestall.

Inprimis the homestall or Scite of the parsonage scituate and lying between the Land of the Lord Windesor and the land of Sir Robert Dormer Knight containing by estimacon half an acre.

Item within the said bounds are contained a garden and an Orchard bothe containing by estimacon twenty poles.

Edifices.

Item the parsonage howse consisting of five bayes built of timber and covered parte with tile and part with thatche, two bayes being chambred over and boarded, and the whole building contrived into two stories, and disposed into seven roomes, *viz.* an hall, four chambers and two other roomes.

Item one barne consisting of three bayes built of timber.

Arrable.

Item one close called the barne close containing one acre.

Item one other close lying betwene the land of the Lord Windesor, and the Land of Sir Robert Dormer East and South, and the parsonage West and North containing one acre.

Item one other close called Litle Bancrofte bounding upon Great Bancroft Northe and Easte, upon Deanes ground Southe and upon Wythie close west containing foure acres.

Item one furlong of arrable lande lying in a field called Great Whitberie, bounding on the land of the Lord Windesor East, and upon the land of Sir Robert Dormer Knight, South, West, and Northe and containeth sixe acres.

Item one parcell of wood ground lying in Common, and boundeth upon the Lord Windesors land on everye part containing by estimacon three acres.

Summa of all   12 acres
Summa of wood ground   three acres

For stocks Implements tenements or anye other thing inquirable by the Canon and not herein before intimated and expressed there is nothing belonging to this Rectorie, as farr as we knowe, or can learne.

per me Georgium Mutley   *Rectorem ibid'*

Nicholas Darvald   Churchwardens
Richerd Wyngrave
William Love Day
Julian Foord
(D/A/Gt/1/18/1)

15. BRADENHAM 1639

A Terrior of all the Gleebe lands belonging to the Rectory and Parsonage of Braddenham in the Countie of Bucks and Diocess of Lincoln made the Twentieth day of July in the Fifteenth yeare of the raigne of our Soverainge Lord Charles by the grace of God Kinge of England Scotland Fraunce and Ireland Defender of the faith etc. *Annoque Domini* 1639.

Imprimis the Parsonage house is tiled and hath fower bay of building in it *viz.* a Kitchin, an hall, A Parlour, one lowe Chamber, and twoe upper Chambers with a studdy.

Item One barne thereunto belonging Covered with Thetch Containeing three bay of building with a Cutt end and a stable ioyned to the other end of the said barne, which house and barne are scituate and being in the middest of a Certain close of Gleebe land Containeing by estimation Fower acres be it more or lesse and butteth uppon the Kings high way towards the West Upon a little Close Commonly Called and Knowne by the name of Mistress Mutley's pickle towards the North, upon a Field Called Greate Bancrofte towards the East and upon a Close Called Martyns Close towards the South.

Item One Greene Lane Containing by estimation one rood, Great Bancrofte on the East and Martyns Close on the West and leadeth South into another Close of Gleebe land Called little Bancrofte Contayning by estimation Five acres be it more or lesse and Butteth upon great Bancroft towards the North and East; Deanes ground towards the South and a Close Called Coppice Close towards the West.

Item Seaven Acres of Gleebe land lying in a Common field Called and knowne by the name of greate Whitbury, and butteth upon the land of the Right Honorable the Lord Windssore towards the East, Little Whitbury towards the South, Deane field towards the West, and the land of the Earle of Carnarvon towards the North.

Item the Churchyard containing by estimation halfe an Acre, and butteth upon the Mannor house towards the East, the Greene Courte towards the South, Braddenham Greene towards the West, and the Dovehouse Close towards the North.

Item Seaven Acres of woodland lying in the Common, Butting upon Chericrofte towards the North, The Willow Coppice towards the East, The Common towards the South and Greate Bancrofte towards the West.   *finis.*

Willelmus Brampton   Rector

John Dorvall   Churchwardens
Richard Dorvall

(D/A/Gt/1/18/2)

16. BOW BRICKHILL 1607

Lincoln Diocesse   Octobris vicesimo Anno Domini 1607 Annoque Regni Domini Regis Jacobi dei gratia etc quinto et Scotie quadragesimo primo.

A Survey or terrour of all the possissions...

Hamstall.

Inprimis the parsonage house and houstall or Scite of the parsonage Sicruate and Lying between the ground of Tho Cooke Jun' on the cast and the kings hye waie on the south and the grownd of Nicholas Cook north and west haveing on Small orchard and on garden.

Edifices.

Item the parsonage consisting of fower bayes where of two bayes built with stone covered with tyle and chambred over and borded with two flowers above contrived into three stories highe *vizt.* a hall and a parlour and the other two baies built with Timber covered with tyle and Chamberd over with bord two stories disposed into two roomes a Kitchin and a pantrey.

Item two barnes consisting of Nyne bayes on stable of two bayes, on hay howse of sixe baies built all with timber.

Item on close of pasture the Common ground lying on the east and north the kings hye waie on the south and the house and ground of Thomas Walton on the west and Conteyneth on Acre.

Arable Land in the North Feild.

In the furlong commonly called Forty furlong two Acres of arable land the Land of Thomas Cooke on the South and William Cooke sen' on the North butting on a hedland of William Chevall on the west and on a Common feild way on the east.

Item three Roodes on short east land the Land of Mr Stanton on the west and the Land of Mr Randall on the East.

Item on Acre Lying on grovehill being a hadland acre the Land of Chevall on the North.

Item on Acre uppon Longe east Land Stanton on the West and Randall on the east.

Item on Acre on Bellowhill:Chevall on the west and Stanton on the East.

Item on Acre on Clay furlong John White on the South and Richard Kirke on the North.

Item on other Acre on Clay furlong Hugh Cooke on the South and Chevall on the North.

Item on Acre on shortcroft furlong white on the east and Randall on the west.

Item two Leyes of Furses at Shrublane end bey and Bellowe slade abutting into Bellowe Slade Randall on the East.

9 acres and On Roode.

Arable Land in the Midell Feild. 17 acres and 2 Roodes.

Item on Acre the nether Dings Randall on the north and Pett on the South.

Item on Acre on over Mowzier White on the North and Stanton on the South.

Item Two Thrrougout Acres on Mowzier Chevall on the North and White on the south.

Item Two Roodes on nether Mowzier William Chevall on the north and white on the south.

Item on Acre on over Mowzier William Chevall on the South and Randall on the north.

Item on Acre on midell Mowzier Stanton on the north and the Lord on the south.

Item Twoe Roodes more shoteing into Rushe slade the Lord on both sides.

Item on halfe Acre in Ditch furlong the Lord on the south and Randall on the north.

Item on hadLey on the same furlong William Chevall on the north.

Item Two Roodes on over Rowloe Pett on the east and Kirks on the west.

Item on Acre on nether Tinkers crofte the Lord on the north and white on the south.

Item on Acre on midle Tinkers crofte Cooke on the north and the Lord on the south.

Item on Acre on upper Tinkers crofts Pett on both sides north and south.

Item on Acre on midle hill the Lord on both sides east and west.

Item Two thorowghout Acres on nameless furlong Randall on the south and north side.

Item on Acre in the same furlong Stanton on the north and Thomas Cooke on the south.

Item on Roode shooteing into watery hadland Pett on the north.

Item on Roode on the same furlong Randall on the north and the Towne baulke on the south.

Item Two Roodes on shorte Bicklow Pett on the East and white on the west.

Item Two Ley Roodes in Collcot Rushe slade Stanton on the north and Randall on the south.

Item Two Roodes moore shooteing in Rushe slade Randall on the south Stanton on the North.

Arable Lond in the South feild 17 acres and 3 Roodes.

Item on Acre on Crowne hill white on the east side and Randall on the west.

Item on Roode on Lang furlong Chevall on the south and the Towne baulke on the north.

Item Two Roodes and on balke betweene them on the same furlong conteyning on Acre Chevall on the north and the Lord on the south.

Item Two Acres on the same furlong Kirke on the south and Stanton on the north.

Item on Acre on small Thorne Stanton on the east William Cook on the west.

Item on Acre on grosse furlonge the Lord on both sides.

Item on hadland Acre on the heiche furlong Stanton on the west.

Item on Acre on the same furlong Tho Cooke Jun' on the east Randall on the west.

Item five Lands and a balke on a furlong called Goodwins hooke conteyning three Acres white on the south and Randall on the north.

Item on Acre on the same furlong William Cooke on the north and white on the south.

Item three halfe Acres on Long bicklowe Randall on the west and the highe waie on the east.

Item on Acre on the same furlong the Lord on both sides.

Item on Acre Lying on a furlong called Litle Hill Pett on the east and the Towne Land on the west.

Item Two Roodes at greene waies end Pett on the south and Chevall on the north.

Item on Acre on brodgate peece furlong Pett on the south and Kirke on the north.

Item on half Acre on fludgate furlong Kirke on the south and white on the north.

The gleabe Meadowe.

Item on Acre of meadowe called the Lamp Acre being hadland Acre to gosse furlong.

Item Two Acres of Meadowe in the more Randall on both sides east and west.

Item on Acre of Meadowe in hacman Dole Pett on the east and white on the west.

Item on Acre of Meadowe in Acrestus Meadowe Pett on the east and white on the west.

Item Two Acres of Meadowe in the meadowe called Tanners hooke the Lord Gray on the south and Stanton on the north.

Item on Acre on the same meadowe called the Checker Acre Randall on the south and Kirke on the north Conteyning by estimacon Tenn pole.

Item on halfe Acre of Meadowe in sperie hooke Pett on the south and Jo:Chevall on the north.

Item on Roode in the Mill homes Randall on the north and the Lord on the south.

Item on halfe Acre on the same Meadowe Pett on the north and the Lord on the south.

Item Three halfe Acres in a Meadowe called Norden Pett on the north and Stanton on the south.

10 acres and 8 roods.

The gleabe Leyes.

Item on Acre of Leyes in Oxe Leyes the Lord on the north and white on the south.

Item fower Leyes being on Acre in gravell pitt Leyes on the nether furlong the Lord on both sides north and south otherwise called fullredie.

Item on Acre of Leyes on gravell pitt Leyes Nicholas Cooke on the south and the Lord north.

Item on Acre of Leyes in the upper furlong of gravell pitt Leyes Kirke on the north and Stanton on the south.

Item Three halfe Acres of Leyes on the same furlong white on both sides north and south.

Item five Leyes in gravell pitt Leyes white on the north William Cooke on the south.

6 acres and 3 roods.

Benjamin Lovell   Rector

Thomas Heider   Churchwardens
Richard White

Thomas Brone   Towens Men
Edmund Chapline

(D/A/Gt/2/1)

17. BOW BRICKHILL 1639

In the County of Buckingham within the Deanery of Newport and Diocese of Lincolne.

A Terreer or Survey of all the Houses, land, Pasture, Meddow, leyes, and arable belonging to the Parsonage of Bowbrickhill, taken this present yeare of Grace 1639: and in the yeare of our Soveraigne Lord King Charles the 15 th by us whose names are subscribed.

House and Homestall.

Inprimis The dwelling House consisting of foure Bayes, one Stable of 3 Bayes, one Hay barne of 6 Bayes and 2 corne-barnes of 9 bayes standing all in one Yarde whereto adjoins a little orchard taken out of the same yarde and lately planted. All which are situate between a

Tenement of William Cooke Junior, on the East, and a tenement of Nicholas Cooke on the West, the highway on the South and a Close called Bow close belonging to the Lord on the North.

Pasture.

One Close called more-close, between the Common, lying East and North, and severall Pightles of Widdow Walton: Richard Crosely and Nicholas Cooke on the west and the highway on the South.

Lammas-ground meddow and leyes, which are Several every yeere, between the Annunciation of the Blessed Virgin Mary and Lammas; and afterwards Common.

Meadow every Yeeres ground.

Inprimis 2 Acres in Tanners hooke the Duke of Buckingham on the South, and Mr Stanton on the North.

Item one Acre in Acre-Stubb; Alexander Brightwell on the East and Richard White on the West.

Item one Acre called Checker-Acre lying at Lockford Mr Randall on the South and William Kirke on the North.

Item half an Acre in Sperry hooke: Mr Chevall of Stratford on the South and Richard White on the North.

Item one Roode in Mil holmes shooting over the River: Richard White South and Mr Randall North.

Item halfe an Acre on the same furlong abutting in the new River: Mr Stanton on the South and Mr Brightwell on the North.

Leyes every yeeres ground.

Imprimis Five Roodes on Gravell pit leyes, shooting towards Lockford Thomas Cooke on the South and Richard White on the North.

Item one Acre in Oxe-Leyes Mr Stanton on the North and Richard White on the South.

Item 2 leyes in neather gravel pit leyes Nicholas Cooke on the South and Mr Stanton on the North.

Item 3 leyes on the upper furlong of those gravell pit leyes shooting into the highway called stow way Richard White on both sides North and South.

Item 2 leyes on the same Furlong Mr Stanton on the South and William Kirke on the North.

Item one Roode on the same Furlong.

Southfeeld, Meddow.

Feeld ground, Fallow every 3 yeare.

Inprimis, one Acre of Meddow called Lamp-acre: being headland to a furlong of Arable land, called Gorse furlong Mr Stanton on the West.

Item 2 Acres of Meddow in the Moore, Mr Randall on both sides.

Item one Acre of Meddow in Hackmandole Alexander Brightwell on the East and Richard White on the West.

Arable.

Imprimis one Acre at Latchmore upon the hitch furlong, being a head acre on the East and Mr Stanton on the west.

Item one Acre on the same furlong J. Cooke on the East and Mr Randall on the West.

Item one Acre on Gorse furlong Mr Stanton on both sides.

Item 2 Acres on long furlong William Kirke on the South and Mr Stanton on the North.

Item 2 Roodes on the same furlong and a baulke between them: Mr Stanton on the South and Thomas Chevall jun. on the North.

Item one Roode on Sallow pit Thomas Chevall jun: on the South and the towne baulke on the north.

Item on Acre on small thorne Mr Stanton on the East and Edward Cooke on the West.

Item 5 lands and a baulke in Goodwins hooke Richard White on the South and Mr Randall on the North.

Item 3 roods on the same furlong. Richard White South and Edward Cooke North.

Item 3 halfe Acres on Long Bicklow the high way on the East and Mr Randall on the West.

Item one Acre on the same furlong Mr Stanton on both sides.

Item one Acre on little hill Thomas Chevall sen: East and towne land West.

Item 2 Roodes at Greenwades end: Alex. Brightewell South and Thomas Chevall junior North.

Item one Acre at Broadgate furlong William Kirke North.

Item halfe an Acre on Hoodgate furlong: William Kirke South and Richard White North.

Item an Acre on Crowhill Richard White on the East and Mr Randall on the West.

Middle feeld.

Imprimis an Acre on Middle hill Mr Stanton on both sides.

Item one Roode on the one side Southward: the towne baulke on the South and Mr Randall on the North.

Item one Rood on the same furlong shooting into watery hadland Thomas Chevall Senior on the south and Thomas Chevall Junior on the South.

Item one Acre on Namoles furlong, called the Acre in the hole J. Cooke on the South; and Mr Stanton North.

Item 2 throughout Acres on the same Mr Randall North and South.

Item 2 Roodes in Bicklow: Alexander Brightwell East and West.

Item a had-ley in ditch furlong South and Chevall jun. North.

Item a land in the same furlong Mr Stanton South Mr Randall North.

Item 2 Roodes on over Rowle William Coles on the East, and William Kirke on the West.

Item one Acre on neather tinkers close Mr Stanton North and Richard White South.

Item one Acre in middle tinkers croft Mr Stanton South and Edward Cooke North.

Item one Acre in over tinkers croft Alexander Brightwell on both sides.

Item one Acre on Midel Mowster Mr Stanton on both sides North and South.

Item 2 Roodes shooting downwaies into Bedford Way Mr Stanton on the south and William Coles North.

Item 2 Roodes on the same furlong Mr Randall South and Mr Stanton North.

Item 2 Roodes in Cawcot over slade shooting upwards into Bedford way Mr Randall on the south and Mr Stanton North.

Item 2 through Acres on over and neather Mowsiers Mr Stanton and Richard White South and Mr Randall North.

Item one Acre on over Mowsier Mr Randall South and Chevall junior North.

Item one Acre at dimmish bush next the Northfield Mr Stanton South.

Item one Acre on neather Ding Alexander Brightwell South and Mr Randall North.

Item 2 Roodes on neather Mowsier Mr Stanton South and Chevall Junior North.

Northfield.

Imprimis 2 Acres on forty-furlong J Cooke south and Edward Cooke North.

Item one Acre on Shortcrofte Richard White East and Mr Randall west.

Item one Acre on clay furlong: Richard White South and William Kirke North.

Item one Acre on the same J Cooke on the South and Chevall Junior North.

Item one Acre on below Hill Mr Stanton East and Chevall junior west.

Item 2 Buts on Adnam leyes Mr Randall East and Mr Stanton West.

Item an Acre on long east-land, being had land to Grove hill East and Mr Stanton West.

Item an Acre on Grove Hill being hadland to short east land South and Chevall junior North.

Item 3 Roodes on Short East land Richard Fish on the East and Mr Stanton West.

George Ashton   Rector

John Laurence   Minister and Curate
Richard Whit   Churchwardens
William Warren
John Walter   mark
William Chevall   mark

(D/A/Gt/2/1/2)

18. GREAT BRICKHILL 1640

A True and perfect Terrier of all the Gleabe Land and meadowes Gardens howses of right belonginge to the parsonage of great Brickhill in the County of Bucks as followeth 1640.

Imprimis on dwelling howse Conteyninge five Bayes with a porch att the Entrance.

One Tyled Barne of Sixe Bay.

One Boarded Barne of five Bay.

One other Barne of fowre Bayes and a Porch.

Two Stables Conteyninge Two Bayes.

One Milke howse of one Bay with Two Bayes adioyninge.

One out howse Called the Olde Kitchin of Two Bayes with a Baye adioyninge havinge in it Gardners to laye Grayne in.

One Garden adioyninge to the Churchyard on the East side The Dwelling howse west.

One close adioyninge on the homestall Conteyninge thre Acres by Estimacon be it more or lese the feilde west the lord North.

One smale Orchard by the street over the way, the Lord West the street North, Mr Meridale South.

Item Thre score acres of Gleabe land in the Common fields lyinge dispersedly as followeth:

Imprimis in Apnam Mead feild.

One Half Acre under Rye Peice the land of Thomas Bett North and Mr Meridale South.

One other halfe acre one the same furlonge the Lord North.

One Roode of the same furlonge the Lord North Francis Hopkins south.

One halfe acre uppon upper wood furlonge the Lord on both sides.

Two halfe acres uppon the same furlonge the land of Richard West Betweene them.

One halfe acre uppon Midle wee furlonge the land of John Duncombe on both sides.

Two Roodes togeather uppon lower weed furlong Thomas Meridale south Mr Burton North.

One acre Togeather shootinge into Mill leyes the Lord south Mr Burton North.

One halfe acre uppon Long Narlonge Mr Jackman West Thomas Betts East.

One other halfe acre uppon the same furlonge the Lord East Markham west.

One other uppon the same furlonge Thomas Meridale East Mr Jackman West.

One halfe acre upon the furlong on this side webes Bush Mr Burton East Robert Seelinge West.

One halfe acre uppon Short Narlonge Mr Meridale West Mr Burton East.

One othe halfe acre uppon the same furlonge next the High Way but one.

Two Roodes togeather uppon Stony furlonge the land of Thomas Meridale south Mr John Duncombe North.

One halfe acre uppon the same furlonge Mr Meridale South the Lord North.

One halfe acre uppon Smeale Hill into Crowes Plott Thomas Bett East Lucke Bush west.

One Roode on the same furlonge Mr John Duncombe East Markham West.

One acre togeather uppon the same furlonge one of them a fore Shorter Mr [...] Colman West Thomas Bett East.

One halfe acre Toward the Northern End of Burge furlonge [...] north Peeter Woodward south.

One other halfe acre on the same furlonge Mr John Duncombe South Markham North.

One other halfe acre uppon the same furlonge into the River [...] south Mr Burton North.

One [...] Mr Duncombes New inclosure uppon Millers [...] the land of Thomas Meridale west.

The Midle feilde.

Imprimis [...] Roodes with some wast ground uppon [...] to the parsonage Close Hedge.

[...] had land Shootinge on to the Headland of Mr [..] uppon Wotten Sandes.

[...] shootinge together North and South next the [...] downe towardes Rich[...] the Land of [...] west.

Two halfe acres togeather on Potten Sandes the land of Mr Merivale west the lord East.

Two Roodes above [...] Luke Bush East the lord west.

Two other Roodes on the furlonge uppon the hill on this side [...] plott, the Lord South Markham North.

[...] grownd on Fish Pond Mr Bowing [...] Lucke Meridale East the highway North.

[...] Leye uppon Clare Bedd Mr John Duncombe North Mr Burton South.

One halfe acre ley uppon the same furlonge Mr Meridale south Mr Burton north.

One Rood of Earable Shootinge into moore Mead uppon Clare Bedd the Lord north Mr Meridale south.

One halfe acre uppon the same furlonge the land of Mr John Duncombe on each side.

One halfe acre on the same furlonge the Lord South Mr John Duncombe north.

Two Roodes togeather by Haltes hole the land of Peeter Woodward South the lord north.

[...] acre uppon wheat Creast the Lord East William [...] Thomas Pitford East.

[...] west.

One halfe acre uppon the same furlonge the Lord East Thomas Meridale west.

One other halfe acre uppon the same furlonge Thomas Meridale East the Lord West.

One halfe acre shootinge into the highway that goes thorough the midel of the Lande by Blacknall bush Mr John Duncombe one both sides.

One Roode uppon the same furlonge next the Churchway Mr Burton South.

One Roode shootinge north and south on this side [...] Bush Robert Seelinge west Luke Bush East.

One other uppon the same furlonge Mr Meridale East William Colman West.

Two Roodes togeather shooting north and South uppon highher Oate hill Mr Meridale East the lord west.

One halfe acre uppon Oate hill William Colman west Mr Jackman East.

One halfe acre uppon the same furlonge Peeter Woodward west the Lord East.

One halfe acre uppon the same furlonge Walter West Mr Burton East.

Five Roode leyes togeather on this side Standbrooke nether gape next the highway Mr John Duncombe East.

One Roode uppon waste ford Mr Meridale North Thomas Meridale south.

One other Rood uppon the same furlonge Thomas Bett south the Lord North.

One headland to the further end of Oatehill Shooeting East and west Thomas Meridale North.

One halfe acre uppon horsepole furlonge in the broade Mr Charlett south the Lord North.

One other half acre uppon the same furlonge William Colman North the lord south.

One halfe acre into swanes neest Thomas Bett South Mr Jackman North.

One other halfe acre into swanes neest Mr Burton on both sides.

One halfe acre headland into the furlonge that shooeteth into marsh Mead with a Rood next to it.

One Rood on the furlonge Betweene water furrowes and Swanes neest furlong Richard Sheppard north Mr Massingberd south.

One other Rood uppon the same furlong William Colman south Mr Meridale north.

One halfe acre in water furrowes the lord on both sides.

One other halfe acre uppon the same furlonge Short north and Robert Seelinge south.

One other halfe acre uppon the same Thomas Bett North Thomas Meridale south.

One Roode uppon the litle furlonge beyound kingshall hill and shooetinge into the highway Richard Sheppard north the lord south.

One other Rood uppon the same furlonge Mr John Duncombe north the Lord south.

One other Rood uppon the same Mr Burton south Francis Hopkins North.

One halfe acre uppon Kingsall hill Luke Meridale west the lord East.
One other uppon the same the Lord on both sides.
One other uppon the same Mr Jackman west Williams east.
One other uppon the same furlonge Mr Massingberd west Markham East.

In Smewnes Feild.

Imprimis att highway lands End on halfe acre Mr Burton north the Lord South.

One halfe acre into Tubes more Mr John Duncombe south Mr Meridale north.

One halfe acre uppon Grase Closes Mr Massingberd north Mr Meridale south.

On other halfe acre next But on Mr Meridale north Peeter Woodward south.

One Rood beyond hanging Baulke Mr John Duncombe north the lord south.

One halfe acre against Cumminges Thomas Meridale North Mr Meridale south.

One other halfe acre against Cummines Luke Bush North the lord south.

One halfe acre against farme Close Mr Meridale North Thomas Meridale south.

One acre att Patredge Bush togeather Mr Meridale North Mr John Duncombe south.

One other acre uppon the same furlonge Luke Bush north Mr Massingberd south.

One other acre uppon the same furlonge William Wright north the Lord South.

One Roode shooetinge into the first Riser of Six acre Mead Thomas Meridale north Robert Seelinge South.

One Roode leye By Rogeres Leyes Luke Bush north the Lord South.

Two Roodes att Bramwell Townes End Mr Massingberd east The Lord west.

Two Roodes next six acre mead Mr Meridale north.

One halfe acre shooetinge into the [...] which are north to it, Richard Sheppard [...]

One Roode likewise into the Leetes Mr Burton south [...] Meridale north.

One Roode on the same furlonge Thomas Pitkine [...] the parsonage Land north.

One acre togeather beinge on halfe acre and two Roodes upp saltwell Mr John Duncombe north Mr Stanton south.

On halfe acre upp saltwell Mr John Duncombe south [...] Meridale north.

One Thoroowte upp to Saltwell and downe to the high[...] at Feny home with on halfe acre next to it: uppon [...] furlonge in the neyther furlong Mr Meridale [...] Luke Bush south; In the [...] south Mr Meridale north.

Three Leyes in Feny home togeather Mr Stan[...] north Mr Burton South.

Two halfe acres leyes in feny home togeather Luke Bush south the lord north.

One other halfe acre ley uppon the same furlong Luke Bush north.

One halfe Acre of Arable upon the same Mr Burton south the lord north.

One Roode upon the same furlonge the lord one both sides.

One Roode on the neyther side the highway that leadeth to Smewnes well Thomas Meridale south Markham North.

One halfe acre next the Russhye way Mr Stanton north.

One halfe acre upon Aliwick hill Mr John Duncombe East Mr Meridale west.

One Roode that headeth the upper way to Smewens mill Thomas Meridale west Markham North.

One halfe acre Beyeond the Letes the lord on both sides.

One halfe acre, on the furlonge above Clarke peice Thomas Meridale north Thomas Bett south.

One halfe acre on this side of holtes hedge Mr John Duncombe south Markham north.

On Rood on this side smewnes Gate into bencrofte Mr Stanton north Luke Meridale south.

One halfe acre with a baulcke and Bushes upp the hill in Strangleden Mr Meridale north Luke Meridale south.

One other halfe acre upon the same furlong Mr Stanton North Williames south.

One Roode into the way beyonde smewnes gate William Colman north Mr Meridale south.

One Baulke beyonde yt into great Dextcombe Thomas Meridale north and the land of the parsones adioyning south Markham south to that Roode.

One halfe acre on the same furlong Markham north Francis Hopkines south.

One Roode Ley in Great Dextcombe John Peryman north Mr John Duncombe south.

One halfe acre on this side Copped moor Mr Jackman north Mr Meridale south.

One halfe acre beyond Coppedmoore Mr Burton north Markham south.

One halfe acre next the highway unto Stableford Bridge Mr Meridale west.

One other halfe acre upon the same Mr Massingberd East William Colman west.

One Roode into the Lordes uper meade Markham East Peeter Woodward west.

One Roode into the parsons meade Luke Meridale north Peeter Woodward south.

One Roode Leye into the lordes upper meade the midle most of the nyne.

One halfe acre on the furlonge beyonde smewnes upp into Copped moore Mr Stanton south the Lord North.

One other halfe acre upon the same Thomas Meridale north Luke Bush South.

One Acre togeather upon the same Mr Stanton north Robert Seelinge south.

One halfe acre ley by neyther lords meade Mr Burton one both sides.

Three Roodes of Stake mead Thomas Meridale north.

Two Leetes in sixe Acre Meade as they Rise by Lot.

Twelve Pole in more meade.

Thomas Jacking   Churchwardens
John Hopkines
Robert Hopkines   his mark   Sidesmen
John Merydale   John Sheppard   his mark
Laurence Merydale
Luke Meridale
Richard Sheppard
Jack Sheppard   his marke

(D/A/Gt/2/2/1)

19. BRILL 1639

November 22 Anno Domini 1639 Annoque Regni Caroli dei gratia 15.

A Terior of all the possessions belonging to the Vickredge and Church of Ockley *alias* Brill made and taken by the Minister and Churchwardens whose names are subscribed.

Homestall.

Inprimis The Homestall of the Vickredge scituate and Lyinge betweene

one close commonly called the Parsonage Close on the North the
Churchyard on the East The streate on the southe and the Orchard
and Garden thereunto belonging on the west which Orchard and garden
Contaynethe by estimacon one Roode.

Edifices.

Item the Vickredge house consisteth of five Bayes built with timber
and thatched in the which are conteined Eight Roomes *viz* Hawle
Parlour dayhouse three Chambers or Lofts boorded and three other
out Roomes.

Pasture.

Item one Close abutting on the orchard aforesayd on the North and
Close aforesayd called Parsonage close on the East and a Lane called
Birdbolts Lane on the West the close conteyning by estimation Halfe
an acre.

Tythes and Offerings.

Item the Tythes belonging to the sayd Vickaredge according unto
what is now and for many years past hath bine payd are the tythe of
milke the Ods of Calfe Woole and Lambe the tythe of Feeding Cattell
and of all such cattell as are not or cannot be tythed otherwise
then monies.

Item the tythe of Woode of Flaxe, of Hempe Bees fruits and all
maner of garden comodities.

Item all the acustomed offerings of the Communicants at
Easter.

Item the accustomed dues that are payd at Weddings Churchings
and burialls.

Item The monies payd out of the Parsonage of Ockley Brill and
Borstall to the sayd Vicar thereof per annum are foure pounds.

Item from Brill two shillings and allso from Borstall two shillings
per annum.

Item to the Mother Church of Ockley *alias* Brill the same two
shillings per annum.

Church land.

Imprimis The Land belonging to the Church of Ockley Lyeth in a
ground called Mile furlong abutting upon Wormall field on the West
and a ground called Tipes hill on the south and part of the foresayd
Mile furlong on the East and another ground called Redweell abutting
upon the Northend thereof which sayd Land conteyneth by estimation
Five Acres and an Halfe.

Item one Acre more (being an a Lotment alowed upon the Disforestation) out of the Kings ground to the sayd Church So the totall
Contayneth Six acres and a halfe.

Thomas Coxen   Vicar *ibidem*
Francis Johnson   *signum*   Churchwardens
Richard Bunts   mark

(D/A/Gt/2/4/1)

20. BROUGHTON 1605

*July 25 Anno Domini 1605 Annoque Regni Domini Regis Jacobi Dei Gratia
3 et 39.*

A Survey or terrour of all the possessions...

Homestall.

Inprimis The Homestall or Scite of the Parsonage scituate and lyinge
betweene a close called Buresteede belonging to Mr Francis Duncumbe
Lord of the Mannor of Broughton on the East, and uppon the Brooke
on the west, abutting north uppon the Highe Way that leadeth to the
Brooke, and Southe uppon a close belonging to Mr Duncumbe
aforesayd and Contaynes by Estimation one acre.

Item within the sayd boundes are conteyned a litle orchard hedged
round about, replenished with a few apple trees and plumme trees
and conteines by estimation one rood plus minus being scituate on
the North side of the Parsonage howse and a litle Pightle conteyning
likewise by estimation one rood plus minus scituate on the Southside
of the howse.

Edifices.

Item the Parsonage howse framed and builded all of timber
crossewayes, consisting of 5 Bayes and a halfe, whereof 4 Bayes are
covered with tyle *vizt.* 2 at the East end and 2 at the west ende of the
howse, the building contrived in 2 storyes and disposed in 8 roomes
viz. 4 upper (with one boarded) and 4 under roomes (with one flowred
with earth) *viz.* a Hall. The other Bay and halfe that standeth in the
middest of the howse is contrived in one storrye and disposed in 2
roomes *viz.* A Kitchin and a Buttrey and is covered with thatche.

Item 2 Barnes (covered with thatche) of tymber building whereof
the one scituate on the northside of the Parsonage howse consisteth of
3 small Bayes and a quillet the other being scituate on the South East
side of the howse consisteth of 5 litle Bayes and a halfe.

Meadowe.

Item 10 roodes and a halfe of meadow (the roode conteyning in breadth 16 foote and a halfe, and the length according to the breadth of the meadow where eache roode lyeth) of the which number 7 roodes do lye in 7 severall doles of the Greate Meade; the other 3 roodes and dimidium do in like manner severally lye in so many severall doles of Awbell Meade the particular places wherein the sayd 10 roodes and dimidium do lye are not alwayes constant in one and the same place but do alter and shift *pro aequalitate et inaequalitate annorum Domini* according as doth the meadowe of the Lord and all the freeholders of the mannor of Broughton, as is particularly expressed in twoe ancient parchement bookes in the custodye of the Lord of the Mannor the one whereof doth particulate the laying forth of the meadow *Quando Anni Domini sunt aequales*, and the other *Quando Anni Domini sunt inaequales*. But howsoever the places and Doles (wherein the sayd ten roodes and halfe do lye) alter and shift, yett the number of roodes belonging to the parson is alwayes certayne, being never more nor lesse then ten roodes and a halfe.

Summa Prati in the Greate)   meadowes is   10 di. roods.
              Awbell)

Item one acre of Meadow leyes Liyng together in Moulsoe crowche Leyes commonly called Meade Leyes, which abutteth East and West and lyeth betweene the Land of Mr Francis Duncombe on the South and the land of Mr Stiles on the north being distinguished from their land by greate stones (which lye hidden in the earth) at the Corners of the sayd aker. 1 acre.

Arrable.

Item 18 akers of arrable (according as they are esteemed) liying dispersed in 3 feildes and do butt and bound in manner and forme following

In Fenfeilde.

In Berry fillans furlong one aker butting East and West lying betweene the Land of Mr Duncumbe on the North and Mr Styles on the South.

In Langland furlong halfe an aker butting South and North Lying betweene the Land of Mr Duncombe on the West, and Mr Pedder on the East.

In the eye furlong one aker butting North and South lying betweene the land of Mr Duncumbe on both sides.

In the furlong under Fillans close hedge, one aker butting North and South, lying betweene the Land of Mr Duncombe on bothe sides.

In Clay Hill one aker butting East and West, lying betweene the Land of Mr Duncumbe on both sides.

In the furlong by the greate Meade on the South Side of Ballandsden, one aker butting West and East, lying betweene the land of Mr Duncumbe on both sides.

Summa acrarum in Fen feild is 5 akers and a halfe.

In Middlefeild.

Under Gillhadland one aker butting North and Sowth lying betweene the land of Mr Duncumbe on both sides.

In Waterslayd Furlong one aker butting North and South lying betweene the land of Mr Duncumbe on both sides.

Item one other aker butting in like manner with the former, lying betweene the land of Mr Styles on both sides.

Item one other Aker butting as the former lying betweene the land of Mr Styles on both sides.

In the furlong butting uppon Clowdes Bushe halfe an aker butting north and sowth, lying betweene the Land of Mr Duncumbe on both sides.

In the Upper furlong leading toward Sawford Pasture gate, one aker butting sowth and north. lying betweene the land of Mr Duncumbe on the East and Mr Styles on the West.

In the nether furlong butting on the Southside of Awbell Meade; one acre butting North and South Lying betweene the land of Mr Duncumbe on the West, and Mr Pedder on the East.

In the furlong under Awbell Meade halfe an acre butting North and South, lying betweene the Land of Mr Duncumbe on both sides.

Summa acrarum in middlefeild is 7 akers.

In Cookes bushe feild.

In the furlong on the North East side of Awbellmeade one acre butting North and South, lyinge betweene the Land of Mr Duncumbe on the East, and Mr Pedder on the West.

In the furlong shooting up into the Greeneway one aker butting North and South, lying betweene the land of Mr Duncumbe on the West and Mr Styles on the East.

In the furlong shooting up to Woddway one acre butting East and West lying betweene the land of Mr Duncumbe on both sides.

In the eye furlong one aker butting north and south, lying betweene the land of Mr Duncumbe on the East and Mr Styles on the West.

In the furlong lying on the north side of the greate Meade one acre butting North and South, lying betweene the land of Mr Duncumbe on both sides.

In Howcrofte halfe an acre butting East and West Lying betweene the Land of Mr Duncumbe on both sides.

Summa acrarum in Cockbushe feild is 5 akers and a halfe.

Summa totalis Arrabili is 18 akers.

For Stockes, Implements, Tenements, Pastures out-tithes or any other thing inquirable by the Canon and not heere in before Intimated and expressed, there is nothing belonging to this Rectory as farre as wee know or can Learne.

Ita testamur   Andrewe [...]   *Sacrae Theologiae professor, et Rector Ecclesiae Parochialis de Broughton.*

John [...]   Churchwardens
The mark of Robert Williams

(D/A/Gt/2/5/1)

21. BROUGHTON 1639.

A Terrior of all the glebe Lands and parsonage of Broughton in the countie of Bucks made the sixt daye of December *Anno* 1639.

Inprimis the dwellinge howse conteyneinge five bayes wherof Fower are tyled and one Thatched.

Item one barne of Five bayes Thatched and one other barne of Three bayes and a stable at the West end of it of two bayes all Thatched.

Item an ortchard a garden the fore yard and backside conteyninge by estimacon Three roods or somewhat more.

Item in Clayehill and Fennfeild Fower acres and an halfe, areable lands wherof one acre Joyninge to barbritch leis the lords land on the East.

One acre upon clayhill the lords land upon both sides one acre at ballance denn bushe the lords land on both sides one acre on the eye furlong the lords land on both sides one halfe acre on Langland the lords land on both sides; one acre more in the same feild formerlie exchanged with wee know not.

in the Midlefeild seaven acres.

Inprimis under gyll headland one acre the lords land on both sides one acre on Waterslade Furlonge the lords land on both sides one acre more on Waterslade furlong the land of Mr Styles on both sides one acre more on the same Furlonge the land of Mr Styles on both sides one halfe acre on hasland butts the lords land on both sides one acre shooting upon Bedford Waye the lords land on the east and the land of Mr Styles on the West one acre shootinge into Abell Meadow the lords land on both sides one halfe acre more shootinge into Abell Meadow the lords land on both sides.

In Cox bush Feild five acres and an halfe.

Inprimis one acre shootinge into Woodwaye the lords land on both sides one acre shootinge into Abell Meadow the lords land on both sides one acre shootinge into greeneweye the lords land on the West and the Land of Mr Styles on the east one acre on the eye Furlonge the lords Land on the east and the land of Mr Styles on the West one acre shootinge into great meadow the lords land on both sides on halfe acre on howcroft Furlong the lords land on both sides.

Item one acre of Leis lyeinge on mead leis the lords leis on the south and the leis of Mr Styles on the north.

Item Tenn roods and an halfe of Meadow ground in the common Meadowes whereof Seaven roods lyeth in the great meadow and three Roods and an halfe in the Abell meadow.

John Parker   Churchwarden

(D/A/Gt/2/5/2)

22. BURNHAM 1607

Octobris 10 Anno Domini 1607 Annoque Regni Domini Regis Iacobi Dei gratia 5 et 41.

A Survey or Terrour of all the possessions ...

Homestall.

Inprimis The homestall or Scite of the Vicaridge scituate and lying on the weste side of the Church yarde and uppon John Ives land on the North, and uppon the Vicaridge lande on the South, and contains by estimation 2 roodes.

Item Within the said Boundes are contained one Garden impailed and a little Courte by Estimation 2 roodes And one Orchard having veri fewe treese in it, with a Doufehous 2 Pondes and a little Pightel adioyning by estimation 2 acres.

Edifices.

Item The Vicaridge house consisting of 16 baies, the wales are all made of Lome, and the roofe covered with tyle, 10 of the saide baies beeing chambred over and boarded, etc. and the whole building contrived in 2 stories, and disposed into 30 roomes, *viz.* the Portch, the entrey, the Hall, a Parler, a Chamber within the Parler, a Stare case, 2 chambers over the Parler, 2 Butteries and 2 Cellers, 2 Kitchins, a Larder, a roome within the Larder, a Milkhouse, 4 upper Chambers, a Studdye, a Bakehouse, a Mault floure, a mault Lofte over it, 2 lodginge chambers for servants, and 3 little Roomes under them.

Item, 2 Barns consisting of 7 little bais and a portch, the walls are all made of Lome, the one of the Barns is covered with Tile, and the other is Thecked. 2 Haybarns contayning 6 veri little Bays and a gatehous 4 of the bais and the gatehouse are covered with Tile, and the other 2 Bays are Theched, 2 little Bais for Stables lofted over and theched all the walls be made of Lome, 2 Pigstis Tiled and the wals made of Boords a Shute with 2 little Rooms the wals are made of Lome and the Roofe is theched the one roome is a Stable and the other a Cowhouse.

Pasture.

Item a peece of Pasture cauled the Dovehouse close with 2 Ponds therin, lying on the west side of the house, it butts uppon the church land on the Este, uppon the Vicaridge Orchard on the North, and uppon Sir Phillip Scudamore's lande on the South contayninge 11 acres.

A peece of Pasture caulled the little Pightel buttinge uppon the Kings hey way on the Est, uppon the Churche lande on the west, uppon Thomas Hutchines his Orchard on the North, and uppon Sir Phillip Scudamoors lande on the South, contayninge 2 roods.

Summa pasturarum   14 acres

Meadow.

Item The Vicaridge meade butting uppon the Vicaridge house on the Est uppon Richard Bainns lande on the west uppon John Ives lande on the North and uppon Anthoni Bainns Orchard on the South, Contayninge 3 acres.

Summa pratorum   3 acres.

Arable.

Item Arable lande lying together in a feelde cauled Menecrofts butting uppon Richard Bainns lande on the est, uppon John Churches land on the west, oppon Sir Phillip Scudamoors lands on the Northe, and uppon John Ives lande on the Southe, contayninge by estimation 7 acres.

Summa Arable   7 acres.

Summa totalis   21 acres 2 roods.

Mesuage.

Item one Tenement neere adioyning uppon the corner of the Church yard, but no lande belonging therto.

For Stocks, Implements, Tenements, or any other thing inquirable by the canon (and not herein before intimated and expressed) there is nothing belonging to this Vicaridge, as farre as we know or can learne.

Randall Wright   Vicar of Burnham   1607

R   This is Robert Hecktons marke   Churchwardens
X   This is Edward Georges marke
[...]
Francis Pound   Sidemen

Paule Wentworth   Inhabitants
[...]
William Goulding
(D/A/Gt/2/6/1)

23. BURNHAM 1639

A Terrier of the Gleabe Lande and Housinge about the vicarage of Burnham in the County of Bucks taken the 22th day of July 1639 by us.

Imprimis A faire vicarage House and in good repaire with a large Hall, a Parlour, A cellar, a Buttery, a Pantry, sixe chambers. a study, and a Closset.

Item a Kitchin, a larder, and a wash-house.

Item one little Tenement standinge by the church yearde, conteyninge two roomes.

Item one feild, Conteyninge xj Acrees.

Item A Doue-House, and a little close by it.

Item one meadowe conteyninge 3 Acrees.

Item one Orchard and two Gardens.
Item sixe Acrees lyinge in a feilde called Many-Crofte.
Item a smale piddle of grounde lyinge by Bonington Hutchins.
Item 3 Barnes, and a Barne yearde.

John Wryght   Vicar of Burnham
Robert White   Churchwarden
The marke of James MacKinson   Churchwarden
(D/A/Gt/2/6/2)

24. CAVERSFIELD 1630

November 3 1630.

A Terrier of the house, Glebe landes, and profitts belongeinge to the Vicaredge of Casefield in the County of Bucks.

Imprimis A Vicaredge howse containeinge three bayes of buildinge devided into Five roomes.

Item one Close adioyneinge to the howse on the North side beinge in quantity about a Roode of land.

Item one parcell of Meadow ground lyeinge in the common field of Stretton Audley beinge in quantitye about one Roode of lande.

Item the Tithes great and smale of Three yard landes and a half lying in the Common fields of Stretton Audley.

Richard Grimes   Vicar

Nicholas Andrewes   his marke   Churchwarden
(D/A/Gt/2/9/1)

25. CHALFONT ST. GILES 1607

Lincoln diocese Buck Chalfont St. *Egidij Rectoria*.
October 10 1607 Anno Regni Domini Regis Jacobi dei gratia Anglie Francie et Hibernie etc. quinto et Scotie 41.

A Survey or Terrier of all the possessions...

Homestall.

Imprimis the Homstall of the parsonage abutting uppon the town street north east and uppon the wast of the Lord south and west and uppon the Land of the Lord northwest and conteyneth about two acres and a half.

Item the parsonage or homestall abovesayd hath within the sayd

Bounds or lymits an ould orchard; and on other new orchard planted by Rychard Smyth the now parson and Incombent – two gardens a parcell of pastur of 3 Rods a yard for Cattell and a small Court.

The church yard half an acre.

Edefices.

The parsonage House consisteth of seaven Larg bayes and covered with Tyle all the sayd bayes being lofted or chambered over (except the Hall) and ar borded and ther ar two other bayes newly buylded this yeare by the now incumbent for a brewhouse and other necessary romes which are not chambered but ar covered with tyle: they sayd hous hath two parlors a hall Kitchin and 7 chambers a buttery a seller Larders milkhouse all tyled and ther is a gatehouse with a loft covered with Tyle.

Item one barne consistinge of 7 bayes besides the thrashing Romes covered with Tyle one other haybarn and stable conteyning about V bayis covered with thatch: ther is a cart house and a cow house conteyning V bayes latly buylded by the sayd Incombent a hous for poultry and for hoggs buylded by the sayd Incumbent.

Arrable lands and woods.

Ther are V closes and two small copes or springgs, Called by the name of the Parsons feylds conteyning about 40 acres all in tyllage bounding uppon out feyld and Beconfeld way ther is one litle close Lying Betwene a common called Mammes and an other comon called Bramles conteyning 1 acre arrable Ther is a peec of arrable in the sayd feyld or common called bramles conteyning half an acre a small peec of arrable about a Rood of Willis Woolmans land betwixt the sayd close and the sayd half acre. Ther are V peeces of arrable in a common called the oute feyld 4 of them do butt uppon the horsway to Uxbridge and the other peec being half an acre abutteth upon [blank].

Meadow.

Ther is half an acre of meadow in a mead called litl Smalde mead inclosed in the occupation of John Dunton who hath 3 half acres in the sayd Meadow. Ther is 3 Roods of meadow in oulde meade half an acre in the lots called church fleets and a Rood in [...] at ould mead gate.

Richard Smyth   Rector.

Arthur [...]   Churchwardens
Ralph [...]

Thomas [...]   Sidman
(D/A/Gt/2/10/1)

26. CHALFONT ST. GILES 1639

A Terrier of the Parsonage of Chalfont St. Giles and the Glebelands thereunto belonginge in execution of [...] 87th Canon made by us whose names are hereunder written the 10th day of July 1639.

Imprimis the homestall of the Parsonage abuttinge uppon the Towne street Northeast and uppon the Waste of the Lord south and West the land of the Lord Northwest and conteyneth about two acres and a halfe.

Item the Parsonage or homestall abovesayde hath [...] sayd bounds or lymmitts one ould orchard and one other new orcharde two gardens one parcell of pasture of 3 roodes a yarde [...] cattle and ij small courts the Churchyarde halfe an acre.

The parsonage house consisteth of seaven bayes all covered with Tyles all the sayde bayes beinge Lofted or Chambered over and are boarded *vizt.* two parlors one Hall one Kitchin a buttry a Cellar larder Milkehouse.

Item 2 small bayes used for a brewhouse and one little house for a wood house.

Item one barne Tyled consistinge of ij bayes besydes the Thrashinge roomes one other hay barne and stable conteyning about five baies thatched one Cartehouse and Cowe house of five bayes.

Item one howse consisting of one bay with a chamber over it.

Item Five closes and two small coppies or springs called by the name of the parsons feilds conteyninge about 44 acres all in tillage bounding uppon out feild and Beckon Feild way.

Item one little close lyeing betweene a [...] called Mames and another common called Brambles conteyninge one acre arable.

Item there is a peece of arable in the sayd Common called Brambles conteyninge halfe an acre.

Item 5 peeces of Arable in a Common called the outfeild 4 of them do abutt uppon the horse way to Uxbridge and the other peece being halfe an acre abutted uppon John Salters land North and uppon the lands belonginge [...] farme called Balstrood south.

Item halfe an acre of Meadow in a Meadow called little Smalder meade.

Item 3 roods of Meadow in ould meade *vizt.* halfe an acre in the Lotts called Church fleet and a rood in the lotts at ould Mead gate next unto Outfeild.

Tho: Valentine   Rector de Chalfont *predict'*
Ralph   [...]

Thomas Barton   Churchwardens
(D/A/Gt/2/10/2)

27. CHALFONT ST. PETER 1607

The xvjth day of September 1607.

A True and perfect Terrar of all gleabes and possessions...

Homestall.

The homestall or scite of the vicarige scituate and lyinge by the river there on the East part of the fielde called the Churche feild on the West and also moundinge upon the Church yard South and a litle meadowe of Sir Henry Drury now in the tenure of John Trybyard upon part of the fielde called the church filde on the North part, within the saide boundes are contayned by estimation ij Acres and a halfe of pasture ground with some fruit trees there upon and also one litle garden ioyninge to the Church yard Contayning by estimation iiij poles and one litle hemp plot on the west side of the house Contayninge by estimation vj poles.

Edifices.

The vicarige house Consistinge of five bayes built with timber and Covered with tiles disposed into viij roomes, a hall, a kichin, a parlour, ij Chambers, which iij roomes last mentioned are lofted over and are iij severall Chambers above.

Item a longe lowe house ioyninge to the Dwellinge house consistinge of iij smale bayes covered with tiles.

Item a barne Consistinge of iij bayes covered with tiles also.

Item a house Consistinge of iiij bayes *viz.* a stable a Cowehouse and a haye house, these are theched.

Dewlande fielde.

Item vj peces in a Common fielde called Dewland *viz.* one peece lyinge by a Close of Sir Henry Drury on the South part and his lande on the Northe part Butting upon the River on the West part and towardes the Kinges High Waye on the East part.

Item one other peece lyinge by the Kinges high waye on the East part and the land of Thomas Winckfielde on the West part Buttinge upon the lands of the saide Thomas Winckfielde on the North part, and the land of Sir Henry Drury on the South part.

Item one other peece lyinge betweene the land of Sir Henry Drury on the West and East parts butting upon his land North and South also.

Item one other peece lyinge by the land of Sir Henry Drury on the East part and the land of one Widow Butterfielde on the West part buttinge upon the River on the South part and a meadowe Called olde Meade on the North part.

Item one other peece lyinge betweene the land of Raphe Downers on the West part and the land of one Widowe Butterfielde on the East part buttinge upon the River on the South part and the olde mead on the North part.

Item one other peece lyinge betweene the land of Sir Henry Drury on the East and West parts, buttinge upon his land on the North and South also all which vj peeces contayninge by estimation ij Acres and a halfe.

Item five Closes called the vicars Close Downes contayning by estimation xxxiij Acres lyinge betweene a fielde called owl fielde on the North part, and a fielde called the common Downes on the South part, buttinge uponm a fielde called the Church fielde on the East part and upon the land of Sir Henry Drury and the Kinges high waye.

Olde meade.

Item one Roode of meadowe grounde lyinge in a Common Mead Called the olde mead which roode [...] hath out of an Acre called the lake and is to have his part by the Cock.

Item iij Closes lyinge together Contayninge by estimation xiiij Acres commonly called Goulde hill Closes buttinge upon the Kinges high way on the East part, and the land of Sir Henry Drury on the West lyinge by the land of Sir Henry Drury on the South part and priest grove, and a fielde called Olde fielde common on the North part.

Item iiij peeces in a fielde Called common Downes *viz.* one peece lyinge betweene the land of Sir Henry Drury on the East and West parts buttinge upon the vicars Downes on the North, and the land of Sir Henry Drury on the South part.

Item one other peece lyinge betweene the land of Sir Henry Drury on the North and South parts buttinge upon the land of Sir Henry Drury on the West part vicars Downes on the East part.

Item one other peece lyinge betweene the land of Sir Henry Drury on the South and North parts buttinge upon the land of Sir Henry Drury on the East part, and the vicars Downes on the west part.

Item one other peece lyinge betweene the land of Sir Henry Drury on the East and West parts buttinge upon the land of Sir Henry Drury on the North and South parts.

Which iiij peces Contayne by estymation iij Acres Moreover to this vicarige of Chalfont St. Peters in the countie of Bucks aforesaide there belongeth a smale Manor called the Vicarig manor of Chalfont St. Peters, in Chalfont St. Peters aforesaid Whereunto is incident a Court Baron And the same manor Consisteth Cheefly *viz.* In rent received of freeholders *per annum* xijd. In Rent received og Certayne Copiholders therein they haveinge estate of inheritance in their severall copyholdes yearly *per annum* xvj s.

Summa totalis redditus   xvij s.
Summa pastura   ij Acres and a halfe.
Summa prati one Roode   *Summa arabilis*   51 Acres and a halfe.

Robert Duck   Inhabitants there
Thomas Winckford
Robert Buckfield

For stockes implements tenements or any other thinge inquirable by the Canon (and not herein before intimated and expressed there is nothing belonging to this vicarige as farre as we knowe or can learne.

Raph Winckefielde   Churchwarden
Edmund Baldwyn
Robert Butterfield   Sydemen
Richard Whitchurch

(D/A/Gt/2/11/1)

28. CHEARSLEY 1639

October the 2th 1639.

A Terar of the Church Landes and of the [...] house which we finde in Chearsley.

Glebe lande.

[...] we have a Churchouse and a little back yard ioyninge unto it the Backside of James Cox adioyninge unto it on the North and the Common Streete on the Southe.

Alsoe there is one Roode of Ley Grounde in the East Fielde the Meadowe of Thomas Hearne lyinge on the East syde.

Alsoe there is in the same Fielde one halfe acre of arrable land Thomas Hearne one the East syde and Mrs Brightwell on the West syde.

Alsoe there is in the same Fielde by Tan Springe a Plott of Ley Ground conteyninge by estimation halfe an Acre Richard Church on the Northsyde and James Cox on the south syde.

Alsoe in the Berrie Fielde we have one Plott of Meadowe Grounde conteyninge by estimation three Roodes the Meadow of Sir Robert Dormer lyinge one the southsyde alsoe we have one acre of Leyground in the same Field Sir Robert Dormer land lyinge one both sydes we have in the same Field alsoe halfe an acre of arrable Land adioyninge to the land of Richard Oliver East and of Sir Robert Dormer West.

Alsoe there is one Baulke in the West Field by hankey bridge conteyninge halfe a Roode Thomas Heborne on the west; alsoe there is one Plott of leyground in the same Field conteyninge halfe a Roode Puttney furlonge abuttinge upon it.

Alsoe there is in the same field one Roode of leygrounde John Parker haveinge a Meadow on the west syde.

Alsoe there is one halfe Acre of arable ground at Hollowmoore in the same Fielde John Parker on the Northsyde.

Jonas Rennols   Churchwardens
John Eustair

(D/A/Gt/3/1/1)

29. CHEDDINGTON 1639

June the 11th day *Anno Domini* 1639. A True Terrier of all the dwelling houses outhouses arrable landes, Rents and meadows belonging to the parsonage of Chedington in the County of Bucks as followeth.

Inprimis in the dwelling house are Nine roomes belowe, and either of them lofted over and the whole roof thereof tyled.

Item one wheate barne of Four baies, thatched.

Item one barley barne of Foure baies, and Two Killis, thatched.

Item one Beane Barne of Three baies thatched.

Item one Hay Barne with stables, and a Cowe house and hogshed Consisting in all of Five baies and one Killis.

Item one Dovehouse.

Item one orchard.

Item one Close called Dovehouse Close butting on the kings high way Mr Combes East.

Item Nine leas butting on the kings high way Martin Colledge land on the West.

Meadowe grounde.

Item, one acre in Astmeade in the lang Furlonge Samuel Fountayne on the North.

Item one Roode in the same Furlonge, Roberte Fountayne on the South.

Item, one other acre in the same Furlonge Mr Combes on the South and Mr Thomas Moule on the North.

Item, one Roode in Astmeade in the short Furlonge Martin Colledge land on the East.

Item, one acre in the same Furlonge Mr Combes on the East.

Item one other acre in the same Furlonge, Mr Combes on the East and Martin Colledge land on the West.

Item, in Smith meade one acre William Kympton on the South.

Item in the same Furlonge three Roodes, John Howes on the North.

Item one acre, and Three roodes in the Moore, by lot.

Arrable groundes.

Item in the Downe Fielde, above the Towne, one halfe acre, Widdow Worster on the North.

Item one other halfe acre in the same Furlonge, William Seare on the East.

Item, one other halfe Acre in the same Furlong, William Seare on the East.

Item Two Roodes in the same Furlonge the highway on the South.

Item in the Furlong Called the Tee.

Item, Two halfe Acres, the Towne land on the North, and the highway on the South.

Item, in the Furlonge Called Overstreate, one acre, John Sawel on the South.

Item one other acre in the same Furlonge, William Seare on the South.

Item one halfe Acre, Widdow Worster North.

Item, in the Furlonge Called Languege one acre, Martin Colledge land on the West.

Item, in the Furlonge Called the Hanging, one Acre, Martin Colledge land on the West.

Item, in the Furlonge Called the South downe linces one acre, Nicholas Seare on the East.

Item in the Furlong butting into Low Crofte, one Acre, John Howes on the West.

Item in the Furlonge Called the Harehole, one Acre, Martin Colledge land on the North.

One Acre more in the same Furlonge, William Seare on the North.

Item in the Furlong Called Gurmon, Three halfe Acres, Mr Combes on the South.

Item, in the Furlong under the Moore, one Acre Mr Combes on the South.

Butting into the Milleway, one Acre Daniel Houghton on the East.

Item in the same Furlong one Acre more, Mr Combes on the West.

Item, one halfe acre more, Barnard Fountayne on the East.

Item in the Furlong called Bangore, one Acre, Martin Colledge land on the West.

Item one halfe Acre butting into Astecrofte way John Howes on the South.

Item, one halfe acre butting into Alisburie way John Sawel on the East.

Item, in the Furlong Called Longe Catsbraine, one halfe Acre betweene the linces, Thomas Fountayne on the North.

Item, one Acre more, Martin Colledge land on the North.

In the Furlong Called Short Catsbraine, one halfe Acre, Widdowe Worster on the North.

South Field.

Item, one Acre butting upon Lowe Crofte, John Seabrooke on the East.

Item, one other Acre butting uppon Lowcrofte, William Seare on the West.

Item, in the Furlong Called Walkhamstead, one Acre, John Seabrooke on the West.

West Field.

Item, in the Furlong butting on the highway, one halfe Acre, Mr Combes on the South.

Item one halfe Acre, Thomas Fountayne on the South.

Item one Acre more Mr Combes on the South.

Item, one Acre more, Thomas Fountayne on the south.

Item, one Acre more John Howes on the South.

Item one Acre more, the Common balke lying on the North.

Item, in the Furlonge Called the Furlong above Smithmeade, one Acre Martin Colledge on the North.

Item Two Acres more, Mr Combes on the North and William Payne on the South.

Item, in a Furlong Called Putnam, one Acre, Thomas Fountayne on the East.

Item one halfe Acre in the same Furlong, Thomas Monke on the East.

Item in a Furlong Called Long Crofte end Five halfe Acres next Woodway, Mr Combes on the West.

Item one Acre more in the same Furlonge, Mr Combes on the West.

Item, one Acre more, Widdowe Seare on the West.

Item, in the Furlonge butting into the Westemeade, one Roode, Mr Combes on the East.

Item one Acre more Martin Colledge land West.

Item, in a Furlonge Called Lang-furlong, one Acre, Thomas Fountayne on the East.

Item, one halfe Acre, Widdowe Worster on the West.

Item, one Acre in the same Furlong, Mr Combes on the West.

In Stichdole, one halfe acre Thomas Stevens on the East.

Item, in the Furlong Called the Hale, one Acre Thomas Seabrooke on the North.

Item one halfe Acre Sir Thomas Hide on the South.

Item in the short furlonge one Acre John Howes on the East.

Item one acre more, Mr Combes on the West.

Item, one Acre more Mr Combes East.

Item, in the Furlonge Called the Furlong butting into the Hale, one Acre, Daniel Houghton on the East.

Item, one Acre more, Mr Combes on the East.

Item, one halfe acre in the same Furlonge Daniel Houghton, East.

Item, Three halfe Acres in the same Furlonge, Daniel Houghton, West.

Item, in the Furlonge Called the Middle Furlonge, one Acre, Daniel Houghton on the East.

Item, in a Furlonge Called Seaven Acres, one halfe Acre, Widdowe Seare on the North.

Item in Pullacre, one Acre, Nicholas Seare on the South.

North Field.

Item, in the Furlonge Called the Short Brach butting into the Highway, one acre Martin Colledge land on the South.

Item one Acre more, Martin Colledge land North.

Item, in the Furlong Called the Greenway Furlong, one acre, John Howes, East.

Item, one halfe Acre more Widdowe Worster on the West.

Item, in the Furlonge Called Short Latchmore one acre, Mr Combes West.

Item, one halfe Acre in the same Furlonge Widdow Worster on the West.

Item, one halfe Acre more, Widdowe Worster on the West.

Item one Roode John Howes on the west.

Item one head land on the same Furlong, Widdow Worster, West.

Item in the Furlonge called Meereway Furlonge, one Acre, Widdow Worster, West.

Item Two acres more in the same Furlong, Thomas Stevens West, and Widdowe Seare East.

Item in the Furlonge Called Short Westhill one Acre, Mr Combes North.

In the Furlonge Called Short Furlong, one halfe Acre, Martin Colledge land South.

Item, one halfe acre more Widdowe Worster on the North.

Item, one acre more, Mr Combes North.

In the Furlonge Called, above Astmeade, one Acre Thomas Stondley South.

Item, in the same Furlonge one Acre more, Mr Combes, South.

Item one halfe Acre more, William Payne South.

In the Furlonge Called Weede Furlonge, Item one Acre Thomas Stondely North.

Item one halfe acre more, John Howes South.

In a Furlonge Called Longe Annat, one Acre, Thomas Stondley East.

Item, one halfe acre more, John Howes on the East.

In the Furlonge Called short Annat, one acre, Mr Combes on the East.

In a Furlonge Called the Weere, one Acre, Thomas Stondley on the North.

Item in a Furlonge Called Horton townes end, one halfe Acre Mr Combes on the South.

Item Two acres more in the same furlonge, Mr Combes on the North, and Thomas Fountaine on the South.

Item, in a Furlong Called Ghosthill one halfe Acre, Thomas Fen on the North.

Item one acre more, Isaac Gurney on the North.

Item one Acre more, Edward Worster on the North.

Item one Acre more, Widdowe Fountayne on the North.

Item in a Furlong Called Horches Furlong, one Acre Mr Combes on the East.

Item one Acre more, Widdow Seare on the East.

Item in a Furlong Called Frogwell, one acre William Payne on the East.

Item in a Furlong Called Hathorne bush, one Acre, William Fountayne on the South.

John Birde   Rector

William Fountayne   Churchwardens
John Howes
(D/A/Gt/3/2/1)

30. CHENIES 1607

October 23 Anno Domini 1607 Annoque Regni Domini Regis Jacobi dei gratia 5 et Quadragissimo primo.

A Survey or Terrour of all the possessions belonging to the rectory of Chynis made and takin by the view perambulation and estimate of the minister Churchwardens and Sides men and other inhabitants there whose names are subscribed etc.

Imprimis the homestall or scite of the parsonage from the east end of the Churchyard downe towardes the towne wood and from the north syd of the Churchyard downe to my Lord of Bedfords banqueetinge house conteyneth in all 2 acres.

Home stall.

Item within the sayd bounds are conteyned, one gardin and orchyard empalled, conteyninge some fowre and twenty pole And within the sayd bounds are two little plotts of grownd conteyneing one acre and three roods.

Edifices.

Item, the parsonage house consisting of fowre bayes build of tymber and covered with tyles beeing chambered and boarded being two storyes high, is disposed into 9 roomes vidilicit a Kichin a milkhouse a hall, a parlour, a buttry and fowre lodgeing Chambers there being adioyned to the end of the Buttrye a litle closet with a study over it.

Item ther is an outward house of 3 bayes built of tymber and covered with tyles disposed into five roomes videlicit an outward Kicthin a milkhouse and a stable over the stable there is a loft and so is there over the milkhouse at the end of which there is an howell for the use of the Cattle.

Item ther is a low barne of six bayes, bounded one the syde and covered with thecth.

Arable.

Item one Arable field of nyne acres called by the name of bottome field abutting one the part of my Lord of Bedford westward and one the ground of Francis Butterfeld westward and one the ground of Lancelot Row southward.

Item another feild by it called by the name of litle feild abutting westward one the park, and northward one the ground of John Barfite conteyning 5 acres.

Item another feild called high feild abutting eastward and Southward one Frauncis Butterfeilds ground, and northward one the ground of John Barefoot and westward one the former litle parsonage feild conteyning in estimation 7 acres all which arable land make, 21 acres.

Medow.

Item one Meddow conteyneing seaven acres abutting westward and southward one the ground of my Lord of Bedford and north one the high way from Chynis to Lattmers conteyning 7 acres.

Quitrent.

Item there belongeth to the sayd parsonage a quittrent of three litle houses or tenements, whereof 2 are now in the tenure of Launcelot Wells and the third in the tenure of James Grimsdell; for every wherof the incumbent is to have yeerely 8d. *summa* 2s.

Composition.

There is also an old composition for certeyne acres of land that were late of the parsonage lands into the new park, for which the incumbent receaveth yeerely fower nobles and is likewise to have his dyet at the Stewards table when there is an house kept there.

Per me   Peter Allibond   Rector

Francis Dell   James Grimsdalle   William Porthesse

Churchwardens

Walter Dolt   Launcelot Rowe   Jhon Dell

(D/A/Gt/3/3/1)

31. CHESHAM LEICESTER 1639

A Terrier of the house and Lands belonging to the Vicaridge of Chesham Leycester in the County of Bucks taken in the yeare 1639.

Imprimis The dwelling house; wherein are thesse Roomes following

1. An Entry with glasse windowes, to the halle
2. The Halle, with a Chymny
3. The Parlour, with a Chymny

4. The Kitchin with a Chymny
5. An entry to the Kitchin
6. A Buttry
7. A little Closett by the Buttry

The upper Roomes are as followeth
1. Over the entry a little Chamber
2. A chamber over the halle, with a Chymney
3. A chamber over the Parlour, with a Chymny
4. A Chamber over the Kitchin, with Chymny
5. A Chamber over the Buttry
6. A garret over the Kitchin Chamber
7. A little Closett in the Kitchin Chamber

The out houses as followeth
1. A barne of 3 bayes tiled
2. An outward Kitchin with a Chymny, Oven and well in it
3. A stable by it pitched with stone

The ground it stands upon about one Acre.

Adam Langley   Vicar

(D/A/Gt/3/4/1)

32. CHESHAM WOBURN 1639

A Terrier of the Vicaridge of Chesham Woborne Com' Buck' taken the 2 day of October *Anno Domini* 1639 by the Vicar of Chesham Woborne and the churchwardens of Chesham.

Inprimis There belongeth to the said Vicaridge, almost one acre of ground on which there is a Vicaridge house with five lower roomes and five upper roomes And also a Barne Stable cow-house and house of office And in which parcell of ground there is a garden and an orchard.

Moreover there belonge unto the said Vicaridge The one Medirtie of the alterage and of the Minute tithes in Chesham aforesaid.

In witnesse where of wee have Subscribed our hands the day and yeare above-written.

Elkanah Gladman   Vicar *de*

Richard Botterfield   Churchwardens
Bernard Breed

(D/A/Gt/3/4/2)

33. CHETWODE 1639

Chitwood The one and Twentyeth day of November 1639

We the minister and Churchwardenes of Chitwood do certifie under our handes That Mr Thomas Riplie Gent is the Impropriator of Chitwood and the impropriation is worth by the yeare Forty three poundes five shillings aighte pence in Chitwood and Mr Phillip Stockes Serveth the Cure in Chitwood and Barton and hath of Mr Thomas Ripley Twenty powndes a yeare for servinge them he beinge Impropriator of bothe the twones and there is now house For the minister to Dwell in neither at Chitwood nor Barton as For any other lande that belongeth to the Impropriation we knowe not and here is as much as wee can certifie.

Philip Stokes   Minister

Signum   Thomas Hawkin
Signum   Tho Bullucke
(D/A/Gt/3/6/1)

34. CHILTON 1639

Chilton this 3 of December 1639.

These are to certifie to the Courte of Alesbury that wee whose names are heare under written haveinge made Diligent Search and enquiry after any parcell of Glibe land which doe or maye be longe to the Church of Chilton Can yet find no discoverye of anye, we supose your owne Rolles can best satisfie.

And so subscribe   Will Squire   Curate
                            his wages   £30

William White   Churchwardens
John Sanders
(D/A/Gt/3/8/1)

35. CHOLESBURY 1639

A Note of the glebe land and Parsonadg hous of Choulsbury in quantitie.

The Parsonadg house Consisteth of two bayes
Item the Parsonadg barne Consisteth of two bayes

Item the Glebeland consisteth of twa acres and an halfe
Item the Church-yearde in *quantitate pariochiae competente*
Item a grove consisting of foure acres by estimation.

Robert Ayre   Church Wardens
Thomas Bachelor

(D/A/Gt/3/9/1)

36. CUBLINGTON 1607

October 26 Anno Domini 1607 Annoque Regni Domini Regis Jacobi Dei gratia Anglia Fraunciae et Hiberniae Regis fidei Defensoris quinto et Scotiae Quadragessimo.

A Survey or Terrour of all the possessions...

Homestall.

Inprimis the Homestall or Scite of the Parsonage scituate and lying between the New Closes on the East and the Kings heigh way on the west and Thomas Lees close on the North and Frauncis Webbes close on the south and contaynes by estimation 3 Acres.

Item within the said bounds are contained one gardin impailed by estimacon halfe a Roode and one Orchard by estimacon a Roode, also three litle closes adioyning to the Orchard contayning by estimacon one acre and a halfe.

Edifices.

Item the Parsonage howse consisting of 4 baies built of wood and with tyle, all being Chambered over and boarded, and the whole buylding contrived in 5 stories and disposed into 10 roomes *viz.* the Hall with A chamber over hit, the Parlour with A Chamber over hit Two nether Chambers with two chambers over them and a Kytchin with A Chamber over hit.

Item one deary howse, two barnes One Stable, One Cow howse: and One Hey howse all consisting of 9 baies buylt of wood and covered with Thatche.

Pasture.

Item one Quadrangular Close called the old Churchyard lying in the midst of A ground called the Hill ground of the possessions of George Leige of Burcott and containes 1 acre.

Meadowe.

Item 6 acres of Meadowe Lying in the Mead field, and one Plott of Meddow abutting uppon Lydcott brooke John Cheny on the north, Richard Bolde on the south, and containes one acre and A Roode One Plott of Meddow lying in Holcombe Hole and containes half an acre.

Summa Pre' 7 acres 3 Roodes.

Arable.

Item one acre of arable lying together in Hogge Leas: John Skelton North John Harle south, one acre lying in brach Thomas Moore north, John Cheny south.

One acre lying in Oate Lande John Cheny north, Richard Broughton south, one acre in Litle Hill William Heyward East John Skelton west, one acre in the lower end of litle Hill John Skelton East, Sir William Willoughby west one acre in Burnwell John Moore East, Frauncis Webb west one acre in Nusledge Richard Broughton north John Chenye south, one acre in Boarn bushe; brooke forlonng north, John Wells south; one acre in brooke furlonng Robert Fincher East, John Harle West, one acre more in brooke furlonng Mr Lee East, Sir William Willoughbye west, one acre called by the name of Butlers acre John Skelton East, John Hart West, one acre in North end William Greene East John Cheny west, two Leas abuting uppon Lydcott bridge, Richard Broughton north, William Heyward south.

Item one acre in Mill Hill Jerom Canfield north Richard Broughton south, one acre called brier acre Thomas Moore East John Thornton west, one acre abutting uppon Nayle Hill end Thomas Moore East, John Thornton west, one acre in steapen Hill John Moore East, Thomas Moore west, one acre in Stone Hades Richard Broughton East, John Hart west, one acre in Vincent Hill Sir William Willoughbye East Thomas Fenn west, one acre in Vincent Corner Thomas Moore North John Moore south; one acre in brooke furlonng John Cheny north Richard Broughton south.

Item one acre in Redmore John Chenye East Thomas Moore west, one acre in Weald Leas furlonng John Hart East gooseaton West, one acre in gooseaten Sir William Willoughbye north John Hart south one acre in Deane furlonng John Hart west William Broughton west, one acre in Pale forlonng John Hart East Richard Jeffes west one acre in New lane end abutting uppon the heigh way John Skelton North, Thomas Moore south:

Item 7 Leas abutting uppon nether Weald gate Richard Bold East John Skelton west.

Item one acre in Deane furlonng John Chenye East, John Moore west, one acre in Fithum Richard Bold East John Moore West. one acre in Codfurlonng John Moore East, William Broughton west, one acre in Gallow furlonnge Richard Bold north Walter Goreing south: one acre in Holcomb hole Thomas Pollen East Thomas Moore west; one Headland and his fellowe in Cod furlonng John Hart East Holcomb furlonng west, one acre in water furrowes Frauncis Webb East, John Hart west.

Item 4 Leas in Penn furlonng John Thornton north west, Sir William Willoughbye South East.

Summa arabilis 33 acres.

Out tythes.

Item the Messuage or Tenement of John Sear of the Cookes within the parishe of Cheddington is liable to the Parsonage of Cublington for payment of all manner of Tythes by Rate accrewing and growing in or uppon the same, nor ever were ther any tythes Detayned so far as we know, saving one close of arable of the said John Sears contayning some 3 acres which is nowe in question betwene Barnard Fountine of Chedington and the Rectorie of Cublington.

Item 66 acres of arabell and 6 acres of meddowe lying in the common fieldes of Chedington are aliable to the Rectorie of Cublington for payment of all such Tythes (payable by custome) growing in and uppon the same.

For stockes, Implements, Tenements or any other thing inquirable by the Canon (and not herein before intimated and expressed) there is nothing belonging to this Rectorie as far as we knowe or can learne.

Thomas Breamer   Rector *ibidem*

John Skelton   Churchwardens
Richard Bolde
Frauncis Webbe
Thomas Broughton   *signum*

(D/A/Gt/3/15/1)

37. DATCHET 1607

September 24 Anno Domini 1607 Annoque Regni Domini Regis Jacobi dei gratia etc. Anglie 5 et Scotie Quadragesimo primo.

A Surveigh or Terrour of all the possessions...

Homestall.

Inprimis the Homestall or Scite of the vicaredge scituate and lying betwene the house and land of Richard Mascall of Datchett aforesaid West and the house of William Phillipps East, and is abbutting uppon the Church there South: with in all which said bounds is One Orchard belonging to the said Vicaredg abbutting uppon the house North and Lyeth betweene the Parsonadge house of Datchett aforesaid weste and the house of William Phillips aforesaid East contayning by estimacon One Acre.

Edifices.

Item the vicaredg house consisting of 5 baies built all of Timber and Couered with Tile being chambered over and boarded three loafts and the whole building contrived into two stories high and disposed all into Eleven smale Roomes *vizt.* the Hall two Parlours 3 Chambers one Buttery Larder with two Chambers over and a Kitchin.

Item one Outroome consisting of two baies one storie high built all with Timber and covered with Tile.

Touching Gleablands pasture Meadow Arrable or any other Tithes there is none belonginge to the vicaredge but A pencon of Eleauen pounds paid by the Deane and Prebends of Windsour and one yerely Anuitye of two shillings sixe pence by Composition Due to the said Vicar and Vicaredge.

For Stockes Implements Tenements or any other thing inquirable by the Canon (and not herein before intimated and expressed) there is nothing belonging to this vicaredg as farr as we knowe or can learne.

per me   Johannes Foster   Vicar *de* Datchett

Richard Hanbery
Morrys Hale
John Reed
John Hale
John Dugglas   Churchwardens
John Nashe
William Phillipes   Sidesmen
(D/A/Gt/3/17/1)

38. DATCHET 1639

July 29th 1639.

A true terrar of the viccaridge house and buildings there and the land to it belonginge *vizt.*

One dwellinge howsse conteineinge three baye of building disposed into a Kitchin a hall and a parlour and three Chambers over them all tyled and walled with lath and loame.

Item one Stable conteineinge a baye of buildinge and a litle roome adioyneinge to it conteyninge halfe a baye tyled and walled with lath and loame.

Item one Orchard and garden plott conteyninge an acre or thereabouts and all these premisses are lett per annum att V li.

Ed Stampe   Vic'

Fra Weast   his marke   Churchwardens
Humfry Nipping
(D/A/Gt/3/17/2)

39. DENHAM 1639

Anno 1639 Jun 12.

A terrier of [...] buildings and lands belonginge to the Rectory and parsonage of the parish of Denham in County of Bucks.

In the dwellinge house a haule a parlor a kichin a seller a pantre a milkhouse applehouse henhouse backhouse kinehouse in the yard gathouse, kowhouse, stable, three barnes one of six bayes, one of four, one of two in good and sufficient reparations.

Lands.

1. *Inprimis* one field of pasture called preists close by estimation five acres: abuttinge one the River one the south and high way one north.

2. Item three litle Crofts with a yard and Orchard about four acres abuttinge in like manner.

3. Item two meddowes seven acres abutting in like manner.

4. Item one pasture close four acres: and a more for pasture fourteene acres abutt: so also.

5. Item a field of Arrable land great sccrcs 12 acres abuttinge one highway to Chesham.

6. Another of Arrable land lesser seers by it 9 Acres.

7. A field of Arrable land called Hudgdens being seven acres and field called fivelands 2 acres dim: nere highway to Uxbridge.

8. Item one halfe acre in a common field called fivelands.

Thomas Vincent   Rector *ibidem*

John Hamptons   mark   Churchwardens
Daniell Cranwell   mark
(D/A/Gt/3/18/1)

40. DINTON 1607

Vicesimo primo die mensis Septembris Anno Domoni 1607.

A Terrior of the Vicardige howses and lands of Dyneton in the Deanery of Wendover.

Inprimis the Meese or Mansion howse of the sayde vicaridge contayneth on hale of two bayes lofted over.

Item one Kittchine of twooe bayes.

Item one other roome called the ncther house contayninge three bayes.

Item a butterie of one bay.

Item one barne contayninge three bayes and a killys.

Item a stable of one bay.

Moreover belongynge to the sayde vicaridge a fore yarde with a ponde therin contayninge bie estimation one acre of ground.

Item an Orchard contayninge by estimation one roode of grownd.

Item in the feelde on acre of grounde in a furlonge called the hale furlonge butting uppon Tame waie north.

Item one land in a furlong called Wyndmill hill furlonge buttinge uppon Tame Way Sowth.

Item one land lyinge in a furlonge called clay butts butting uppon Tame way sowth.

Item one acre in a furlonge buttinge uppon Goosy Way East commonlie called Vicars Pittes.

Item one lande lyinge in a furlonge called Goosie furlong buttinge uppon Goosy Way Sowthe Weaste.

Item one land lying in a furlonge called hange lands.

By me Edmund Poulter   Viccor of Dynton

Edmund Robyns   mark

William Moore
John Fulkes   mark

John Lawrance   Churchwardens
Anthony Goddyn
(D/A/Gt/3/19/1)

41. DORTON 1639

A true Terrier of Dorton   1639.

Vicaridge.

Vicaridge house we have none.

Glebe lands we have none nor Church land. Sir Robert Dormer is the Farmer.

The Parsonage is *impropriat'*.

The Curate hath 10 li per annum from Christ Church College in Oxon.

Robert Rogers   Curate

Jacob Watson   Churchwarden

(D/A/Gt/3/21/1)

42. DRAYTON BEAUCHAMP 1607

Octobris 27 Anno Domini 1607 Annoque Regni Domini Regis Jacobi Dei gratia 5 et 41.

A Survey or Terrour of al the possessions...

Homestall.

Inprimis The homestall or scite of the parsonage scituate and lying betweene the Comon Wicke or towne greene on the Eastsid of the churche lane on the west and abutting upon a common lane or highway on the north, and upon the parsonage piece on the south, and containes by estimation 2 acres.

Item within the said Bounds are contained one little garden inclosed partly with the parsonage house and partly with wound walls about 3 poles long but not so broade: also a dovehouse tiled, on the westside of the house.

Edifices.

Item the parsonage house consisting of thirteen bayes (wherof eleven bee very small ones) covered all with tile excepte the wellhouse end wherof 9 are chambred or lofted over and boarded and the whole building disposed into 15 roomes *viz*; the hall, the parlour, a lower chamber and a buttery and three chambers anonswerable to them above, the Kitchen, milkhouse ashehouse and welhouse, with 4 lofts over parte of them: builte partly with raggestone from the foundation partly from the foundation as al above the wall plates with wound walls.

Item a barne of 8 bayes with a killice for a stable all thatched.

Meadow.

Item in a lott meade called draitonmeade containing in all 44 acres there are 6 acres of glebe belonging to the parsonage *viz* in eche quarter of the meadowe divided into 4 partes one acre and an halfe, in this sorte: the whole acre in the lott called, the Crosse, in eche quarter, and a yard or 4th part of an acre in every lott called the wheele in eche quarter: and a yard likewise in eche quarter in the lott called the weedehooke.

Summa pratorum   6 acres.

Arable.

Item, a piece of 4 acres call'ed the parsonage piece bounded by newbarne close on the Easte, the churchlane, churchyard and a picked piece of the lord of Draiton on the west, and the homestall of the parsonage on the north, and an highway on the south.

In Golfeild.

Item, one halfacre in Draiton Golfiede abutting north on Egleway and south on John Mallards hedland: Thomas Plummer lying on the Easte and John Dracott on the west.

Item an whole acre lying together in the same furlong abutting as the nexte before: Thomas Plummer lying on the west, and Thomas Eliot on the Easte.

Item one halfe acre abutting Eastward into the Shyreway, and west into an head-acre of Thomas Plumer having Eglenway on the north and William Gregory on the South.

Item, another halfacre in the same furlong, abutting as the next before, William Gregory lying on both sides.

Item an halfacre in the same fielde abutting north on William Gregoryes hedland, and Southward, on Robert Bates hedland: William Gregory lying on both sides.

In Foxhedge feilde.

Item an halfacre lying in Foxhedgefielde, abutting westward into woodway and Easte into Londonway: William Gregory lying on the north, and Thomas Arniat on the South.

Item an halfacre in the same furlong abutting west into woodway and Easte into Robert Bates hedland: Walter Norwood lying on the north, and Thomas Kilpin on the South.

Item, an halfacre in Foxhedgfurlong abutting at the picked end southward on a foreshooter of William Gregoryes and north on John Dracots land: Henry Clarke lying on the Easte, and William Gregory on the west side.

Item another halfacre in the same furlong abutting South into Stonhils hedland, and north into Walter Norwards hedland: Richard Arniat lying on the Easte and Stonhill on the west.

Item an halfacre in the same field abutting west into woodway and Easte into the Shyreway: John Mallard lying on the north and Roberte Bate on the south.

Item, another halfacre in the same furlong abutting as the nexte before Roberte Bate lying on the north and John Dracott on the South.

Item another halfacre in the same furlong abutting as the nexte before William Haile lying on the north and Painesland on the South.

Item another halfacre in the same furlong abutting as the nexte before John Dracott lying on the north and Robert Bate on the South side.

In Turret field.

[*incomplete*]

(D/A/Gt/3/22/1)

43. DRAYTON PARSLOW 1639

A Terrier of the gleabe known to be long and appertaine to the Rectorie or parsonage of Drayton Paslowe in the County of Bucks and Deanry of Mursley taken and made upon the twentyth day of June in the fifteenth year of Charles the first King of England etc. defendor of the fayth *Annoque Domini* 1639.

Imprimis a Dwelling house of five bayes of building and a half where of two bayes [...] and three and half thacht a barne of three bayes and half thacht [...] stable in it of three bayes.

Item an orchard garden and yard more half an acre of ground An orchard and pitle late John Ocklayes lying on the East thereof the street and hyghway on the West. Also on close below the barne John Lanes Close Caled Illands on the East and Stones Diggins on the west [...] an other little close with a building of two bay there in Edward Thornton the Elder lying on the North and Edmund Thornton the Younger on the south: the street on the East. On little pitle with two bayes of building [...] the street lying between the Church yard on the West and Thomas Cookes Orchard on the East. Land Lying in the Common feilde Commonly taken for a yard land haveing thereunto belonging Common for a yard land.

In the feild next Salden.

One Land shooting to Oate close hedge Edmund Thornton lying East and Oliver Thornton Lying west.

Item Sixteen Lands lying all together with their [...] Edmund Thornton on the South west and Johnson Lying on the North East butting on the South East toward the towne.

Item Six Roods and a slipe of grasse grownd Running Downe by the brook Edward Hall Lying on the west and [...] South butting on a hadland of Francis Stone.

Item half Acre Lying on the West of Almeade Roger Parrett lying [...] and Francis Stone on the North.

[...] land More on that furlong John Bould Lying on the South and [...] on the North.

Item on [...]hill Eight lands lying betweene backes Francis Stone lying West [...] East.

[...] shooting into the great slade with Hades Edward Taylor lying either side north and south.

Item on the same furlong six lands togeather Edward Hall lying south, and [...] hades belong unto them.

Item [...] furlong Robert Crowley lying on the South: and [...] on the North.

[...] lying below Crosse way Francis Stone lying South [...] on the North.

In the [...]

Imprimis [...] abutting into the slade on the North hades belong there unto Jeffry Thornton Lyeth East and West thereof.

Item fower other acres Lying on the furlong North of Foxall Heade togeather the Constables Rood on the West and Michaell Parrett lyeth on the East.

Item in that furlong a fore[...] and the fallow both lye for an acre Michaell Parrett [...] on the West.

Item on Sand Hill [...] lands togeather shooting towards Stewkley brook, and butting on Midsummer grownd of John Thornton William Bradshaw lyeth on the South and Randell Huxley on the north.

Item fower lands More on that furlong towards the lower End of Sande Hill Roger Parrett Lyeth South of them and Edmund Thornton Junior on the North.

Item one Land on Lancatts Hill being an half acre Oliver Thornton Lyeth South and John Barley on the North.

Item one other half Acre on Lancatts Hill Furlonge Thomas Bond South and Edward Taylor lyeth on the North.

Item two Lands on the furlong Called Balan Pitts Edward Taylor lyeth East and West.

Item A platt of Midsummer grownd Commonly Called the parsons

Pott by Estimacon Neare an acre Butting on the South East on Stewkley Brook on the North west on seven lands end of John Lane John Thorntons Midsummer grownd lyeth South west and Mr Henry Waltons Midsummer grownd on the North East.

In the feild Next Stoke Hamond.

Imprimis On the furlong Caled black pitt on half Acre a land lately John Ockleys South West and Edward Thornton senior North East.

Item On Prisendale furlong: on thurrowout William Bradshaw on the south west and Edward Taylor North East.

Item in the same furlong a but William Bradshaw lyeth south west and on the North East Lyeth Michaell Parrat.

Item a land more on the same furlong William Bradshaw Lyeth on the south west and on the North Lyeth Edward Tayler.

Item a land shooting into Wickhils way beyond Debdin Francis Stone Lyeth North East and Roger Parrett South West.

Item [...] Mr Henry Lyeth South West and on the North [...] Edward Taylor.

Item in Dibden there lye Six other lands togeather with hades Roger Parrett Lyeth on the south East and Michaell Parrett North West.

In the furlong Caled above Broad Way fower lands togeather Oliver Thornton lyeth [...] and on the south west Lyeth Randall Huxley.

Item [...] Furlong on [...]land Edward Kempes fore shooter lying North East there of and Edward Tayler on the south west thereof.

Item on other land lying on the furlong Caled Hogstie furlong Edward Thornton senior Lying South West thereof.

Item on Acre on Langhad furlong Thomas Bond lying on the North West thereof and on the South East lyeth William Temple.

Item on butt more on that furlong lying by the balk leading into broad way Edward Tayler lying on the North West there of and Edward Thornton Senior south East.

Item an other acre Lying in the furlong Caled above broad way Robert Crawley lyeth south west thereof and Michael Parrett on the North East thereof.

Item one Rood of Medow grownd in Hey Meade Edmund Thornton Senior lyeth north East and a rood of Edward Kempe lyeth South west.

Item [...] Leyes att the Narrowes with severall Hades belonging to them: a ley Lately John Oakleys lyeth south west and Edmund Thornton junior North East.

Item a platt of Layes and severall hades belonging On fursen Hill shooting to Hollonden brook in number att on end twenty three: att the other twenty Nine Francis Stone lyeth south west and Edmond Thornton Junior North East.

In testimonie that this is a true terrier of the gleabe belonging to the Rectorie of Drayghton aforesaid we have hereunto sett our hands.

William Bradshaw   Churchwardens
Richard Cooke   mark
(D/A/Gt/3/23/1)

44. DUNTON 1639

A note or terrier of all the glebe lande meadowes gardens [...] houses stocks Implements Tenements and portions of tithes rightes in the parrishe or out of the parrishe belonginge to the parsonage of Dunton in the County of Bucks *Anno Domini* 1639.

Imprimis there is an dwellinge house contayninge one parlour one hall one Kitchin One buttery, One lower Chamber one Milk house with lofte and chambers over them And a brewhouse with a Well and a plumpe belonginge to it whereof 3 bayes of it is for the mor part tiled and the rest thatched it stands over against the Churchyarde on the south side of the Church.

Item there is one barne of 4 bayes thatcht with a hoggstie leaning to it.

[...] one Stable One Cowhouse with another out house all thatcht [...] 5 baies of building.

Item here is a garden ande an orchard of some halfe an acre of ground adioyning to the house upon the south side of it with a yard on the other side of a like quantitie.

Item there is one home close of Pasture of some fower acres of grounde By common estimation adioyninge to the garden And a close of one Thomas Millers on the west side and the Common feilde upon the East.

There is a meadow close of an acre of grounde adioyning to the Comon feild upon the north and a meadowe nowe in the occupacon of William Barton upon the south west and a part of the Comon field Called Michenden upon the south east.

Item there is one Acre of arable lying in the Comonfeild in meade had furlong Lying next unto a land of Samuel Carters on the west [...] next unto a land of Edward [...] upon the East and upon the Common at both endes.

Item there is two yards of [...] lying in the meade feild by Meade baulke being bounded with the land of Samuel Carters on the east and an lande of Henry [...] on the west with 2 hades of greensward belonging to them and reaching downe unto the Ham.

Item there is halfe an acre of arrable in the meadfeild lying in [...] being bounded with a land of Edward Mallards [...] land of William Friars on the West with a had of greensward belonging to it reaching downe unto the mead hedge.

Item there is half an acre of Arrable in the mead feild lying in [...] furlong being bounded with a land of William Friars on the east and a lande of Samuell Carters on the west having a hade of greensward belonging to it reaching downe to the mead hedge.

Item there is one laye of grasse in the further [...] which lye next [...] arrable on the west side and next to a lay of Edward Mallards on the east.

Item there is halfe an acre of arrable lying in the upper Colewells which [...] next unto the Cowpasture on the south and a land of Thomas Millers on the north.

Item there is halfe an acre of Arrable in Hartwell furlong being bounded with a land of Edward Mallards on the south and a lande of Richarde Tharbox on the north and shootes up to spamers bushes on the East with a hade of greensward belonging to it which may be plowed up if the Incumbent please.

Item there is halfe an acre of Arrable in Stakehill tree furlong being bounded with a land of William Friars on the West And a land of Thomas Millers on the east And is iust against the pitt by stakehill tree.

Item there is halfe an acre of arrable in Windmill hill furlonge being bounded with a land of Mr Clutterbucks on the north, and a land of Samuell Carters on the south.

Item there is one laye of grasse on fallow layes bounded with a laye of Samuell Carters on the West, And a laye of Henry Fenners on the east and is the third laye from the bushe.

Item there is One yard of laye grasse in Crosse layes being bounded on the West with a lay of Thomas Millers And on the east with a laye of Richard Tarbox and is the 5th lay from the land that shoots to stakehill tree.

Item there is one yard of Arrable in the west feild that shootes downe to the highway being Hogshou hedg and is bounded with a lande of Edward Mallards on the West And a land of Henry Fenners on the East and goes up to a laye of grasse of glebe land which shootes up to the hedge Corner.

Item there is one laye of grasse in West layes which shootes up to Creslowe hedge [...] and is bounded with a laye of Thomas Wallers on the west And Henry Fenners on the East.

Item there is one yard of arrable in West layes furlong that shootes down the highway by Hogshow hedge and is bounded with a land of Edward Mallards on the West and a land of Richard Tarboxes on the east [...] upon the fursen bushes in West layes.

Item there is a Lay of grasse in west layes bounded with a lay of Richard Tarboxes on the East and a laye of William Friars on the west which shootes downe to the stile in Hogshou hedg.

Item there is a laye of grasse in Furzenhill, which shootes up to the Cowpasture And is bounded with a laye of Edward Mallard on the West and a laye of Richard Tarboxe on the east.

Item there is halfe an acre of Arrable in the Upper Royalls which is bounded with a Laye of Edward Mallards on the north and a land of Samuell Carters on the south and lyes about the middle of the furlonge.

Item there is halfe an acre of Arrable in the Lower royalls bounded with a land of Richard Tarbox on the north and a land of William Friars on the south and is the 7th land from Comon close hedge.

Item there is another halfe acre of Arrable in the Lower Royalls bounded with a land of Henry Fenners on the south and a land of Edward Mallards on the north and is the first land that shortens in stakehill waie.

Item there is halfe an acre of Arrable in Townesend furlong and is bounded with a land of William Friars on the west, And a land of Richard Tarboxes on the east, and is the second land next unto the hedge.

Item there is halfe an acre of arrable in Windmill way furlong [...] land of Edward Mallards east and west and [...] upon the baulke.

Item there is halfe an acre of arrable in Wood way furlong and [...] land of Samuel Carters upon the north [...] downe to the highwaie by Nuttparke hedge and is [...] and a ridge beyond the baulke.

Item there is halfe an acre more in Woodway furlong with a [...] of grasse at the West ende which goes as farr as [...] Crosse land with halfe the baulkes on eyther [...] with a lande of Thomas Millars on the south [...] of Henry Fenners on the north and is the third [...] beyond the long yards.

Item there is halfe an acre more in Woodway furlong with the baulke and is bounded with 2 lands of Edward Mallards upon the north and south. It lyes on the home ward side of a greate baulke that goes almost quite through the furlong.

Item there is halfe an acre of Arrable in Flixland furlong with a hade of grasse at the south end of it reaching to the next Crosse land and is bounded with a land of Edward Mallards on the weste and a land of Samuell Carters on the East and is the [...] land that shortens there.

Item there is half an acre of Arrable in Woodway furlong bounded with 2 lands of Samuel Carter on the north and south And shootes downe unto the parsonage plott by Willmatch hedge.

Item there is a plott of grasse by Wallmatch hedge bounded on the north with blackland hedge and on the West with plowde land and on the east with Wellmatch hedge.

Item there is halfe an acre of Arrable with a hackin in Willmatch furlong with hades belonging to them upon the north end reaching unto Wallmatch hedg and are bounded with two lands of Thomas Millers upon the East and West.

Item there is halfe an acre of arrable in Churchway furlong bounded with a land of Samuell Carters on the East and a land of Thomas Millers on the West, and shootes Downe stonellpond gate and is the fourth land from barley feild hedge.

Item there is halfe an acre of arrable in Water furlong and bounded with a land of Richard Tarboxes on the West and Henry Fenners on the east, and shootes unto Church way and lyeth next to the Hadlam.

Item there is a laye of grasse that lyes under Lidcot hedge upon the east side [...] in Michenden.

Item there also belongs unto the parsonage as many beast Comon and shepe Comon and Horse Comon as are Comonly allowed to a yard land.

Th Tithe of the farmer are paid in kind The tithes of the [...] pastures are paid by the tenth penny of the rest there is for every [...] paid to the patron there is 10 li paid to the parson.

William Burton

(D/A/Gt/3/24/1)

45. EAST CLAYDON 1607

A true and perfecte surveye or terroure ot all the possessiones... October the xxiij *Anno Domini* 1607.

In *primis* the homestall or scite of the vicarage scituate and lyinge betweene the kinges highewaye on the Northeast and the Lords grownde in tenure of John Stephenes on the Northe and southwest and conteynes by estimatione three quarters of an acre.

Item within the sayde boundes ar conteyned one garden impayled by estimatione eight yardes square.

Item the vicarage howse consistinge of three bayes buylte of tymber and covered with tile all lofted over and disposed in six roomes *viz.* the hall parlour and [...] above three small loftes.

Item one [...] house consistinge of fowre bayes buylt of tymber and covered with strawe some parte thereof servinge for a derie howse the residue for [...] and fodder.

Item ther hathe bene longe sithence one yard land belonginge to this vicarage the which of Longe [...] hathe bene lost, by whose fault wee knowe [...] neyther do we knowe in whose possession it is.

Item out tithes belonging to the [...] there is nothinge belonging to this vicarage as far as we knowe or can Learne.

Aven Gleyme   Minister there

George Scottes   mark   Churchwardens
William Biginells   mark
Thomas Bishoppes   mark   Sidiman
William Millwards   mark
John Stevenes   mark

(D/A/Gt/3/10/1)

46. EAST CLAYDON 1639

East Claydon *Cum Membris Com'* Bucks.
A terriar made December 6 *Anno Domini* 1639.

Imprimis now in the vicars posession a dwelling house of three bayes lofted over and a leane thereunto annexed all covered with tiles.

Item one bay sett on hovell postes used for a milke house Covered with Thatch.

Item one barne of three bayes and one other bay adioneing there unto being lofted over, all covered over with thatch.

Item one litle Close and a yard with that ground which the houseing standeth on Containeth in all about an acre of ground abutting on the land of Agnes Stevens widow towards the north and on the Streat of East Claydon towards the east.

We doe also herein mention some other parcells of land which hath beene reputed vicaredge ground but we have never knowen nor have hard that any vicar there was ever posessed therof.

Item in the Common mead belonging to the parish there lieth eighte yerds of meadground called by a terrier thereof (made in the 37 yeare of King Henry the eight) the vicaredge yeards which yerds lie not Constant in one place but doe move every yeare but are Constantly in the occupation of Thomas Hicks and John Hicks, Ellinor Line or Agnes Stevens Widows.

Item there is in the field Called Woodfield One hadland in a furlong Called Sandhill which is Called by the name of the vicaredge haddland now in the occupation of Thomas Hicks or John Hicks abutting uppon a sladd Called Hickwell Sladd towards the north and on [...] long Called hanging land towards the South the land of Thomas Millward on the East side thereof.

Item in the north field in a furlonge Called stony land reportedly Thomas Webb senior to be a land Called the Vicaredge ley now in tyllage abuttinge on a land of William Tame towards the north.

Item one vicar saith he hath in his Composition from the prior of Byssam Abbey one whole yard land in the parish of East Claydon Com' Bucks.

[...] Gryffyth   Vicar *ibidem*

John [...]   Churchwarden

(D/A/Gt/3/10/2)

47. EDGCOTT 1639

A terrer of all glebe.

Imprimis on the [...] of the Church of the sayd [...] Mansion house and other houses [...] parsonage situated and built upon a plott of ground conteyning by estimation about an acre streeted round about.

Perry field.

Item three lands the farme ground one the North syde and the highway one west syde.

Item two yeards shooting towards Dunstall hill a land of John Mayo one the west syde and a yeard of farm ground one the east syde.

Item 1 rod arable in short perry furlong a rod of William Abbott one the North syde and acre of Martin Mayo one the South.

Item in the sayd furlong two butts or picks the lordship of Charden one the North syde and two picks of Joh Longlys on the South syde.

Middle feild.

Item three leyes one Bidcott furlong the farme grownde one both sydes.

Item in the same furlong i land arable a land of Edmund Wallington one the South syde and a land of the farme grownd on the North.

Item i land in nether bidcott a land of the farme grownd one the south syde and a land of John Mayo one the North.

Item one the same furlong i Land arable Edmund Wallington one the North and Widdow Martin one the South.

Bartlits furlong.

Item 4 rods arable Widdow Martin one the North syde and bartlets bush one the South.

6 acre furlong.

Item two rods arable Freeswid Slaymaker one the North syde and William Abbott one the South.

Item an acre and the farme grownd on both sydes.

Item one land arable William Abbott one the South and Freeswyde Slaymaker one the North.

Item a land in longland furlong William Abbott one the North and John Folleatt one the South.

Lackamstead furlong.

Item 1 land Thomas Clark one the east syde and William Hughes one the west.

Item one land with a foreshooter hade the farme grownde one the west and John Holmes one east.

Webbed furlong.

Item one ley the farme grownde one both sydes.

Item another Ley John Folleatt one the North and widdow Marten one the South.

Item i butt arable Joh Mayo one the North and the farme growd one the South.

Item i land shooting one Widdow Martens hadland Edmund Wallington one the North and Marten Mayo one the South.

Item one land arable a rod of Thomas Clarke one the South and a rod of Mayo on the North.

[eight lines illegible]

Item 1 land arable Marshway one the North and Edmund Wallington on the South.

Item 4 ley yeards one the west syde of Webbed the farme grownde one the South and John Folleatt one the North.

Item 1 hadland shooting one Marsh way Thomas Clark one hadland on the east.

Item at long furlong end 1 butt Thomas Clark one the east and Joh Mayo on the West.

Item another land Marten Mayo on the east and Thomas Clark one the West.

Item another in the same furlong the farme growd one the east and William Abbott one the west.

Item another land Thomas Clark one the east and the farme grown one the west.

Long furlong.

Item one land arable Joh Mayo one the east and the farme grownde one the west.

Item another land Edmund Wallington one the east and Thomas Clark one the west.

Gumbell furlong.

Item two butts arable shooteing to Kings ditch the farme grownde one the South and Widdow Marten one the North.

Rannell furlong.

Item 1 land arable Widdow Marten one the South and William Abbot on the north.

Item anther land William Abbott one the South and Joh: Langly one the north.

Item 3 land arable the farme grownd one both sydes.

Item one plott of Medd: grownd Called Rannell hook two poole one the North and iiij poole in the middle belonging unto the farme.

Hyll feild.

Imprimis 1 acre arable one bigberry hill the farme grownd on the East and Joh Mayo on the west.

Hare shoote furlong one land arable Edmund Wallington one the west and Thomas Clark on the east.

Item another land John Folleatt on the west and the farme grownd one the east.

Blackwell furlong.

Item 1 land arable the farme grownde one both sydes.

Item a rod of farme grownd one the east and a ley of Thomas Clarkes one the west.

Item a ley in the sayd furlong a ley of Thomas Clarks one the east and a ley of the farme grownd on the west.

Item two rod leyes shooteing to blackwell William abbott one the west and Thomas Clark on the east in *predict'* furlong.

One rod of Meddow grownd the town dole meade one the west and a rod of farme grownd one the east.

Item in the dole Meddow 9 Leetes on every leete one pole *et di'* the farm grownd on both sydes.

Redland furlong.

Inprimis 1 land arable Thomas Clark on the north and 1 land arable Joh Mayo one the South.

Item ij yeard arable William Abbott on the North and 1 Land arable Joh Mayo one the South.

Item vij buttes together one butt on the North in tenure Marten Mayo and William Abbott on the South.

Grene hill furlong.

Imprimis one land arable Thomas Clark one the North and allsoe on the South.

[*seven lines illegible*]

Nether purlpitt.

Imprimis 1 land arable [...] on the South and 1 land Thomas Clark one the North.

Item one land arable in *predicto* furlong Thomas Clark on the North and Joh Mayo on the South.

Longe leye.

Inprimis 1 land arrable Joh Mayo one the east and Thomas Clark on the west.

Item 1 butte arable Mr Humphrey Mayo one the east and the farme grownde one the west.

Hill meede Leis.

Item four leyes together Thomas Hicke one the South and Marten Mayo on the North.

Woolland furlong.

Item 1 land arable Thomas Hicke one the east and 1 land arable the farme grownde on the west.

Small mede.

Item one rod arable east and west in the sayd furlong one rod Marten Mayo one the east and Humpherey Mayo one the west shooting to Kinges pasture.

West feild.

Langland furlong east and west.

Inprimis 1 land arable end east and west one land William Abbott one the North and the farme grownd one the South.

Nether bottomn furlong North and South.

Item 1 land arrable butting one London way widdeow Marten one the west and 1 land Marten Mayo on the east.

Castel furlong North and South.

Item 1 land arrable in *dicto* furlong Joh Folleatt on the east and ij rods William Abbott one the west.

Twelve acre east west.

Item 1 land arable in *dicto* furlong William Abbott one the south and on land arable John Langly one the North.

Item at the end of Rannell hooke iiij butts ending North and South broad [...] hooke one the west and iiij leyes John Folleatt one the east.

Long brech furlong east and west.

Inprimis 1 Land arrable Marten Mayo one the North and William Abbott one the South.

Item two rods arable 1 land Joh Folleatt one the South and the farme grownde one the north.

Item one land Freeswid Slaymaker one the North and William Abbotts one the South.

Short hill furlong east and west.

Inprimis two butts Joh Folleatt one the North and farme grownde one the South.

Item two butts in *dicto* furlong William Abbott one the South and farme grownde one the North.

[...]

Inprimis a hadland south and north one had ley of Thomas Clark one the west syde.

Item on land arrable butting on the sayd hadland William Abbott one the South and William Harres one the North.

Item 1 land shooting in land of William Abbott on the north and [...] on the South.

[*17 lines illegible*]

Inprimis on ley [...] and ij rods William Abbott one the west.

Item ij leyes in the same furlong farme grownd on both sydes.

Nether ham and over flax land.

Inprimis one ley north and south William Abbott on either side.

Item one ley in [...] flaxland William Abbott one the east and John Langly on the west.

Item one ley in the sayd flax land William Abbott one the east syde and Widdow Marten one the west.

Street furlong east and west.

Inprimis one ley widdow Martin one the South and William Abbott one the north.

Item in the said furlong one ley William Abbott one both sydes.

Street furlong east and west.

Item on ley William Abbott one the south and farme grownde one the north.

Item one land farme grownde one the south and Joh Folleatt one the north.

Item iiij butted Leyes farme grownde one both sydes.

Addmans furlong east and west.

Inprimis 1 land arable William Abbottt on the south and John Langly on the North.

Item acre arable farm grownd on [*three lines illegible*].

West more longland east and west.

Inprimis acre arable in the sayd furlong John Folleatt one the north and farme grownde on the South.

Item one land arable Thomas Clark on the North and William Hewes one the South.

Water furrowe.

Inprimis one ley John Longly one the south and William Abbott one the north.

Item 1 Land arable Jo Langly one the south and William Abbott one the north.

Bann furlong east and west.

Inprimis ij rods arable William Abbott one the north and Humphrey Mayo one the south.

Item 1 land arable Widdow Marten one the north and William Abbott one the South.

Item one ley in the sayd furlong William Abbott on the North and William Hewes one the South.

Item 3 leyes there adioyning William Hewes ley one the South and Thomas Clark one the north.

Bygglebred east and west.

Item in the sayd furlong one ley land Humphrey Mayo one the South and John Folleatt one the north.

Grendon mede furlong arable all and haded.

Inprimis the farthest land in the sayd furlong William one the north and John Folleatt one the South.

Item the next butt in the sayd furlong John Folleatt one South and William Abbott one the north.

Item the third butt homeward William Abbott one the north and Humprey one the South.

Item the fourth butt homeward William one the North and John Folleatt one the South.

Item two yeards *di' acr'* William Abbott one the north and one land John Folleatt one the South.

November 23 *Anno Domini* 1639.

Richard Atwood   Rector *de* Edgecott

Surveyed by Hugh Hart *Juratt'*
Marten Mayo Thomas Clark John Folleatt William Mountague
[...]   Haynes   Churchwardens
John Langly
(D/A/Gt/4/1/2)

48. ELLESBOROUGH 1639

A Terrier of the howse outhowses and glebe Lands belonging to the parsonage of Ellesborough in the County of Bucks within the dioces of Lincolne taken the 18th of September 1639 by those whose names are subscribed.

Imprimis the Parsonage howse containing fower bayes of building wherin five lower roomes five Chambers besides garrets and Closets.

Item the Moyitie or half part of the great barne containinge six bayes of buildinge.

Item the Moyitie of another newe barne containinge fower bayes of buildinge.

Item one Stable with a garden plott.

Item the Moyitie of the yard or backside containing by estimation one acre.

Item 3 acres and halfe of arrable lying next unto the great barne Mr Egleton on the west end and [...] Packington on the North side.

Item one acre bounded by Sopers balke on the est side and Mr Egleton his land on the west side.

Item eyght yeards in the feild called the Mawme contayninge by estimation two acres bounded by Sir Henry Crookes land on the west side and the Priory on the est side.

Item 4 acres called Hart [...] bounded Mr Egleton on the Northe side [...] Crooke on the south and est sides.

[two lines illegible]

[...] in Tenn acres furlonge bounded by Sir John Packington on the west [...] on the east.

Item half an acre in the upper Mawme bounded by Mr Hills Land on the [...] syde and [...] on the [...] side.

Item two acres in the upper Mawme bounded by Mr Egeton on the [...] and Acknell way on the Northe side.

[...] lying under [...] shooting North and south [...] the east.

[...] the severall parcels of Land befor mentioned lye in the feild [...] called the Mawme.

Item the Southe feild in Butlers cross furlong on half acre bounded by Sir John Packington on the west end and Mr Egleton on the est.

Item [...] acres containing by estimation on acre and a half [...] Sir John Packington on the North and the Priory on the southe.

Item [...] of Land bounded by Mr Egleton on the Northe side and the Priorye on the south side.

[two lines illegible]

Item on acre shooting southe and north along by the woodwaye on the east side.

Item on half acre bounded by the Priorie on the south and John Packington on the Northe side.

Item on acre of arable bounded by Mr Hill on the west Sir Henry Crooke on the east.

Item another acre in the same furlong bounded by Edward Wade on the east and Sir John Packington on the west.

Item on yard liing at the end of the acres shooting east and west Sir Henry on the southe side.

Item on acre on the east side on the wood waye bounded on the Northe and the Priory Land on the south side.

Item one yard of ground in prior furlong bounded by Mr Hill on the east side and Sir Packington on the west.

Item one acre by pennings corner bounded by Sir Henry Cooke on the south side shooting east on pennings.

Item one acre belowe pennings bound by Sir John Packington on the east and west sides and shooting upon Acknell [...] est.

Item one acre in Moore furlong bounded by the Priorye [...] and Nicholas Abridg on the south.

[*two lines illegible*]

Item one Swathe in Litle Meade bounded by Sir John Packington on the North and Mr Egleton on the south.

Item one half acre [...] midsummer acre bounded by the Priory on the southe John Packington on the north.

Item on half acre in the feild called the backside bounded by the Priorie on the east and Edward Wade one the west.

Item one half acre in Lee field bounded by the Priory land on the south and Edward Wade one the North.

Item one yard in Winniatt feald bounded by the Priory land on the east and Kimble feild one the west shooting upon the [...]

Item one Butt in Stonye feild Lake and the Priorye on the est.

Thomas Blanchflower   Rector *ibidem*

William Fenners   Churchwardens

[...]

John Neighbor

and Smith   The mark of Thomas Baylie

(D/A/Gt/4/3/1)

49. EMBERTON 1640

A Terrier of the Glebe land belonging to the Rectorie of Emberton taken and made the xij th day of February 1639.

In Stonie feild.

Imprimis ij halfe Acres lying together in the furlong called Whitecroft in Maudlin Furlong Mr Tyringham East and West.

Item i halfe Acre in Long Stones furlong Raph Smith West Prentice East.

i halfe Acre on the furlonge above Coopers Close the land of Mr Tyringham East and John Boswell West.

ij Sellions lying together on Shales furlong by estimacon half an Acre the lande of Raph Goodwyn East and Mr Tyringham West.

Half an Acre on further Caswell Mr Tyringham East and West.

Half an Acre and 4 Roods together on Moore furlong Mr Tyringham East and West.

i Roode lying on Barrells furlong John Boswells land East Mr Tyringham West.

i Acre lying beneath the towne hedland Raph Smith East Mr Tyringham West.

In Middle feild.

Inprimis half an Acre next the way of hall peice furlong Mr Tyringhams land East and the Kinges highway West.

ij halfe Acres on the same furlong Mr Tyringham East and West.

i halfe Acres and i Roode lying together in holystreete Furlong the land of John Boswell North and Mr Tyringham South.

iij halfe Acres lying in hollingdon Furlong Mr Tyringham East and West.

i throughout Acre and a halfe [...] Mr Tyringham East Widdow Goodwin West.

i half Acre lying on gravell pit furlong Mr Tyringham East and West.

i half Acre and 4 Roodes lyeing on West halfe, the lande of Raph Smith East and Widdowe Goodwin West.

viij Roods on the same furlong Mr Tyringham East Raph Smith West.

i Roode on vij Acres furlonge Mr Tyringham west and Raph Smith East.

ij Acres together on vij Acres furlong Mr Tyringham East and West.

In Crosse Albons feilde.

Inprimis v Acres lyinge together called Parsons peice the Close of Edward Cooper West and James Greatheade East.

i halfe Acre lying on the furlong called Hempsons den Mr Tyringham South and Widdow Goodwin North.

i Roode on Abbington hill Widow Goodwin South the foresaid half Acre East.

ij halfe Acres in the furlong called short longdon the lande of Mr Tyringham West and Thomas Boswell Est.

ij halfe Acres together Vate through furlong Mr Tyringham North.

ij halfe Acres together on the same furlong Mr Tyringham South Glovers heyres North.

i Roode on the same furlonge Mr Tyringham North Raph Smyth South.

i Rood on the same furlong Mr Tyringham South Thomas Boswell North.

i Roode lying on Smithen hill furlong Mr Tyringham South and Raph Smith North.

ij halfe Acres lying on the same furlonge the Common baulke North.

ij Acres lying together on Crosse Albons furlong Mr Tyringham East and Raph Smith West.

i halfe Acre lying in the furlonge Called Neather Thornes betweene the land of Mr Tyringham's East and West.

i halfe Acre lying on Smithen hill furlonge Mr Tyringham South and Raph Goodwin North.

One Roode of Meddow in the East Meade lying after the first stone betweene Thomas Boswell East and West.

One Roode in the same Meddowe after the third stone Raph Smith West and the heyres of William Boswell East.

One Roode in the West Meide betwixt Raph Smith West Jo: Phillips East.

Two acres of lease in the Cowpasture with iiijer beast commons belonging thereunto.

Simon Youngers   Rector

Anthony Smith   Churchwardens
John Campian
(D/A/Gt/4/4/2)

50. FARNHAM ROYAL 1607

Septembris xv⁰ Anno Domini 1607 Annoque Regni Domini Regis Jacobi dei gratia Anglie etc Quinto et Scotie xlj⁰.

A survey or Terriour of all the possessions...

Inprimis the homestall or Scyte of the parsonage with divers parcels of ground to the same adioyning bounding uppon the landes belonging to the parsonage of Stoke Poges on the est part the highwaye leading from Beconsfild towards Farnham on the west parte, And the lands of Andrewe Umbervile gent on the South and north parts.

Within which bounds are conteyned one conveniente dwelling house built with tymber and Tiled over of Two stories high disposed into Eleven roomes *vizt.* a hall two parlors lofted over, a stodie, a kytchen lofted over, a butterie a milke howse and a boulting howse.

Item A barne of iiij bayes thetched with ij Coote endes.

Item a Carte howse Thetched.

Item a haye Barne a stable a gate howse and a brewe howse adoiyning being tyled.

Item ij yerdes or Courtes a garden ij orchards one little pitle and ij closes of pasture adioyning Conteyning all by estimacon xx acres.

Arable.

Item Syxe acres of arrable lande lying together in a peece called the xxiiij acres on the south side of the same peece And Syxe acres more on the North side of the same peece called the xxiiij acres   xij acres.

Item Fyve acres lying together in the Comon feild Feild called Farnham feilde butting uppon Wyndesor waye on the west, and the land belonging to Farnham Courte est v acres.

Item Three acres lying in the Upper ende of the same feild at the parke Corner butting uppon the lande belonging to Farnham Courte on the est and North iij acres.

in toto of arable xx acres

Summa totalis xl acres

Item one acre in Bidwell adioyning uppon the foote waye going from Farnham towards Windesor on the west called the Parsons Acre, deteayned and taken awaie by Eustace Maskall deceased late fermor to Farnham Courte i acre detayned.

For Stockes implements Tenements or anie other thing inquirable by the canon and not herein before intimated and expressed there is nothing belonging to the Rectorie as farre as we knowe or can lerne.

Matthewe Browne   Rector   *Ecclesiae de* Farnham Riall

Thomas Ingelle   Churchwardens
Roger Gate

In toto the Homestalle yerds orchards and garden and closes adioyning xx acres.

(D/A/Gt/4/5/1)

51. FARNHAM ROYAL 1639

Terrier of the gleabe land and house belonging to the Parsonage of Farnham Royall in Bucking' July 26 1639.

Inprimis a house consisting of five bayes of building and roomes over all the first floores in very good and suficient repaire.

Item two barnes one but small the other a faire large one with a stable at the end of it.

Item one brew-house and an out house for to lay wood in or other uses.

Item one Pidgeon-house standing afore the dwelling house at the end of the lesser barne.

The land belonging.

Inprimis twenty acres inclosed by and neere adioyning to the house, divided into severall closes and parcells after this manner.

Inprimis an Orchard and garden, and yard with 2 little Pitles of land by the barne, all containing 2 acres.

Item 3 closes ioyning to the lane leading from the parsonage to the church butting on Stoke-brooke East on the said lane West.

The first, ioyning to the yard of the house, containing 4 acres, the second sixe acres, the third, sixe acres.

Item a fourth close, containing 2 acres, butting on the said Stoke-brooke, East and upon the third close of sixe acres West.

Item twenty acres in the Common feild liing in foure severall peices.

The first next to the towne of Farnham containing 3 acres butting at one end on the field called the Parke, North at the other end, on a field called Bidwell South.

The second Peice, containing sixe acres, liing in a part of the field, called 24 acres, butting at one end, on Stoke-Park East, at the other end on the land of Andrewe Umphrevile and Richard Hanwood West.

The third peice containing sixe acres, liing at the end of that part of the field called 24 acres before named, butting on the foresaid Stoke Park East, at one end, at the other on the land of Andrew Umphrevile and John Peryman, west.

The fourth peice containing five acres, butting on a part of the common field called 18 acres, East one way, and another on the Roade Way to Windsor, West.

Item one acre of meadow ground in Farnham Meade called the Parsons acre, liing neere to the gate, entring the meade.

Item one close at Hedgly, containing one acre, butting on the Roade Way to Beaconsfield, East, and upon the land of George Salter West, commonly called and knowne by the name of the Parsons acre.

Thomas Daniel   *Cura' ibid'*

Thomas Crips   mark   Churchwardens
John Waters   mark
Thomas Floyd
William Ingle
John Clinton

(D/A/Gt/4/5/2)

52. FAWLEY 1639

A Terrier of the howsing and lands belonginge to the Rectorie of Fawley in Com' Bucks taken and exhibited the 5th day of October *Anno Domini* 1639.

Inprimis One dwelling howse, one Barne, a Stable and an outhowse.

Item a garden, an Orchard and a yarde, conteyning by estimacon one acre.

Item One Close called the Arbour conteyning by estimacon Six acres, abutted on the North West, with the highway on the Southwest, with a field of Edward Chards called Pit Close on the East with midle field on the North East with the garden, orchard and yard.

Item one field called Midle field (by estimacon Eight acres abutted on the West, with the Arbour on the south, with a ground of Edward Chards called Stone Close on the East, with a field of Edward Chards called Bittams on the North with a field of Ralph Randalls called home Close.

Item one field called Lower Close conteyning three acres abutted on the south with Bittams on the East, with a field of John East called Lotts on the North, with a field of Ralph Randalls called Round Close on the west with midle fielde.

Item one Close called litle Close by estimacon one acre abutted on the West and South the garden and orcharde on the North with the highway on the East with midle fielde.

William Kitson   Rector

Abraham Randall   Churchwardens
Thomas Carpenter

(D/A/Gt/4/6/1)

53. FOSCOTT 1639

A true note and Terrier of the [...] house with all other houses, and with [...] Land *viz.* Gardaines Orchyards [...] Pasture and Meadow belonging [...] of Foxcot as it is now in the use [...] me James Stilton Rector of [...] October 19 *Anno Domini* 1639.

Inprimis the dwellinge house having three roomes *viz.* a parler Kichin and dayrie house [...] Lofted and having three Chambers over them.

Outhouses.

Item a Barne adioyning to the said dwelling house conteyning three Bay of building with a stable adioyning to the sayd Barne and an old hay house set upon posts in the ground with a yard conteyning by estimacon one Roode of Ground with a Kilne [...] standing and being at the over end of the yard unto a pasture and enclosed ground belonging to Elizabeth Walcot one the west.

Item a litle garden Plott and a litle Court neare unto the dwelling house East.

Pasture and Areable.

Item a litle close of Pasture with an Orchyard lying and being close and adioyning unto the dwelling house yard one the North conteyning by estimacon halfe an acre of ground or there about.

Item An enclosed ground of Pasture abbutting upon the litle close of Pasture and Orchyard aforesayd North, and [...] Elizabeth Walcot Widdow one the west and Thomas Shert East and South Conteyning by estimacon Eight Acrees.

Item Fourteene of Areable land and Pasture Lying and [...] In an enclosed ground commonly called Cater Peice [...] abutting one the common Layne West and Stratford High Way South and Edward Greenefeeld Gent North.

Meadow.

Item Two Acres and a halfe of Meadow Lying and being in a meadow commonly called Bowbridg Meade Abutting upon Leckhamsted Common Pasture North and the river South and the Rales or partition of the meadow betweene Leckhamsted and Foxcott East the sayd Two Acres and a halfe being of an Equall breadth from Leckhamsted Common Pasture and the river aforesayd.

Areable and Meadow in the Parish of Maydsmorton.

Item One Acre of Areable Land within the Parrish of Mayds Morton abutting upon an Enclosed ground in Foxcot commonly called fish close East and a slayd of Grasse ground West and John Easton of Mayds Morton North.

Item One Acre of Meadow at the over Part of Maids Morton deep Meadow abutting upon the feild that is areable north and the river South.

Item An other Acre and a pole and a halfe of Meadow Lying and being in Mayds Morton Middle Meadow Abutting as aforesayd viz. the Tilled feild North and the river south.

James Stilton   Rector

Thomas Cowley   Churchwarden
his mark
Robert Warner   Sidsman

(D/A/Gt/4/10/1)

54. FULMER 1639

A True Terriarr of the Parsonage in the County of Bucks and all belong unto it made the [*blank*].

Inprimis the Parsonage howse Consisting of [...] Halle Parlor a Kitchin and a little Buttry. In upper chambers a milk howse and another Butry [...] howse for Buttery and a square green court befor the dore att [...] into the Howse and a plesant walk uppon the Sowth west syd of it.

Item Behind the Parsonage Howse another square greene court and a garden and orchard with a litle cloase [...] unto them About an Acker [...] is used for Medow.

In the Backyeard there is A Barne

There is moore over one close of Pasture adioyning to the little meddow uppon the Sowth sydd of it [...] a Hundred peeces except one by the Parson and churchwarden ther to the use only of the Parson and his successors.

John Brigges   Rector *Ecclesiae ibidem*

[...] Brigges   Churchwardens
John [...]
[...] Standench   mark
(D/A/Gt/4/11/1)

55. GAYHURST 1639

December 6 1639 A Terrier of the glebe lands of belonging to the Rectory of Gayhurst *alias* Gothurst with the appurtenances thereunto belonging [...] by the Churchwardens [...] and yeare above written *viz.* December the 6th 1639.

Inprimis a mansion house consisting of 3 bayes and a Milke house and yarde an orchard a Garden and a [...] Pickle in all about an acre of ground.

Item i barne of three bayes and arable.

Item i halfe acre of meddow in the meadow called [...] the Lady Digby on the North, and Lathbury meadows East and South.

Item ij acres and an halfe in [...] of arable and by [...] leas on the South and the lande of Richard Wakeling on the North.

Item 1 acre of arrable on stoke feilde side Everard Ellis his lande on the west and the lande of Mr Hampden on the East.

Item 1 acre on high oke furlonge the lande of Hughe Baguley beinge East and West.

Item l peice called Peters [...] the grounde of the Lady Digby lyinge West and John Smithe East.

In the Millfeilde.

One acre above the mill way the ground of Hughe Baguley on the South and Edward Tompkins on the North.

Item j halfe acre on Wren furlonge the Lady Digbye on the south and John Smithe on the Northe.

Item j but on the same furlonge a roode, the grounde of John Smithe on the South and the higheway on the North.

In the Hoofeild.

One acre on Barley furlonge Hughe Baguley West and John Smith East.

Item l halfe acre of greensorde on Midle hads the grounde of the Lady Digby West and of John Smithe East.

Item l acre on Ditch furlonge the grounde of the Lady Digby North East and of John Smithe South West.

Item l acre more on the same furlonge the lande of Richard Wakelin North East and Hughe Baguley South West.

Item l peice at the Mortar Pitts Hughe Baguley lyinge North, and the higheway sowthe.

Lastly 1 half acre lying at Hamonds bushe ditchfurlong shooting upon it North, and Hughe Baguley his grounds South With Commons in the Common feildes of Gothurst and Bunstie leas in both the parts of them for nine great cattell and thirty sheepe.

Robert Wallis   Parson

Nicholas Morton   his mark   Churchwardens
John Carter   his mark
(D/A/Gt/4/12/1)

56. GROVE 1607

The terrer of the Rectorie of Grove parva in the countie of Bucks the sixten day of October in the Fifte yeare of the Raigne of our Soveraigne lorde by the grace of god James Kinge of England Fraunce and Ireland and of Scotland Fourty one etc 1607.

The parsonage standeth est and West, tow baies the Hall and one chamber both lofted over, one barne tow baies at the west end of the parsonage howse.

Inprimis one halfe yeard of Arable land lying in the Fields of Mentmore, the common for tenne sheepe a horse one cowe and A weenyer and hoggs.

In Bidborowe Feilde.

1. Item one halfe Acre in brooke Furlong north and south landmaks Richard Wigg.
2. Item one halfe Acre in hin stone furlong buting est and west landmaks Richard Thood north and John Steven southe.
3. Item one halfe Acre in barke furlong butting north and southe Landemaks Richard Thood West and Thomas Davers est.
4. Item one halfe Acre butting upon hewetts yeard West Landmaks William Wigg south and Thomas Fenne north.
5. Item one halfe Acre in dole-meede furlong butting est and West Landmaks Thomas Godman south and Thomas Batchiler north.

The middle Feilde.

1. Item one halfe Acre in Whadden Furlonge buttinge est and west Landmaks Thomas Davers north and Richard Wigge south.
2. Item one halfe Acre in Rowden Furlonge buttinge north and south Landmaks Robert Parrat Est and Richerd Wigge West.
3. Item one but in short furlong Buttinge est and west land-makes Robert Parratt North and Thomas Batchiler south.
4. Item one lande in Lange furlonge buttynge est and west Land-makes Robert Parratt south and Richard Wigge north.
5. Item one Lee in brightingoo furlong butting north and south Landmaks Thomas Davers West and John Thord est.
6. Item one halfe Acre in neither brightingoo furlong butting est and west londmaks Thomas Davers north and Richard Wigg south.

The 3 feilde next Mentmore.

1. Item one lande in Bumber furlonge butting est and west lande makes Thomas Batchiler north and William Thard south.
2. Item one halfe Acre in longe furlonge buttinge est and West Landmakes Thomas Davers north and Richard Wig south.
3. Item one halfe Acre in Walden furlong north and south Landmaks John Steven est and Richard Thood west.
Item these 3 feildes common for tenne sheip one cow one Weanyer A horse and hoggs.
Item out of Broughton in the parishe of Grove A Rate tith of Sir Robert Dormer Knight cxvj s. viij d. A yeare and the smale tithes of the howse standing in broughton.

Item tithes out of tow meddowes in Grove-bury.

Item out of Mantels mood five shillings and grasse for a cowe the moneth of October the v s. to be paid on midsomer day.

Item paid oute of somerlees six shillings and eight pence everi yeare on midsomer day and A moneth grasse for A gelding every year.

By me   John Facer   Parson *ibidem*

Robert Coxe   Churchwarden
signum Robert Coxe

(D/A/Gt/4/14/1)

57. GREAT HAMPDEN 1607

September 25 Anno Domini 1607 Annoque Regni Domini Regis Jacobi Dei gratia Anglie Francie et Hibernie Regis 5 et Scotiae 40.

A survey or Terrier of all the possessions...

Edifices.

Imprimis the Parsonadge house consisting of five bayes and a halfe (Wherof two were built from the grounde by the now incumbent) built of timber and covered with tiles all chambred over and boarded all the which buildings contrived in two stories (excepting the Kitchen which is but of one storie) and disposed into 9 roomes *viz.* the parlor and hall with chambers over them the Kitchin two other lower roomes for necessarie uses and chambers over.

Item one old barne consisting of sixe small bayes and a halfe and one stable of one bay.

Item one yard or hayse lieng before the house with a lane conteyninge 0 acres 25 poles.

Item the garden orchard and a little pightell adjoyning therto inclosed with a hedge conteyning by estimation 1 dim' acre 28 poles.

Medow.

Item a close called meade close conteyning by estimation 5 acres 32 poles.

Arable.

Item a close called the Kitchin close parted by the now incumbent neere the middle with a quick hedge containing by estimation 6 acres.

Item a close called the further close parted likewise neere the middle by the now incumbent with a quick hedge conteyning by estimation 7 acres 11 poles.

Wood.

Item one grove of wood conteyning by estimation 12 acres.
Summa totalis   32 acres and 16 poles

Bounded.

This whole glebe lyeng together and adjoyning to the Parsonage house aforesaide hath on the South west in length one close called Tarie close belonging to the Lord of the mannor and one close called the Parsonage close belonging to the Lord of the Mannor and the land of Henry Milward and one close of Philip Bourd called Bourders hill and on the Southeast in breath the land of Philip Bourd *viz.* Lanes field Stony close and the end of his grove on the North east in length the highway leading to Chipping Wickomb and on the Northwest in breadth one little coppice and one close called Mawdelines belonging to the Lord of the Mannor.

Out Tythes.

One little close within little Hampden conteyning by estimation foure acres commonly called Little Hanger Close belonging to Litle Hampden farme oweth all maner Tithes to the Rectorie of great Hampden which never hath bene denied.

For Stock implements Tenements or any other thinge inquirable by the Canon and not before intimated heerin there is nothing belonging to this Rectorie as far as we know or can learne.

Ricardus Woodcote   Rector

Philip Mores   Churchwardens
Henry Wetherhead

Thurstane Harding
Philip Bourde   Inhabitants therc
John Hore
(D/A/Gt/5/3/1)

58. HARDWICK 1605

July 25 Anno Domini 1605 Annoque Regni Domini Jacobi Dei gratia 3 et 39.

A survey or terrour of all the possessions...

Homestall.

Inprimis The homestal or scite of the parsonage, being in the Est towardes the greene 8 pole 11 foote on the west towardes the highway 28 pole 5 foote on the North, by a close in the tenure of Widow Miller 21 pole 5 foote on the South by a close in the tenure of William Marcham 18 pole.

Edifices.

The parsonage house consisting of 19 bayes whereof 10 lofted and tiled, 2 tyled but not lofted being a brewhouse and kichin the other thetched and ij bayes lofted being a malte house.

Item one barne consisting of 4 bayes thetched.

Medow.

Item in the Estmede one halfe acre, Jeames Rothwel East and Bennett Harris Lyinge West.

Item in the same meade one yard, widowe Est, lying Est and bennett harris lying on the west.

Item in litle Est meade one swath.

Item in munke meade 5 swathes next the highway Est.

Item in Masgar hookes, a hooke on the home side from the Ladshend to the broke.

Item in Dane meade one acre nexte the hedge which is for al the medow known by the name of Dane meade.

Item in the west feld on hooke nexte pichecott brooke being Ihon Reding Est and the Lees West.

Item one platt of Marse hedge v poole 8 foote and halfe Ihon Reding sowth Ihon Duncombe West.

Item in lichegrove it is the wheat feld at the semer end 17 pole 10 foote and halfe when it is the beane feld 17 pole 10 foote and halfe in the middest betwixte the 2 farmes and when it is fallow 29 pole 9 foote at the farther end nexte berry feild.

Itcm in Wedon feld one plat next [...] dole in [...] in Michel meade Ihon Doncombe on the north 15 [...] east and sowth.

Item on other plot the homer side hedged and diched the other compassed with bearten broke called tithemeade

Arable.

Item in hardweke felde one halfe acre in hidefurlong the lande of Ihon Duncombe Est, and Thomas Reding west.

Item in bredred furlong one halfe acre being the seventh lande from Chadwelley the colledge ground on other syde east and west.

Item on other halfe acre, the 5th land from the former, Sir Lee Lyinge Est and the colledge grounde west.

Item in Long [...] one half acre being the 6th from wodshed lade Sir H Lee ground East, and the colledge ground west.

Item in straglad furlong one land nexte the highway side on the North and Sir H Lees ground on the southe.

Item 2 yerds next Bragman Way on the north and Sir H Lee on the south, shething in to theupping ij heades.

Item in Over frog land one acre, Sir H on the Easte and the colledge ground on the west.

Item at Windmil knappe one Land next the headland the colledge ground lying on both sides.

Item at Wedon hil on plott called the old churcheyarde the watercourse Est the higheway sowth, Calecutt North and the farmers lees west.

Taken the 20th day of August 1607 by

William Tame   Churchewardens
Herry Basen
William Bowdon   Assistants
William Doncomb
Jhon Redinge
Leonard Hobs
Richard Harris   *ibidem*

(D/A/Gt/5/7/1)

59. HARDWICK 1639

A perfect terrior of all the gleibe lande belonginge unto the parsonage of Hardwicke taken the 20 day of June 1639.

Imprimis in the East feilde one halfe acre of arable in hide forelong betwene the land of James Duncombe one the East side and Thomas Reading one the west.

Item in the East feild in breadred furlonge one halfe acre beeing the seaventh lande from Chadwell ley the Colledge ground lying one either side East and West.

Item one other halfe acre in the same furlonge which is the fift land from the other towards the east lyeing betweene Sir Henry Lees ground one East and the Colledge ground one the west.

Item in longe.oo.one half acre beeing the sixth from Wood ead land one the East and Sir Henry Lees ground lyeinge one East and the Colledge ground one the west.

Item in strangland furlong one land lyeing next the high waye side one the north and Sir Henry Lees Ground one the sowth.

Item in the west feilde two yards with heads shooting into the uppings hedge next bragmane way one the north and Sir Henry Lees ground one the sowth.

Item one acre in averfroggelands lyeing beetwixt the ground of Sir Henry Lees on the east and the colledge ground one the west.

Item one land at the windemill knape next the headland the Colledge ground lyeing one both sids.

Homstall.

The Homestall or scite of the parsonage beeinge one the East towards the greene Consistinge 8 polle a ii foote one the west towards the highway side 18 pole 5 foote one the sowth by a cloase in the tenner of William Marcham 18 pole.

The parsonage Howse Consisting of 19 bayes where of 10 are Lofted and tiled 2 tiled but not Lofted Beeing a Kitching and a Brewhouse.

The other theched and two bayes thereof being a Malt Howse Lofted.

One barne Consisting of five bayes thetched and 1 wheate barne Consisting fowre bayes thetched.

Edward Lee   Rector

Bennett Hall   Churchwardens
Thomas Brookes

(D/A/Gt/5/7/2)

60. HARTWELL 1639

A terrier of the pleas Land and houseing belonging to the Rectory of Hartwell in the county of Bucks made *Anno Domini* 1639.

Imprimis A dwelling house consisting of 4 bayes of building of which two dormer windowes are tyled the other part of the house thatched.

Item neare the dwelling house on the west side thereof a kitchen of 3 small bayes of building covered with thatch.

Item two Barnes and a stable consisting of 11 bayes of building covered all with thatch.

Item two little garden plotts on the East side of the dwelling house.

Item an Orchard conteyning about half an acre of ground on the west side of the dwelling house.

Item in Stockam-dich furlong 1 Land.

Item in Long Wardes 2 Landes.

Item in short Wardes 1 Land.

Item In church furlong 3 yarden.

Item in the same furlong 1 land.

Item in Green furlong 3 yarden

Item in Clay furlong next the way save one 1 yard

Item beyond Maynes whete acre in the same furlong 1 Land

Item shooting against Cleydons ash 1 Land.

Item at broad way end 1 butt.

Item in Hatch furlong shooting towardes Lumses close 3 yarden

Item in Lang furlong 3 acres.

Item in Middle furlong 3 yards.

Item in the same 1 Land.

Item one foreshotting acre butting on Long Leyes 1 acre

Item in Heiford furlong 3 yarden.

Item in the same 2 Landes.

Item in Witherstub furlong 2 Landes.

Item in Wadborow furlong 2 Landes.

Item in the same one land 1 Land.

Item in the Ward feild 4 Landes.

Item shooting upon Asen Hill furlong 3 yarden.

Item in Asen Hill furlong 1 Land.

Item in Whaddon feild in the Hanghill 3 yarden.

Item in the same next save one land 3 yarden.

Item in the mill feild 2 Landes.

Item of Ley ground in Long Leyes furlong next to the gutter 2 Landes.

Item in the Butts 4 butts.

Item the chickacre next to the little feild 1 acre.

Item two hooks or closes of Meddow 2 acres.

Item one Ley in Row leaes 1 land.

Item a close lying in Little Hampden 8 acres.

Guilielmus Braig   Rector *ibidem*

John Barnard   Churchwardens
Allexsander Mayne
William King

(D/A/Gt/5/8/1)

61. HAWRIDGE 1639

A terrier of the parsnidge house.

A note of the house and landes belonging to the Parsnage of Hawridge September 4th 1639.

A hall and kitchin and two Buttreys below and two Chambers And 5 chambers above. Two barnes containing 3 bayes apeece. A stable. A hay house; A hen house A hog sty. Five and twenty eakers by estimation lying in 5 closes altogether, joyneing upon the house.

Allsoe at Marsworth in the Common feilds thirty eaker.

Elidad Blackwell   Rector *ibidem*

Robert Furth
Thomas Patman   Churchwardens

(D/A/Gt/5/10/1)

62. HEDSOR 1639

A terrier of all the Gleebe Lands and profits belonginge to the parsonage of Hedsor in the County of Bucks made the sixe day of June 1639.

Imprimis the church yeard of the same parrish Church and Chancell ther beinge no other Gleebe Lands nor parsonage howsse belonginge to the said Parsonage.

Item all the Tythes of Corne Heay Wood and all the Privy Tythes proper to the said place and belonginge to the said parsonage to the locall Custome of Tythinge.

Item the Church duties *Viz.* for Churchinge six pence for Marriage with bands two shillinges with Licence According to the Custome for burrial without a Coffine sixe pence with A Coffine twelve pence and for Mortuaries according to statute in that behalfe belonginge the parson of the said Church. All which according to the estimation of the Incombent nowe beinge doe amount to the yearlie Valuewe of twentie Pounds per Annum or ther a bouts more or lesse. In witnesse hereof the said Incombent and Churchwardens with the rest whose names are hereunderwritten have setto their hands the day and yeare above written.

per me   Ed. Horwood Parsonn

mark   Richard Dymes Churchwarden
mark   Johannes Burcot

(D/A/Gt/5/12/1)

63. HITCHAM 1607

Octobris 1 Anno Domini 1607 Annoque Regni Jacobi dei gratia 5 et 41.

A Surveye or terriour of all the possessions...

Homestall.

Imprimis The homestall or Scite of the parsonage scituate and lyinge betwene the land of Sir William Clerke Knighte commonly called and knowne by the name of Hunts coppice northeast and Cutlers pitle With the lane leadinge from Taplowe to the comon woode called Whittage lane west and the Land of Sir William Clerke aforesaid called Colegrove South with two severall grounds of Henry Manfyld gent called Colgrove and Nightinge crofte upon the Southwest and the common feild upon the Easte conteyninge by estimation 26.

Item within the sayd boundes are contayned one garden impayled by estimation 7 poles and one orchard sufficiently replenished by estimation 1 acre.

Edifices.

Item the parsonage house consistinge of 7 bayes buylte all of tymber and covered with Tyle being all Chambered over and boarded and the whole buyldinge contrived in 2 stories and disposed into 15 roomes *viz.* the halle the parlour, the Buttrie the celler the Larder the boultinge house, the Kitchin, two entries, the studie, two bedchambers a corneloft and two other litle rooms above for other uses.

Item one barne consistinge of 3 bayes buylt of tymber and covered with tyle, one fodder house and a stable thatched consistinge of 3 bayes a peece.

Item within the sayd bounds are conteyned 15 acres of arable ground called the pitle the barne cloase and the further cloase boundinge upon whittage lane west, and other broomy cloases boundinge upon the comon feild [...] cloase, and holybush cloase contayninge by estimation 9 acres and nowe lyinge for grasse.

Pasture.

Item pasture none savinge those two broomie cloases within the bounds above mentioned.

Item one coppice lyinge betwene the said holybush cloase East and the barne cloase west and a coppice of Henry Manfyll gent south, conteyninge by estimation 1.

Medowe.

Item 5 acres of medowe and one roode lyinge in Hicham meade whereof one halfe acre next the Marshe lane, lieth betweene the land of Sir William Garrard Knighte, South and the land of Sir William Clerke Knighte North 2 acres and a halfe betwene the land of Henry Manfyld gent South and the land of Sir William Garrard North with one hedhalfeacre abuttinge on the land of Sir William Clerke west and an other hedhalfe acre boundinge on the land of Sir William Garrard South and the land of Henry Manfyld gent. Sir William Gerrard Sir William Clerke Knighte aforesaid North, one halfe acre betwene the land of Henry Manfyld west and the land of Sir William Garrard East one half acre betwene the land of Sir William Clerke South, and the land of Sir William Garrard North and the yeard betwene the land of Sir William Garrard North and Sir William Clerke South.

Item in Taplowe Meads 2 acres and a halfe whereof one halfe acre in smale meade and an other halfe acre in sladmeade both lott meads and the other 3 halfe acres in longemead whereof the myddest lyeth betwene the land of the parson of Taplowe north and the kings land south, thother two half acre betwene the land of the said parson North and the land of Heny Manfyld gent' South.

Summa pratorum.   7 acres 3.

Arable.

Item in the field betwene the parsonage house and the church one peece of arable ground boundinge upon the parsonage cloases west and upon the land of Sir William Clerke Knighte North East and south contayninge by estimation 21a.

Item in Warren field 7 acres arable *vizt.* one lyinge betwene the land of Sir William Garrard north and the land of Sir William Clerke south abuttinge upon longe lane West, one acre betwene the land of Henry Manfyld gent' south and north a buttinge on longe lane west, halfe an acre abuttinge upon Wyndesor waye south and boundinge upon the land of Sir William Garrard West and the Abbey land east, one acre abuttinge on Windesor way south and Burnham field north and betwene the land of Sir William Clerke east and west one acre betwene the land of Sir William Clerke East and the land of Mr Butler of Burnham west one halfe acre betwene the land of William Butler East and the land of Sir William Clerke west one acre boundinge upon the land of Sir William Garrard West and the land of Sir William Clerke East abuttinge upon Burnham field north The seventh betwene the land of Sir William Clerke East and Butler of Burnham west.

Item in hicham field 7 acres and a halfe *viz.* three halfe acres betwene the land of Sir William Clerke East and west abutting upon Windesor Way 3 acres lyinge together on Marsh hyll boundinge on the land of Henry Manfyld gent' East and on Taplow field west abuttinge upon the land of Sir William Garrard North and the land of Sir William Clerke South one acre called the groundfall acres betwene the land of

Richard Howe West and the land of Henry Manfyld East one acre betwene the land of Sir William Garrard west and the land of Henry Manfyld gent' east and abuttinge upon Windesor way towards the north the seaventh betwene the land of Sir William Clerk east North and south abuttinge on Windesor way west and on longe lane east   7 acres 2 roods.

Item belowe London waye 8 acres *vizt,.* the furthest acre of the parishe in Dorney fielde the furthest acre in Midle lease. the furthest acre in Westowne field and one acre in Neewecroft bounded with the land of Sir William Garrard East and west. 4 acres.

Summa arabilis [blank].

Out tythes.

Item all the tythes of George Clarks arable within Taplowe and all other [...] he hathe any quittrente commonly called Clerke land, belonginge to Henry Manfyld gent' nowe in the tenure of some of his tenants whereof never tythes were yet denied to the parson of Hicham.

As for stocke tenements and other implements enquirable by the Canon and not expressed here in as far as we knowe there is none belonginge to this Rectorie.

Robert Lloyd   Parson of Hitcham

Harry [...]   Churchwarden his mark
[...]   his mark
John Paile   his mark
Christopher [...]   his mark
William Crayne   his mark

(D/A/Gt/5/14/1)

64. HITCHAM 1625

Hitcham Patron Mr William Clark Esq. *May decimo tertio Anno Domini 1625.*

A Survey or Terrar of all the possession belonging to the Rectory of Heecham made amd Taken by the view perambulation and estimate of the Minister and Churchwarden and other inhabitants their whose names are subscribed beinge therunto nominated and appoynted by the Generall surveiour of Church Gleabes and possessions within the Diocese of Lincolne by a Commission Decreed by the Reverend Father in God William Lord Bishipp of Lincolne *Anno* 1611 And now by the Reverend Father in God John Lord Bishopp of Lincolne the

Right honorable Lord Keeper of the Great Seale of England for the further execucon of the Cannon in that behalfe recalled and established.

Homestall.

Imprimis the homestall or Site of the parsonage scituated and lyinge between the Land of Mr William Clarke Esq. Commonly called and knowne by the name of hunts and Parkers pitle west and north and the lane that leadeth from the said hunts to the parsonage barne closse, East and South by estimacon 1 Acre 1 Rood.

Edifices.

Item within the said bounds are contayned on garden impaled by estimacon seaven poles, And on orchard suffitiently replenished by estimacon 1 Acre.

Buildings.

Item the parsonage house consisting of Seaven baies built all of Timber and Covered with Tiles being all Chambered over and boarded, and the whole buildings Contrived in Two stories and disposed into Fifteen Roomes *viz.* the hall the parlour the buttery the Celler the larder the boulting house the Kitchin two entries the Study two bed Chambers a Corne loft other two little Roomes all above, to make upp the number.

Item one Barne consisting of three baies, built with timber and Covered with Tiles, one fodder house and a stable thatched consisting of Three baies a peece.

Pasture.

Item Pastures Nine Acres of rossie broomy ground which for the mosse and growing the same is sometimes, dared lying between the Lands of Mr William Clarke called hunts north and the land of the said Mr William Clarke called colegrave South and haveing the Common feild east and the parsonage house west and devided into two severall closses called new close and holy bush close contayning by estimacon 9 Acres.

Item one Coppice lying between the said holy bush closse east and the barne closse west and a Coppice of Mr Henry Mansfeild gent. South contayning by estimacon 1 Acre.

Meadow.

Item Five Acres of Meadow and one Roode lying in Hicham Meade wherof one halfe acre next the Marsh lane lieth between the land of

Thomas Garrard Esq. South and the Land of Mr William Clarke north two Acres and a halfe between the Land of Henry Mansfeild gent South and the land of Thomas Garrard Esq north and one head halfe acre a butting on the Land of Mr William Clarke Esq. west, one other head halfe acre on the Land of Thomas Garrard South all along and the Lands of Henry Mansfeild Thomas Garrard Mr William Clarke north, one halfe acre between the Land of Henry Mansfeild west and the land of Thomas Garrard east, on halfe acre betweene the land of Mr William Clarke South and the Land of Mr Thomas Garrard north, and the yard between the land of Thomas Garrard north and the Land of Mr William Clarke South.

Item in Taplow Meades two Acres and a halfe wherof one halfe acre in smale Mead and on other halfe acre in slade meade both lott meades, and other three halfe acres in Long meade wherof the Midest lyeth betweene the Land of the parson of Taplow north and the Kings land south the other two halfe acres between the Lands of the said parson of Taplow and the Lands of Henry Mansfeild gent north and south.

Arable.

Item fifteen Acres of Rossie arrable ground inclosed and bounding uppon whytage lane west and a ground of Henry Mansfeild gent South upon the parsonage Coppice and holly bush close aforesaid east and the parsonage barne on the north devided into four severall closes or Pitles, the Tow barne closes and the further close contayning by estimacon 15 Acres.

Item in the feild between the parsonage house and the Church one peece of Arable ground bounding uppon the parsonage closes west and uppon the land of Mr William Clarke north east, and south Contayning by estimacon 21 Acres.

Item in warren Feild seaven Acres wherof one acre lieth between the land of Thomas Garrard Esq. north and the land of Mr William Clarke Esq south and a butteth upon longe lane west one acre between the lands of Henry Mansfeild gent south and north abutting upon the same lane west, one halfe acre abutting upon windsor way south and bounding upon the land of Thomas Garrard Esq north and upon the Abbey land east one acre abutting upon Windsor way south and Burnham feild north and lieth between the Lands of William Clarke east and west, one halfe acre between the land of Absalon Butler east and the land of Mr William Clarke west and abutting upon Burnham Feild north one acre between the Land of Absalon Butler of Burnham west and the land of Mr William Clarke east and one acre between the land of Thomas Garrard Esq west and Mr William Clarke Esq east and the last acre between the land of Mr William Clarke east and the Merebanke adioyning upon the land of Absalon Butler of burnham west 7 Acres.

Item in Hicham feild Seaven acres and a halfe wherof three halfe acres ly together upon Windsor way between the lands of Mr William Clarke east and west three acres lying togeather bounding upon the land of Henry Mansfeild gent east and Taplow feild west abutting upon the land of Thomas Garrard north and the land of Mr William Clarke Esq south and one acre between the land of Richard How west and the land of Henry Mansfeild gent east one acre between the land of Henry Mansfeild South and the land of Thomas Garrard north and upon Windsor way east and upon Taplow feild west and lastly one acre abutting upon long lane east and Windsor way west bounding between the lands of Mr William Clarke Esq north and south.

Item below the highway from Bristow to London four acres *vizt.* the furthest acre of all the parish of Dorney feild the furthest in Midle lease, the furthest in westowne feild, and one acre in new Croft abutting upon Marsh Lane between the land of Thomas Garrard Esq east and west and north 4 Acres.

Quite Tithes xiiij Acres and a yard.

Item Certaine Lands of Mr William Clarke Esq that sometimes belonged to the farme house being all the Arable that hee hath in that parish of Taplow that belongeth to the said farme scituated in Hicham and alsoe certaine Lands in Taplow beelonging to Henry Mansfeild gent now in the tenure of some of his Tennants wherof Mr William Clark receiveth quitrents amounting to xiiij acrs and a yard wherof Tithes were ever paid to the parson of Hicham, but wee Compt them in the parish of Hicham within the precincts of Taplow.

Stocks Tenements or any other thing inquired by the Cannon and not expressede, wee have none as farr as wee know. No lands Rents or stockes for the poore, but what Mr William Clarke gave at his Death which is given them as they have need, that is five Pounds.

No Catechism taught but that in the Common Praier.

Robert Lloyde   Parson

Jasper Grave   Churchwarden
John Poole
Christopher Bovingtonn
Abraham Stone.

(D/A/Gt/5/14/3)

65. HITCHAM 1639

July the eight 1639.

A Survey or terrer of the possessions belonging [...] rectory of Hitcham.

Inprimis the housestall or site of the parsonage situate and lieing and beinge betweene the land of John Clerke esquire knowne by the name of Hunts and Pooles pigythle west and north and the lane that leadeth from the sayd Hunts to the parsonage [...] orchardes yardes backsides [...] contayneinge by est[...].

Item the parsonage house [...] back disposed into these severall [...] a parlour a chamber over the Sellar a stare case leadeinge up to 4 chambers, with a studdy: an entry to the Kitchin a meale house, one litle buttery a Kitchin a brewhouse a milkehouse two litle larders and a sinkehouse leaneinge to the brewhouse a chamber over the Kitchin a Corne loft over the brewhouse and cockloftes all over the hall and the parlour.

Item two barnes the one tyled consistinge of 3 bayes and a portey, with a stable thetched leaneinge thereunto: one other barne thatched consistinge of 4 bayes and a portch.

Item one hay-barne consistingwe of 4 bayes all thatched.

Item two closes of arrable or pasture, the one called new close, the other holy bush close contayneinge by estimation 12 acres lyeinge between the landes of John Clerke esquire called Hunter North and the landes of the sayd John Clerke caled Cole grene south.

Item 5 acres of meadow and one roode, lyeinge in Hitcham meade and one halfe acre betwene the land of Sir James Palmer south and the land of John Clerke north: 2 acres and a halfe betweene the land of Sir Edward Manfeild south and Sir James Palmer north, one head halfe acre abuttinge on the land of Mr John Clerke west and one other head halfe acre boundinge on the land of Sir James Palmer south and Mr John Clerke aforesayd north: one halfe acre betweene the land of Sir Edward Manfeild west and of Sir James Palmer east, one halfe acre betweene the land of Mr John Clerke south and Sir James Palmer north, and the yeard betweene the land of Sir James Palmer north and John Clerke south.

Item in Taplow meades two acres and a halfe whereof one halfe acre in small meade and an other halfe acre in slade meade both Lott meades and other three halfe acres whereof the middle most lyeth between the land of the parson of Taplow north and the kings land now in the tenure of John Hampson esq south the other two halfe acres betweene the landes of the sayde parson and the lands of Sir Edward Manfild north and south.

[...]
[...]

Item in the feild betweene the pasture [...] one peice of arable ground boundinge upon [...] [...] closes west and uppon the land of Mr John [...] and south contayneinge by estimation [...] whereof one acre lyeth between the land of Sir John Parsons north and Mr John Clerke south and butteth uppon longe lane acre betweene the landes of Sir Edward Mansf[...] south and north and abuttinge on the lande aforesayde west. one halfe acre buttinge uppon Windsor way south and boundinge on the land of Sir John Parsons north: and uppon the Abbey land east one acre abuttinge uppon Windsor way south and [...] feild north and lieth betweene the land of John Clerke [...] west and one halfe acre by the land of John [...] buttinge on Burnham feild [...]tweene the land of Rob[...] and the land of Mr John [...] betweene the land of Sir John [...] Mr John Clerke east, and the last acre [...] the land of Mr John Clerke east and [...] banck west [...].

Item, in Hitcham feild 7 acres and a halfe [...] 3 halfe acres lye together uppon Windsor [...] betweene the landes of Mr John Clerke [...] three acres lieinge together boundinge [...] land of Sir Edward Manfield east and [...] feild west, abuttinge on the land of Sir John [...] north and the land of Mr John Clerke south. [...] acre betweene the land some tymes of Richard [...] west and the land of Sir Edward Manfield east, one [...] betweene the land of Sir Edward Manfeild south [...] the land of Sir John Parsons North: uppon [...]sor way east, and Taplow feild west and lastly one acre abuttinge uppon longe lane west and windsor way west, and betweene the lands of Mr John Clerke north and south.

Item below London highway 4 acres *viz.* the futhermost acre in all the parish in [...] the farthest [...] towne feild, and one acre in New crofte abuttinge uppon Marsh lane betweene the land of Sir John Parsons East and west.

The marke of John Grove   Churchwarden.

(D/A/Gt/5/14/6)

66. HOGGESTON 1639

A Transcript of a Terrier of our Glebelands and houses belonging to the Church and Rectorie of Hoggeston in the county of Bucks and Diocesse of Lyncoln taken from a copie dated July 9 1639.

Imprimis One Pasture ground containing by Estimation fifty and six Acres lying and butting East and south upon the lands of the Right Honorable Robert Earle of Caernarvon and now in the tenure and occupacon of Joseph Busbie Gent and West and North upon a common high way leading from Murseley town to Hoggeston aforesaid.

Item one close Pasture ground containing by Estimation Eleven Acres adjoyning to the abovesaid Fifty and six Acres East and south and West upon a lane leading from the town to diverse of the inhabitants grounds and North upon the aforesaid Highway from Murseley.

Item a little peice of ground commonly cald the old Churchyard at the Townesend West.

Item a Parsonage Mansion house convenient with a barne and stable.

£2172 11s. 4½d.

Ben Jones   Rector

Thomas Short   Churchwardens
William Short

(D/A/Gt/5/15/1

67. HORTON 1639

A True Catalogue of all the houses orchards Lands and possessions belonging to the parsonage in Horton *in Comitatu* Bucks.

The Dwellinge House together with out Houses adioyninge within the Moate Consiste of Twenty one bayes all Covered with tiles.

The barne Consists of five bayes Covered with Strawe.

The Medow orchard and gardines aboute the Houses Containe Two acres and a halfe Buttinge west upon the Common and South North and est upon the Land [...] Bulstrod Esquire.

One acre of Medowe in Celly Meade butted and Bounded round with the [...] Henery Bulstrod Esquire.

One acre in Colbrooke Feild buttinge west one the Common Called [...] and North [...] one South with the Lande of Henery Bulstrode.

Two acres in Lome Feild Buttinge Southward one the Lands of John [...] and east one the Lands of James Homer and west one the Lane that [...] from Langly to Welly.

One Have acre Lainge in Turkey Shott buttinge est one a Cloce [...] Esq and all soe bounded South North and West with the Lands of [...].

One Rood in the sayd Shott Buttinge east one Close of the [...] and west one the Lands of James Haines.

One acre Lainge in a feild Called Homers acre [...] Lands of John Ives West one a Lane Leading from Langely to Welly [...] with the Lands of Henery Bulstrode Esq.

One three yeard Lane Lainge in Hie Feild buttinge North [...] bounded east west and South with the Lands of Henery [...] Three Halfe acres wherof one three yard butts North and south one three roods more belonginge to the parsonage [...] the Landes of James Haines one west with the Lands of Henery [...] the other three Yards buttinge South one the Lands of Henery Bul[...] one North one West one the Lands of Henery [...] Esq. one east one the Lands of James Haines.

Edwarde Goodall   Parson of Horton

James Heine   Churchwardens
Robert Biddell
signum   [...]   Michell
signum   Thomas   [...]
(D/A/Gt/5/17/1)

68. HUGHENDEN 1607

October [...] Anno Domini 1607 Annoque Regni Domini Regis Jacobis dei gratia 5 et 41.

A Survey of all the possessions...

Homestale.

Inprimis the homestale or scite of the vicaridge scituat Lying and being betwene the hye Waye on the northeast and Southeast and the Lords land belonging to his manner and parsonage of Hutchenden on the Northwest and Southwest.

Item within the said bounds are conteyned one litle Court or garden besett on every syde with the house and Wales, by estimate two pooles and one orchard partelye paled and partly hedged by estimation half an Acre.

Edifices.

Item the Vicaridg house consisting of sixe bayes built all of tymber work and wals plaistered with earth morter and the house covered with tyles fower bayes lofted over and borded the whole building contryved and disposed into sixe Roomes *vizt.* the haule one under chamber two litle butteries one Kitchin one old house for wood or other lyke th[...] thereto adioyned one litle barne of two bayes covered also with tyles.

As for pasture medowe arrable owttythes or any other thing inquyrable by the Cannon there is not any as farr as we knowe or canne Learne.

Hugh Lane   Minister

Robert Lane   Churchwardens
Thomas Lane
Christopher Weden
Gyles Randall   Sydman   mark
John Coo   mark
Jefferie Stevens   mark
(D/A/Gt/5/19/1)

69. HULCOTT 1639

A Terrier of all the glebe land belonging to the Rectori of Hulcott in the County of Bucks made the seaventh day of August *Anno Domini* 1639 by us whose names are hereunto subscribed.

In Fenne feild x ridges of arable.

In short hasteads Furlong one halfe acre lying betwene the land of Bernard Norcott on the Southwest side and the Land of Alexander Walker on the North east side.

In Long acre furlong one halfe acre lying betwene the land of Bernard Norcott on the South side and the land of Mr Thomas Fountaine Esq on the north side.

In Lang Furlong one yard with a head lying betweene the land of Bernard Norcott on the south side and the land of Mr Thomas Fountaine on the Northside.

In high heads Furlong one halfe acre lying betweene the Land of Bernard Norcotte on the south side and the land of Mr Thomas Fountaine on the North side.

Item upper pease furlonge one halfe acre lying betwene the land of Bernard Norcott on the South side and the land of Mr Thomas Fountaine on the North side.

In midle pease furlonge one acre lyeing betwene the land of Henry Stratford of Beorton on both sides.

In Fenne furlong neere Turpine hedge one butt with a head lyeing betwene the land of Bernard Norcott on the South side and the land of Mr Thomas Fountaine on the North.

In the same furlong one yard butt with a head lyeing betwene the land of Bernard Norcott on the South side and the land of Mr Thomas Fountaine on the north side.

Item woodway Furlong att green wayes end one butt lying betwene the land of Bernard Norcott on the South side and the land of Mr Thomas Fountaine on the North.

In Midle Feild xij ridges of arrable and one ley.

One headland heading Church Furlong on the south side and the land of Henry Strattfold lying on the North.

In the poole one halfe acre lying betwene the land of Bernard Norcatt on the south side and the land of Mr Thomas Fountaine on the North side.

In long Bennell one halfe acre lying betwene the land of Mr Thomas Fountaine on the west side and the land of Bernard Norcatt on the east side.

In the same Furlong one halfe acre lyeing betwene the land of Mr Thomas Fountaine on the west and the land of Bernard Norcatt on the east side.

In short Bennell one halfe acre lyeing betwene the Land of Bernard Norcatt on the east side and the land of Mr Thomas Fountaine on the west side.

In the same furlong one acre lying betwene the land of Mr Thomas Foutaine on the east side and the land of the earle of Carnarvan on the west side.

In the Rewe one halfe acre lying betwene the land of Bernard Norcatt on the east side and the land of Mr Thomas Fountaine on the west side.

In Mare Furlong one butt lying betwene the land of Mr Thomas Fountaine on the North side and the land of Bernard Norcatt on the south side.

In long Lowe one acre lying betwene the land of Mr Thomas Fountaine on each side.

In high honds Furlong one halfe acre lyeing betwene the land of Bernard Norcatt on the South side and the land of Mr Thomas Fountaine on the North side.

In Borsdene one ley lying betwene the land of Mr Thomas Fountaine on the west side and the land of Bernard Norcatt on the east side.

In Hoods Feild viij ridges of arable and one ley.

In Hulcott houghills one acre lying betwene the land of Mr Thomas Fountaine on the South side and the land of the Earle of Carnarvon on the north side.

In the same furlong one halfe acre lying betwene the land of Bernard Norcatt on the south side and the land of Henry Strattfold on the North.

In the furlong shooting upon sideling plott one halfe acre lying betwene the land of Bernard Norcatt on the east side and the land of Mr Thomas Fountaine on the west side.

In short hill one halfe acre lyeing betwene the land of Mr Thomas Fountaine on the west side and the land of Bernard Norcatt on the east side.

In the butts shooting into hoods one butt with a head lying betwene the land of Thomas Webb on the east parte and the land of the Earle of Carnarvan on the west side.

In short furlong one halfe acre lying betwene the land of Bernard Norcatt on the South and the land of Mr Thomas Fountaine on the North.

In churchway furlong one halfe acre lying betwene the land of Mr Thomas Fountaine on the North side and the land of Bernard Norcatt on the South side.

In hoods one leye lying betwene the leyes of Bernard Norcatt on the East side and the Mercers hold on the west.

In Hulcott nether leyes one acre of leyes being Michaelmas ground lying betwene the leyes of Bernard Norcatt on the west side and of Mr Thomas Fountaine on the east side.

In upper hulcott leyes one ley lying next unto the hedge of Ruth Crosse Bernard Norcatt and John [...] on the east side and the leye of Mr Thomas Fountaine on the west side.

One halfe yard of meadowe in the Fenne and Blackhedge lyeing in the lott Called the three score and pitt.

One Mansion house thatche Containing five bayes and one thatche barne Containing fower bayes with a yard a garden plott and a litle orchard.

One Close adioyning to the house and lying betwene the leyes of Mr Thomas Fountaine on the South east side and the highway leading unto Beerton on the Northwest side.

William Bell

Henry Gurney   *Gardianes*
Benedict Rash

A Terrier of all the land belonging to the Church of Hulcott made the seaventh day of August *Anno Domini* 1639 by us whose names are hereunto suscribed.

In Fenne Feild one halfe acre lying betwene the land of Henry Gurney and the land of Thomas [...] on the South.

In Midle Feild one halfe acre lying betwene the land of Bernard Norcatt on the South and the highway leading to Beerton on the [...].

In the [...] two acres of ley ground lying betwene the landes of Mr

Thomas Fountaine on the east side and the land of Thomas Harding one west.

In Brooke furlong one halfe acre lying betwene the Mercers land on East and the land of the Earle of Carnarvon on the weste.

One house Containing [...] dwelling house and [...] barn with a litle backside adioyning [...].

William Bell

Henry Gurney
Benedict Rash   *Gardianes*
(D/A/Gt/5/20/1)

70. IVER 1607

Octobris 9 Anno Domini 1607 Annoque Regni Domini Regis Jacobi Dei gratia 5 et 41.

A Survey or Terrour of all the possessions...

Homestall.

Imprimis The Homestall or Scite of the Vicaridge scituate and lying betweene the Kyngs Majesties high waye on the East and the common feilde Called the Moore on the west; and abutting upon the ground of Henry Britrydge gent. on the North and upon the ground of the said Brytridge South and contaynes by estimation one roode.

Item within halfe of the sayd roode is contained on garden and in the other halfe an orchard hedged and ditched.

Item the Vicaridge house consisteing of a haule a Kitchin and a [...] ioyned to the Kitchin and two [...].

John Atkins   Vicar

Nicholas Clarke   Churchwardens
William Willde
John Brooke   Sidemen
John Hunte

For Stockes Implements Tenements or any other thing inquirable by the Canon (and not here in before intimated and expressed ther is nothing belonging to this Vicaridge the churchyard Crisomes and burialls excepted) as farre as wee know or can learn.

William Wheeler senior
William Wheeler junior
John Stanley
John [...]
(D/A/Gt/5/23/1)

71. IVINGHOE 1607

Octobris xvij Anno Domini 1607 Annoque regni Regis Jacobi Dei gratia 5 et 41.

A Survey or Terrior of the possessions...

Homestall.

Imprimis the homestall or Scite of the same vicarage scituate [...] uppon the streate, Betwene a Copyhold tenement belonging to [...] the parsonage on the East syde nowe in the tenure of Thomas [...] And a Copiehold Tenement belonging to the Mannor of Ivinghoe [...] nowe in the tenure of Josyas Hebbes And one yard adioyning belonging, All which conteyning in length from the strete northwards [...] polles and ix foote, and in bredth at the strete twoe polles and iij [...] and in [...] at the northe ende two poll iij foote and [...] or ther abowtes.

Edifices.

The Vicaridge dwelling howse consisting of fyve bayes all of timber buylding, and covered with Tyles being chambored over and boorded [...] story high, disposed into x roomes, *vizt.* a Hall [...] a Kechin, a buttrey, and fyve chambers above.

Item one lyttle barne anexed conteyning [...] small Baye and an halfe.

Item one Lenetoe.

Tythes.

The other possessions of the same vicarage consisting of all mortuaries and offerings in the said parish Excepte tythe grayne and Tythe haye. also customable dutie of iiij d. for everie yard land [...] yard land which is Copiehold of the Mannor of Ivinghoe and [...] was bond tenure within the said parish with divers [...] owte of dyvers tenements Messauges and groundes [...] and customary [...] Seabrooke, Chedington, Horton, Cooperend St. Margaretts [...] Nettleden, Except all Tithes of corne and hay.

For pastures Meadowes arrable landes stocks Implements Tenements or any other things enquired by the [...] and not herein before nomynated and expressed [...] at this tyme possessed or enioyed to this vicar [...] ben for tyme of remembrance as farr as [...] us certenlie knowe or can perceive or learne [...].

Robert Bostock   Mynister
with the addicon endorsed

Henry Sandys
John Payne   mark   Churchwarden

[...]   Hannell
Edward Sawell   mark   Sydeman
Michael Serre   mark
George [...]
(D/A/Gt/5/24/1)

72. GREAT KIMBLE 1639

A terrier of the gleabe land belonging to the Vicarage of Kimbell
magna *in comitatu* Bucks 1639.

Imprimis two acres of arrable land whereof one lyeth in the Little
field in a furlong named Nittens hill the land of John Hampden
Esquier on the east side, and the land of Sir Walter Pie on the
west side.

Item one other acre lyeth in a field called Hoorestone the land of
John Hampden Esquier on both sides.

Item one slip of grasse ground lying on the east side of the lane that
leadeth from the church towards the Lintch contayninge by estimacon
a roode of ground be it more or lesse.

Item one parcell of ground lying south, from Bulpittwood, which
formerly hathe beene wood grownd, contayning by estimacon two
acres be it more or lesse.

Item the Churchyarde contayning by estimacon three roodes be it
more or lesse.

Item the Vicarage house contayning these roomes.

Imprimis a hall and entrie, not lofted over.

Item three roomes from the entrie eastward, all lofted over.

Henrie Silvester   Vicar

Peter Aldridge   Churchwardens
Francis Clarke
(D/Λ/Gt/6/1/1)

73. LITTLE KIMBLE 1607

*October v Anno Domini 1607 Annoque Regni Domini Regis Jacobi Dei gratia
5 et 44.*

A Survey or terrour of all the possessions...

Home-stall.

Imprimis the homestall or Scite of the parsonage contaynes by estimation one acre within the bowndes whereof are conteyned one garden plott hedged, by estimation one pole, and 2 orchards hedged by estimation one half acre.

Edifices.

Item the parsonage howse consisting of 2 bayes built all of tymber and covered with thatch whiche are chambred over and booreded disposed into ij Roomes *viz.* a hall and a parloure.

Item one barn consistinge of two bayes Joyned to the parsonage howse and a Leento to the end of the barn for a stable.

Pasture.

Pasture none gleebe none.

Arable.

Arable none.

Medow.

Medow that hath in plots *viz.* one plott in the moore conteyninge by estimation one half acre one plott in Apsley meade by estimation one acre one plott in Apsley dryclose by estimation one acre one plott going over the end of all Normeade by estimation one greate acre one plott in Normeade by estimation one acre.

Item yt hathe all manner tythe corn and hey withall other pryvy and smale tythes accrewinge and growing in or uppon the said parish.

Item yt hath one plott of grownde having wood and box groing in yt, Lying uppon the topp of the boxwood next unto the hill thereto adioyninge.

For Stocks implements tenements or any other thing inquirable by the Canon (and not herein before intymated and expressed) there ys nothing belonging to this Rectory as far as we knowe or yeat can Learne.

Thomas Prowde   the Parson there.

Thomas Limtayne   Churchwardens
Francis Stadam
Christofor Franklyn   Inhabytants
William Bampton

(D/A/Gt/6/2/1)

74. LITTLE KIMBLE 1639

A Terryer of the glebe land belonging to the Rectorye of little Kymble *Anno Domini* 1639 July 27.

Inprimis A plat of ground upon which the house stands which conteynes two Acres of ground more or lesse on the north side bounding upon a close belonging unto a farme of Richard Braceye, and on the other side upon the Widowe Stathams Farme.

Item the Churchyard conteyning an acre of ground more or lesse.

Item woodground conteyning 2 Acres more or lesse, lying in boxe Wood on the south side bounding upon the Common, on the North side on the wood of Richard Bracey and the Widowe Statham; on the East upon the Wood of Christopher Eggleton, and on the West upon the highway.

Nicholas Cantrell   Rector

The marke of William Allen   Churchwardens
The marke of Gregory Price

(D/A/Gt/6/2/2)

75. LAVENDON 1607

October 5 Anno Domini 1607 Annoque Regni Domini Regis Iacobi Dei gratia quinto etc.

A Inivey of all the possesions belonging to the Viccarech of Lavendon made and taken by the viewe perambulation and estimate of the minister, churchwardens sidesmen and other of inhabitants thes whose names are Subscribed and appoynted by William Folkingham Gent generall surveiour of church gleabes and possessions within the Diocesse of Lincon as followeth.

The home stale.

The home stale or vicearch sett and Joyned unto the church yearde on parlor with a lofte an halle with a loft on Kytchin with a loft on Dery howse with a loft on smale orcharde a little backside and a barne.

Land.

Arrable firste in Tenacke feilde iiij lands 1 acre abuttinge south into howbrookeslade and north upon a hadland of on Anthonie Bird.

Causleyfeild.

Item theire three Landes on acre west towards a close Called gussitts and East towards a waye called gussets waye.

The Mill feild.

Item theire three Lands on acre the land of Mistriss Norwich lyinge on the southe side and the Land of one John Lauton on the north side.

Item in the same feild foure Landes by estimacon on acre abuttinge eastward upon the Lande of the Lorde Mordant and westward upon the Lande of John Haywarde esquier.

Thomas Newton   Viccar theire

Edmonde Man
Richard Sibtharp
Thomas Man
Edwarde Morgan   mark
Anthonie Birde   mark   Churchwarden
William Norman   mark   Sidesman
Christopher Buchar *alias* Sibtharp   mark   Churchwarden

(D/A/Gt/6/6/1)

76. LILLINGSTONE DAYRELL 1639

Glebe Landes belonging to the Rectory of Lillingston aforesaid the Rector and Churchwarden thereof, know of None, one by the Parsonage house itself and round about it in garden, yard and ground next to it six and thirty poles in all, or there about in compasse.

Samuel Wastell   Rector *ibidem*

The x marke of John Knight   Churchwarden

(D/A/Gt/6/9/1)

77. GREAT LINFORD 1607

Octobris vicesimo primo 1607 Annoque Regni Domini Regis Jacobi dei gratia Quinto et Quadragesimo primo.

A Survey or Terriour of all the possessions...

Inprimis The homestall or Scite of the parsonage aforsaid scytuat and lyinge betwene the Strete on the east syde and the feild called the [...] west and the close of Henry Cowley on the South and a farme house belonginge to the Lord of great Linford on the North and [...] 1 acre.

Item [...] said bound are contayned one Orchard and a garden lyinge together fenced about with quicksetts contayninge by estymacon two roodes [...] which compass of ground standethe a dovehouse made of stone.

Item [...] howse consistinge of syxe bayes buylt all of stone and Tymber and covered with tyle all beinge chambered over and bourded etc. [...] of the said syxe being in height three storyes and the other three bayes in height two stories and disposed into xij roomes *viz* an hall [...] a kitchin etc. [...] consistinge of v small bays unto the which adioyninge one other litle barne contayninge two bayes buylt etc. [...] stable contayninge two bays buylt etc.

Item one haye howse adioyninge to the said stables contayninge two bayes buylt etc.

[...] adioyninge to the aforesaid orchard and garden on the east syde and the common feild on the West and contayneth by [...] 1 acre.

Item there doth belong to the said parsonage in the common meadow of great Linford one halfe yard of meadowe which lyeth by lott and contayneth by estymacon two roodes of ground 2 roodes.

Item [...] belonginge to the said parsonage in the said Meadow in respect of the tithe of the meeadow aforsaid one pece of meadowe beinge bounded [...] lyeth alwayes certen contayninge by estymacon 5 acres.

Summa pratorum 5 acres 2 roodes.

The Woode Feild.

Imprimis nyne roodes lying together upon the furlonge called westhill shotinge east and West the land of John Blundell on the south and the [...] ditch on the North.

Item one other halfe acre shotinge westward towardes Stanton hedge the Lord on the south and [...] on the north.

Item one half acre on the furlonge called Whitson path shotinge West towards Stanton hedge John [...] north and the land of Sir Anthonye Tyeringham Knight on the south.

Item one halfe acre on the Myddle furlong [...] and west the land of John Nycholls on the south and the Lord on the north.

Item one half acre lyinge on Rowlowe [...] west the land of John Rufhead on the north and Henry Kent on the south.

Item one half acre on North hill shotinge east and [...] William Malins on the north and Robert Nycholls on the south.

Item eight half acres lying together on the furlong called lytle hoe shootinge North and south the land of John Blundell on the West and the land of Sir Anthonye Tyringham east.

Item two roodes lyinge together on a furlonge betwixte Ridgeway and Lye Way shotinge east and Weste the land of Sir Anthony Tyringham on the south and the furlonge called Aerfurlonge on the north.

Item one half acre under Ridgeway shotinge east and west William Hopkins on the north and Sir Anthonye Tirringham on the south.

Item one halfe acre shootinge into Nereham brooke the lord on both sydes.

Item one halfe acre lyinge upon Bryer Ridge shootinge east and West the lord on both sydes.

Item one half acre lyinge upon Crane Hill shootinge east and West the land of Thomas Roughead on the south and William Malins on the north.

The Middle Feild.

Imprimis one halfe acre Lying at Malsmeade furlonge shootinge north and south Thomas Roughead on the east and the common on the West.

Item one half acre lying at under streete shootinge north and south Thomas Roughead on the West and the lord on the east.

Item one half acre shotinge into the lea feild betwixt [...] William Campion on the west and William Hopkins on the east.

Item one roode lyinge by Drove Way shotinge north and south the lord [...].

Item one halfe acre Lyinge upon the same furlonge nere unto hatchett way William Malyns on the east and Sir Anthonie Tyringham on the west.

Item one halfe acre on the furlonge under Picknutts shotinge north and south the lord on the east and Sir Anthony Tyringham on the west.

Item one half acre under Stonehill hades shotinge North and south the lord on the east and William Hopkyns on the West.

Item [...] shotinge north and south William Campion on the east and the lord on the west.

The Feild next Newport.

Inprimis two half acres and two Roodes lyinge together upon a furlonge called Downe head shootinge north and south the land of the Lord Mordaunt on the west.

Item one halfe acre lyinge on Pennyland shotinge towards the fourd north ward John Blundell on the east and the lord on the West.

Item two roodes lyinge near to pennyland bushe shotinge north and south William Marten on the west and a balke next unto Calcott feild on the east.

Item one halfe acre being a lea land on the further syde of Calcott brooke shotinge north and south John Blundell on the west and William Hopkins on the east.

Item one half acre lyinge upon Fulwell hill shotinge north and south John Nycholls on the west and Henry Kent on the East.

Item one roode lyinge on the same furlonge John Blundell on boothe sydes.

Item one halfe acre lyinge on Beane hill shotinge east and West the lord on the north and John Blundell on the south.

Item one roode lyinge on Drynes furlonge shotinge north and south John Blundell on the east and John Hull on the West.

Item one halfe acre on Porthill shotinge east and west Sir Anthonye Tyringham on the south and Henry Kent on the north.

Item one halfe acre lyinge on neither lance furlonge shotinge east and west William Malins on the north and the lord on the south.

Item one half acre lyinge on over launce furlonge shotinge east and West John Nycholls on the north and Sir Anthonye Tyrringham on the south.

Item one half acre lyinge on a furlonge called over the pathe shotinge north and south John Blundell on the West and Richard Sandye clarke on the east.

Item one roode lyinge on the further syde of [...]ong ends shotinge east and west the lord on the south and the balke that Devideth the feildes on the north.

Summa arabilis 22 acres.
Summa totalis 30 acres 2 roodes.

Tithes.

There is not any belonginge to the parsonage aforesaid.

For Stocks Implements tenements or any other thinge inquyrable by the Canon and not herein intymated and expressed there is nothing belonginge to this parsonage as far as we knowe or can learne.

Richard Sandye   Parson of Linforde

Richard Wetherhed   Churchwardens
John Byrde
Henry [...]
John Uvedail
John [...]
(D/A/Gt/6/10/1)

78. GREAT LINFORD 1640

A Note of the buildings and houses upon the parsonage of Linford Magna And a Terrier of Glebe-land belonging thereunto February 6 1639.

The dwelling house containing five bayes; the Lord North, Mr Wellis south.

The barnes four bayes.

Stable and other houses three bayes.

One close, containing an Acre.

One piece in the woodfield four acres lying in peare-tree forlong, the Lord south and East Thomas (*modo* Edmund) Roughhead north. Another piece in the same field in West hill furlong, being nine ridges the Lord East Richard Smith south.

Three Roodes in the forlong called betwixt Ridgeway and Lay-way, the Lord South.

An halfe Acre in Head-ditch the Lord South, Richard Smith west.

An halfe Acre in Weston-path.

An Acre putting in Stanton slaid.

An halfe Acre in long-Rolow.

An halfe Acre in Ridge-way.

An halfe Acre in Lay-field forlong.

In the middle-field.

An halfe acre in over-pig nite forlong

An halfe acre in nether-pignite forlong.

An halfe acre in Stonell-heads forlong.

A piece containing three roodes in under-street.

An halfe acre shooting in lay-field.

An halfe acre in spring-hill.

In Neoport-side field.

An Acre in downe-head forlong.

An halfe Acre in over-penny land.

An halfe acre in Nether-penny land.

An halfe acre in fulwell-hill.

One roode more in fulwell-hill.

An halfe acre in Beanhill.

An halfe acre over the path.

An halfe acre shooting in the Morter pit.

An halfe acre at Neeport-Willowes.

An halfe acre shooting Martials hadland.

One roode in Mare-forlong.

Theodoricus Gravius   Rector

John Uvedale   Churchwardens
William Wetherhed

(D/A/Gt/6/10/2)

79. LONG CRENDON 1639

We Certaine of the parishioners of Longe Crendon whose names are hereunto subscribed; doe Certyfie to all those to whom these presents shall come or appertaine That the house wherein our Mynister doth usually dwell is no Vickeridge house neither is there anye Gleibe land or other lands or Church land belonginge or appertaininge thereunto soe far as wee knowe or beleive And conserninge our Parsonadge it is an Impropriacon and belongs to Mr Edward Wraye Esquier and the right honourable the Ladye Elizabeth his wife farmed from them by Mr Thomas Sterne of Crendon aforesaid gent. And Conserninge our Ministers meanes are sume small privye tythes which amounte to the value of forty pounds per annum or thereaboutts And thus much in effect hath heretofore beene Certified into the Bishopps Court. In witness whereof wee have put to our hands this presente Tenth daye of December *Anno Domini* 1639.

Thomas Burnard
John Greening
Thomas Canon   mark
Richarde Harris   mark
Thomas Clarke
John Standell

(D/A/Gt/6/13/1)

80. LOUGHTON 1639

A true Terrar of all the Gleabe landes belongeinge to the Rectorie of Loughton in the Countie of Buck made *Anno Domini* 1639.

Inprimis the homestalle with all the buildings thearupon And the Pightell adioyninge to it conteyninge two acres the land of Richard Somner east the streete southwest.

Item one other Pightill or Close called the Crosse Close containinge by estimacon twoe acres the Brooke south and the streete easte-weste.

Item one inclosed meadowe in the Moore feild conteyninge by estimacon Five acres the land of Thomas Hopper south and the land of Henry Whitebread northe.

In Priors Marche Feild.

Item one land upon unset inlands the land of John Crane Esq[...] land of Charles Kinveton gent. north.

Item upon Banland one halfe acre Henry Whitebread east Valentine Moretofte west.

Item upon Stangell one acre Henry Whitebread east Thomas Hopper west.

Item upon longe Willowe bedd one half acre Thomas Hopper south Valentine Moretofte gent. north.

Item upon shorte willowe bedd one halfe acre Valentine Moretoft gent. north and South.

Item upon the same one acre the land of John Lane north and the land of Henry Whitebread south.

Item three half acres shootinge into Broadwell Deane Valentine Mortofte gent. east John Crane Esq. west.

Item one acre more on the same furlonge Valentine Mortoft gent. east and William Abbot west.

Item twoe roodes at Foxeholes John Binion west Mr Moretofte east.

Item one rood of Ley shootinge upon the Abbye hedge Mr Crane west Mr Moretoft east.

Item one acre under the Furses Sir John Fortescue north and Thomas Hopper south.

Item one halfe acre more upon the same Furlonge Henry Whitbread north John Binion southward.

Item one half acre upon Turnhill Henry Whitebread eastward Mr Moretoft west.

Item one acre more upon the same Furlonge Mr Crane eastward Mr Moretoft westward.

Item one half acre more upon the same Furlonge Mr Moretofte westward John Binion eastward.

Item upon Shorte Crowne hill one half acre beeinge a Foreshooter at one end Thomas Hopper eastward Mr Moretofte westward.

Item upon longe Crowne hill one land and one rood togeather Thomas Hopper westward Sir John Fortescue Knt. eastward.

Item one roode more upon the same Furlonge Thomas Hopper eastward Mr Moretofte westward.

Item one halfe acre upon Pinderfurs in exchange for one land at Stratford gapp John Binion southward Richard Somner north.

Item one acre togeather buttinge from over downe waye towards Pindersfurse the lande of William Abbot on both sides.

Item one acre togeather upon Windmill hill Thomas Purney south John Crane north.

Item one land more on the same furlonge Mr Crane north Mr Moretofte south.

Item one acre togeather on Specland John Lane on both sides.

Item three half acres togeather upon Overdowne Sir John Fortescue Knt. south Henry Whitebread north.

Item one acre togeather upon Netherdowne Sir John Fortescue north Mr Moretofte south.

Item one half acre more on the same furlonge John Bynion south Mr Moretofte north.

Item one acre at Eleis Robert Goodred north Sir John Fortescue south.

Item one acre under the Furze togeather Henry Whitebread south Sir John Fortescue north.

Item at Posterne gate one half acre the close of John Crane Esq southward Valentine Moretofte gent north.

Item by the Towne side at Cawdell Lane end Fower half acres Sir John Fortescue north the lane from the Church south.

Item one Ley crossinge the northeast end of the Fower shootinge northwest betwixt the waye on the south west side and Mr Moretofts Close.

The whole some of the arable land and leys in this Feild is twentie fower acres one roode.

The Moore Feild.

Item in Whitelande one land John Simon east Charles Kinveton west.

Item at Ricks hedge twoe Lands Thomas Hopper north Sir John Fortescue [...].

Item Fower lands next on the same Furlonge Thomas Hopper north Sir John Fortescue south.

Item on the same furlonge twoe roods William Abbot north Thomas Hopper south.

Item above the Moore Fower half acres one of them beeinge a hadland John Lane west.

Item in Shorte Okehill twoe lands one of them a hadeland to the lands buttinge into London waye the other lyeinge next to Sir John Fortescue east.

Item in the same Furlonge twoe half acres more Thomas Hopper east Sir John Fortescue west.

Item on Ash Pill one half acre Thomas Hopper on both sides.

Item in longe Okehill one land Henry Whitebread on the one side the towne land on the other.

Item one the same furlonge one throughout acre William Abbot east Thomas Hopper west.

Item one land more on the shorter Furlonge theare Mr Crane on both sides.

Item on Redland one half acre Henry Whitebread north, Mr Moretofte south.

Item one rood buttinge into Childe Waye William Abbot east Mr Moretofte west.

Item in Shorte Prettige three lands togeather next John Lanes hadelande west Mr Moretofte est.

Item on the same Furlonge one halfe acre more Sir John Fortescue on both sides.

Item, on lower Prettige one half acre Mr Moretoft on both sides.

Item two half acres more togeather on the same Furlonge Thomas Purnye west.

Item one Winterne hill twoe half acres togeather buttinge into Winterne Deane William Purney east William Abbot west.

Item twoe half acres more above on the same hill abuttinge on John Parratts hadland south Hugh Lyne east Thomas Hopper west.

Item one roode on the shorte Furlonge upon the same hill buttinge on the breach Mr Moretoft north Thomas Hopper south.

Item on the hommer side of the gutter comeing from the moore one roode Mr Crane west the comon balke east.

Item on the other side of the said gutter twoe roodes more Sir John Fortescue west the towne rood east.

Item on Okehill slade one half acre beeing a hadland to parte of shorte Okehill.

Item in Winterne Deane one half acre beeinge a hadeland to longe Prettidge.

Item on Winterne hill twoe roods buttinge into Winterne Deane John Binion east Mr Moretofte west.

Sume total of this Feild   xix acres.

In Secloe Feild.

Item twoe half acres togeather abuttinge into the brooke on the hommer Cost: Riddye Thomas Purnye east Mr Moretofte west.

Item one roode on the Feilder side of Cost: Riddye a hadeland to [...] Furlonge theare buttinge into the brooke Thomas Parrat east.

Item one half acre buttinge from Portwaye to Cost:Riddye Mr [...] Sir John Fortescue east.

Item Fower half acres togeather abuttinge from Portway to Ditche Furlong Thomas Parrat east Richard Somner west.

Item on the Homer Coombes twoe half acres togeather buttinge into Crosse waie John Binion north Mr Moretofte south.

Item on the Feilder Coombes one half acre buttinge into Potters way land the towne land west Mr Moretoft east.

Item one half acre betweene Portwaye and Potterswaye Henry Whitebread west Mr Moretofte east.

Item twoe half acres more togeather theare Sir John Fortescue west John Bynion east.

Item one half acre more theare William Abbot west.

Item one half acre more on Buckridge Mr Moretofte east Henry Whitebread west.

Item three half acres more on the same Furlonge Mr Moretoft west John Parratt east.

Item one Longe Ditche Furlonge two half acres Mr Moretofte west John Lane east.

Item in Shorte Ditche Furlonge one half acre Mr Moretofte west Sir John Fortescue east.

Item on the Middle Furlonge one half acre Mr Moretofte west Thomas Hopper east.

Item on the same Furlonge twoe half acres more Thomas Hopper west Henry Whitebreade east.

Item one Horridge twoe half acres togeather Mr Moretofte west Mr Crane easte.

Item three half acres on Langage William Abbot east Thomas Hopper west.

Item in Symons Moore one half acre Thomas Hopper south Henry Whitebreade north.

Item in Somerwell three half acres buttinge into Bradwell feild the Common on both sides.

Item on Rookes Ley three half acres the Towne ley west Henry Whitebreade east.

Item on the same furlonge one half acre more Thomas Hopper west Sir John Fortescue east.

Some total of this Feild   xviij acres Three roodes.

Edward Baker   Rector *ibidem*

Thomas Purney   Churchwardens
Robert Goodared   mark

(D/A/Gt/6/14/1)

81. LUDGERSHALL 1634

Taken october the 3 1634.

A Terror of the Rectory house And the gleeb Lands of Ludgarshall.

Inprimis the dwelling house Containing seven bayes of building And six bayes of barning and stable with Cowhouses.

The [...] Cloose [...] house by Estimation five Acres Fryers Close [...] north side and [...].

There is one yard Land Lying in the Common feild of Ludgarshall.

Inprimis in the mill feeild Eighteen Lands of erable.

of Lea ground in the mill feild six Leas besides one att the end of the home Close.

of Meadow ground in the mill feild three yeards.

The erable Land in the Middle feild.

twelve Lands Little and great.
of Lea ground their five Leas.
ten years of meade ground in this feild.

In Titchwicke feild.

twenty six Lands Little and great.
Lea ground their 3 Leas.
seven yeards of meadow ground.
The Commons [...] to the Lands twenty six sheap and 2 Cow Commons at may day and at Lamas day 1 more and two horse Commons.

Thomas Hayward   Rector of Ludgarshall

Thomas Sherly   Churchwardens
William   [...]
(D/A/Gt/6/15/1)

82. LUGERSHALL 1637 [?]

Ludgarsall Rectorie *in Comitatu* Bucks 1637. A Terrier answerable to a Survey or Terrier of the possessions belonginge to the rectorie of Ludgarsall made and taken 1607 by the vew perambulacon and estimate of the minister churchwardens Sidemen and other inhabitants there being thereunto nominated and appointed by William Folkingham gent' general surveyor of Church gleabes and possessions within the diocese of Lincolne by Virtue of a commission decreed by the Reverend Father in god William Lord Bishop of Lincolne in execucon of a Canon in that behalf established.

Homestall.

Imprimis the homestall or Scite of the parsonidge scituate and lying at the bell end (a cart way going between) contayning by estimacon with a garden 1 acre.

Edifices.

Item the parsonidge howse and other buildings consisting of 14 bayes the walles ruffecast and covered some with tyle and the rest with thatche.

Pasture.

Item a little close upon the backside of the parsonage contayninge by estimacon 3 acres.

Meadow.

Item 2 peeces of meadowe lying upon Tetchwick syde and 20 yards of meadowe more within the meadowe of Ludgarsall.

Arable.

In the mill Feilde 17 ridges and 9 leyes.
In the middle Feilde 11 Ridges and 6 leyes.
In Tetchwicke Feilde 26 Ridges and 2 leyes.

For stocks implements tenements or any other things inquirable by the Canon and not heerin before intimated and expressed there is nothing belonging to this Rectorie as farre as we knowe or can learne.

Richard Edmondes   Rector of Ludgarshall

Richard Speir   Churchwardens
the mark of John Miller

(D/46/152)

83. MAIDS MORETON 1607

October 24 *Anno Domini* 1607.
A Survey or Terrior of all possessions...

Homestall.

Imprimis the homestall or Scite of the Parsonage house scituate and lying betweene the Causeway to Buckingham and the North and Holloweway feild and the South abutting upon the Churchyard on the

East and upon Piffeline grove on the west, and it contains by estimation 2 Acres.

Within the said Boundes is conteined one garden hedged in with a drie hedge by estimation one roode.

Edifices.

The Parsonage house consistinge of Foure bayes built of stone and covered with tile the whole building contrived in three stories and disposed into 10 roomes *viz.* the Hall, Kitchin and Butrie 4 Chambers and three cocke loftes.

Item two Barnes one of five bayes the other of foure, and one Hovell of three bayes.

Medowe.

As it is lotted by the Medow booke.

In Deepe Meade.

In the Short Dole two pole and the Residue varyinge in mesure 2 Poles.

In the Longe Dole two poles 2 poles.

In the Tith Dole, two poles, and sixe poles 8 poles.

In Middle Meade.

In the Woe dole two poles 2 poles.

Besides in next dole two poles 2 poles.

In the halfe dole one pole 1 pole.

In Buckefurd one pole 1 pole.

Summa pratorum 4 acres.

Arable.

In Chatwell Feild.

In Coppedmore betweene Mr More and William Scott 1 land.

Shooting into Wullford slade betweene William Lamberte and R.Warre 1 land.

In Wullford slade between Mr Eston and Mr More 1 rood.

Against Mr Dorrells gate betweene Mr Eston and William Lambert 1 land.

In Nele betwene William Lambert and Robert Warre 1 land.

In Longe Chatwell between William Lambert and John Phillpott 1 rood.

In Pratchell betwene William Lambert and John North 1 land.

In Short Chatwell betwene Simon Lambert and Sebroke 1 land.

Shooting in Allmeade betwene William Lambert and John Smith 2 roods.

Lyinge utmost in Woodway furlonge 1 land.

Against Windemill hill bush betwene William Lambert and Mr Eston 1 land.

At Windemill hill betwene the wayes six butts containing 1 acre 2 roods.

One Lea land in Windemill hill next Richard North 1 land.

In Townsend furlonge betwene the Lambertes 1 land.

In Mearepitt furlong betwene Mr Eston and William Lambert 1 land.

In the Upper Feild.

Shootinge uppon the Church Hadeland 1 land.

In Water slade betwene William Lambert and Mr Eston 1 land.

In Yenchsell betwene William Lamberts landes 1 land.

Neere Hell close betwene Thomas Kemps and Mr More 1 land.

On the further side Radewell amidest William Lambertes 1 land.

In the neere side Radewell betwene the Lambertes 1 land.

At Dripley gate betwene Mr Eston and William Scott 1 land.

Shooting into Richway betwene Shreine and Robert Warre 1 land.

Betwene Mr Eston and Shreine in Ridgeway 1 acre.

Shootinge into Wellmoore betwene the Lambertes 1 rood.

In the Lower Feild.

By Foscott brooke betwene John Whitmell and Shreine 2 acres.

By Foscott brooke betwene William Lambert and Mr Eston 1 land.

In the brooke furlonge betwene William Lambert and Rive 1 land.

At Hidegate in Winterfurlong betwen John North and Robert Warre 1 land.

In Long Sharely betwene John North and Shreive 1 land.

In Holloway feild.

In the Short Flexelandes betwene William Lambert and Rive 1 land.

In Short Flexelandes betwene William Lamberts and Bradshewe 1 acre.

In Longe Flexelandes betwene William Lambertes landes Behinde the Church 1 land.

In Holloweway hill betwene Simon Lambert and Clemson 1 acre 1 land.

In further Holloweway betwene the Lambertes 1 land.

In Full pitt betwene William Lambert and Richard North 2 roods.

At Ducbills crosse betwene William Lambert and John North 1 land.

At Ducbills crosse betwene the Lambertes 1 land.

On Pagehill betwene William Lambert and Thomas Moore of Buckingham 1 land.

At waytinge tree bush betwene William Lambert and John Smith Lea landes 2 roods.

In Causeway.

Shootinge over durtie way betwene Richard Gill and William Lambert 1 rood.

Shootinge into durtie way betwene Mr Eston and William Lambert 1 rood.

Summa arabilis 24 acres 1 yearde.

Summa totalis 28 acres.

For stockes Implements Tenements, or any other thinge inquirable by the Canon (and not hereing before intimated and expressed) there is nothing belonginge to this Rectorie as farre as we knowe or can learne.

George Bate   *Rector Ecclesiae de Maides Morton*

signum   Richardi Atwood
signum   Johannes Robothom
(D/A/Gt/6/16/1)

84. GREAT MARLOW 1607

Anno Regni Jacobi dei gratia Anglie 5 etc 41.

A Survey or terrour of all the Possessions of the Vicarage of great Marlowe in Lincoln Diocesse and Wicombe Deanerie Made and Taken the tenth of October 1607...

Scituation of the vicarage howse.

Inprimis the vicarage howse is scituatt and Lyinge in the Highe streat of Marlowe Abovesaid on the West syde of the same streate betweene the tenement and land of Thomas Farmer of Cookham in the Countie of Berks Esquire on the south; wherein now dwelleth one Rychard Pasmore Baker And the tenement and land of one Cotterill of Eastamsted in the Countie of Berks yeoman on the North side and wherein now dwelleth one William Switser Jerzey Dresser: The said vicarage howse is of buildinge twoe stories highe: Covered with tyle consistinge of theise Romes Followinge:

Item A halle paved A Citchine and twoe other low romes A shopp and A Sellor under yt: And Sixe Chambers: Boarded: A square Courte betweene the howses with a well in yt: all the roomes beinge in number twelve romes 12.

Item half an Acre of Land Whereon the house standeth part of yt beinge A garden Palled in and the other part beinge Arable: this is all that wee doe knowe or can learne that dothe be Longe to the vicarage land dim'acre.

Richard Langley   his marke

John Bloxsome
John Little
Thomas Hoskines   Churchwardens

(D/A/Gt/6/17/1)

85. LITTLE MARLOW 1607

Novembris 5 Anno Domini 1607 Annoque Regni Domini Regis Jacobi Dei gratia 5 et 41.

A Survey or Terrour of all the possessions...

Homestall.

Inprimis The Home-stall or scite of the vicaredge scituate and lyinge on the East upon the parsonedge close, on the west upon a tenement of Syr William Borlas, on the Northe upon the church high-waye, on the South upon the common moore and conteynes by estimacion one acre.

Item within the sayde boundes are conteyned one garden hedged about by estimacion a yard of grounde with the backside, and one orcharde diched about by estimation a yard of ground, and a little pycle or close by estimation halff an acre.

Edifices.

Item the Vicaredge house conteyninge one Hall a buttrie 2 Chambers one gate house.

Item one barne conteyninge two small bayes.

Pasture.

Item No pasture save the halff acre before named.

Meadow.

Item two acres in the Comon Meade.

Coppis.

Item two acres, one called Wheatley hill bounded East North South with the grounds of Syr William Clerke, on the West with the grounde of Sylvester Hill: the other acre of Coppis named Short croft lyinge upon the East and North *vis.* the ground of Syr William Clerke on the west and south upon the grounds of Syr William Borlas.

Arable.

Item 8 acres of Arable lyinge in Church feilde, 2 acres in Westfielde, 7 acres and a halffe in preistecroft, 3 acres in Gibbs wherof Mr Jno Borlas by the consent of the Vicar then beinge Mr Tylbie tooke in one halff Acre into Roughdell, in recompense wherof Mr Borlas bade the sayd vicar take as much ground ioyninge by the same, but the sayd vicar neglected to take it but now present and full satisfaction is promissed to bee made.

For out-tithes, stock, implements, tenements or any other thinge inquierable by the canon ther is nothing belonginge to this Vicaredge as farr as we know or can learne.

Summa Arabilis 20 acres.

Summa totalis 25 acres.

Thomas Buckley   *ibid Vicarius*

John Hind   Sydeman
William Hunt   Churchwardens
Androw Nebbery
John Brady   his marke
John Tame   his marke

(D/A/Gt/6/18/1)

86. MARSWORTH 1639

A true Terriar of all the Land belonging to the Vicaridge of Marsworth.

In the ChurchFeild.

Item One halfe acre in neather westcrofts Edward Sale Lying on the south side.

One halfe acre more in the same furlong William Whitchurch Lying on the southside.

One halfe acre in the upper westcroftes William Duncombe Lying on the south side.

One halfe acre more in the same furlong William Duncombe Lying on the southside.

One Acre in middle furlong Edward Sale lying on the south side.

One halfe acre in the same furlong Thomas Allen lying on both.

One acre in Bourne furlong [...] Lying on the south side.

One halfe acre in West Stonhill Thomas Allen Lying on the south side.

One acre in the water slade Michael Seere Lying on the East side.

One halfe acre more in the same furlong William Whitchurch Lying on the East side.

One halfe acre in Ecknill furlong William Ives Lying on the East side.

One halfe acre more in the same furlong Edmund Sale Lying on the East side.

One Acre in Woodway furlong Edmond West Lying on the south side.

One halfe Acre more in the same furlong Edmund West Lying on the south side.

One halfe acre more in the same furlong Thomas Allen Lying on the North side.

One halfe acre more in the same furlong Thomas Allen Lying on the south side.

One halfe acre more in the same furlong Michael Seere Lying on the south side.

One halfe acre in Elderne Stubb Michael Seere Lying on the North side.

One halfe acre more in the same furlong Thomas Allen Lying on the south side.

One Acre in Long Stonhill William Ives Lying on the East side.

One halfe acre more in the same furlong Michael Seere Lying on both sides.

One Acre in Pease Furlong Thomas Allen Lying on the west side.

One Acre in Stubb Furlong Thomas Allen Lying on the East side.

In the Long Feild.

One Acre in Ecknill furlong the Hewards ground Lying on the East side.

One halfe Acre more betweene Streight Edmond West lying on the south side.

One halfe acre more in the same furlong Michael Seere Lying on the southside.

One halfe acre in Woodway furlong Michael Seere Lying on the Northside.

One Acre more in the same furlong Michael Seere Lying on the North side.

One halfe acre in Short Whorrage Thomas Allen Lying on the East side.

One halfe Acre in Long Whorrage Michael Seere Lying on the East side.

One halfe Acre in Crabtree furlong William Ives Lying on both sides.

Three halfe acres in the same furlong Thomas Allen Lying on the south side.

One head Acre in middle furlong Edmond West Lying on the North side.

One acre more in the same furlong Edmond West Lying on the South side.

One head Acre more in the same furlong Michael Seere Lying on the South side.

One halfe acre in Endland Furlong Edward Sale Lying on the East side.

One halfe acre more in the same Furlong Michael Seere Lying on the East side.

One halfe acre in Strampitts Furlong Edmond West Lying on the West side.

One Acre in Shoote Langers Furlong Edmond West Lying on the East side.

One halfe acre in hollowtree Furlong Michael Seere Lying on the West side.

One acre in Banfurlong shooting up to Pitston Greene Thomas Allen Lying on the south.

One acre more in the same furlong Edward Sale lying on the North side.

One halfe acre more in the same Furlong Humfry Paine Lying on the North side.

One halfe Acre more in the same Furlong Roger Brewer Lying on the North side.

One headacre in middle furlong Roger Brewer Lying on the South side.

One halfe acre more in the same furlong Humfry Paine Lying on the North side.

One Acre more in the same furlong widdow Glenester Lying on the North side.

One halfe acre more in the same furlong Thomas Allen Lying on the South side.

One halfe acre at Damwell Hedge Thomas Allen Lying on the South side.

In the North Feild.

One halfe Acre under Downe Michael Seere Lying on the South side.

One halfe acre more in the same furlong William Seere Lying on the North side.

One Acre more in the same furlong William Sale Lying on the North side.

One halfe acre more in the same Furlong Edmond West Lying on the North side.

One Acre in Northhill furlong William Sale Lying on the North side.

One halfe acre more in the same furlong Edmond West Lying on the South side.

One halfe acre in Allens furlong Michael Seere Lying on the East side.

Two Acres in middle furlong William Ives Lying on the South side.

One halfe acre more in the same furlong Thomas Allen Lying on the South side.

One halfe Acre in the Brach William Duncombe Lying on the South side.

One halfe acre more in the same furlong Edmond Hodson Lying on the South side.

One halfe acre in Lollimeade furlong William Hawes Lying on the East side.

One halfe acre in the next Lollimeade furlong William Hawes Lying on the West side.

One Acre more in the same furlong William Ives Lying on both sides.

One Acre more in the same furlong William Ives Lying on the East side.

One halfe acre in Merchant furlong Richard Sale Lying on the East side.

One Acre more in the same furlong William Ives Lying on both sides.

One halfe acre more in the same furlong William Ives Lying on the South side.

One Acre more in the same furlong William Ives Lying on the North side.

One Acre more in the same furlong William Duncombe Lying on the North side.

One Acre more in the same furlong Widdow Norwood Lying on the North side.

One halfe acre of Laies lying at North hill Willowes Michael Seere on both sides.

One acre more in the same furlong the Howards land lying on the south side.

One halfe acre more in the same furlong Michael Seere Lying on the Southside.

Three Acres in the Slade Michael Seere lying on the North side.

Two Acres in More Meade Michael Seere Lying on the North side.

[four lines illegible]

This Terriar was made on the twenty six of July in the yeare of our Lord God 1639.

Roger Wilford   Minister

Thomas Theade   Churchwardens
John Saylle
(D/A/Gt/6/20/1)

87. MEDMENHAM 1605

July 25 Anno Domini 1605 Annoque Regni Domini Regis Jacobi dei gratia 3 et 39.

Homestall.

Imprimis The home stall or Scite of the Vicaridge scituate and lyinge betweene the land of Mr Frances Duffeild Esquier on the Easte and the same Frances on the South The Kinges hie waye on the West and North and contaynes by estimation 1 Acre halfe Roode.

  Item within the said bound are contayned one garden impaled by estimation 4 poles and one orchard well replenished.

Edifices.

  Item the Vicaridge house consistinge of 2 baye built with mudd walles and rough cast and covered with tyle, both bayes being chambred over and boarded, porched and a studdy over that.

  Item one barne consistinge of 2 bayes built etc Ayled.

Meadow.

  Item on lotted halfe acre lyinge in charle meade contayninge dimid.

Arable.

Item on land of Arable lyinge in a feild called great West feild contayning, the land of William Borlas knight lyinge East West North dimid 1.

Item on other land lyinge in great feild abuttinge upon a more called the Lady Pedam more on the North and the land of William Borlas Knight on the East South and West contayninge dimid. 1.

For Stocks, Implements, tenements, or any other thinge inquirable by the Canon (and not herein before intimated and expressed) ther is nothing belonginge to this vicaridge, as farre as we Knowe or can learne.

Robert Lewin   Minister

Silvester Deane   mark   Churchwardens
John Ebsonn   mark
William Readinge   mark
John Plumridge   mark

(D/A/Gt7/1/1)

88. MEDMENHAM 1639

A Taryouer of the vicrige howse and the Glibe Land that appartaines to it 1639.

Belonginge to the vicridge on Dwellinge Howse one barne one churchyard and gardene Containeinge halfe one acer and allso one acer Land lyinge in a Ground of Mr John Burlaces Called west feeild buttinge one a ground called wineshaken pecce one the east a nothere acre of land land lyinge in a Ground of Mr John Burlaces Called new pastuer butinge one a more called Cisseles more one the North and one halfe acre of meddow lyinge in Charle meadow butinge one the Tames one the South.

Thomas Deane   Church Wardins
Jeffrey Barne   his marke

(D/A/Gt/7/1/5)

89. MIDDLE CLAYDON 1639

A true Terrier of the gleabe Land and Tythes of the parsonage of Midcleyden in the County of Bucks made by the parson Churchwardens and certayne other parishioners of the towne of Midcleyden November 19 1639.

Imprimis a dwelling house of 5 bay a stable and woodhouse of 3 bay a barne of 4 bay with a garden at the North and East of the house and an orchard South.

Item a Little Cloase on the west side of the house neare half an Acre bounded by a lane on the south called the parsonage lane west with the streete north with a cloase of Sir Edmund Verney.

Item by the Barne a cloase above a roode of ground bounded with the barne on the North on the East with a lane, on the South with a little Pitle house and orchard which is sayed to be long to the parsonage yeard and then the bounds is Sir Edmund Verney his orchard palle south the west end is bounded with the parsonage orchard and the end of a lane.

Item in Whithard feild 19 ridges areable togeather with hades at the south ende of them three of which ereable ridges beeing esteemed an Acre bounded South with Riffam Barr North the hades are bounded with Harepit East and west with two high wayes.

Item 23 ridges areable (with hades to them) called rie peece Lichburrough Leas and Lands on the East ende the Bull meade and a meere way on the west end the Butts called Riffam Barrs on the North side Roger Warnes land now in the occupation of Henry Knapp on the South side.

Item in Boughton feild eight ridges areable shooteing into the Deane Meade beeing the North Ende Barden furlong on the South end a high way on the east side Thomas Hix his Land on the west.

Item on Long Boughton foure ridges by esteemation four Acres half that ridge that lyes Northward was given (as is sayed) for half an Acre of the parsonage Lands which lies incloased of late in a parcell of ground called Charlwell in the occupation of one Hall which parsonage Lea thus incloased is bounded with a gutter on the West with a common Lea on the East Leanards Leas on the South Common Leas on the North end) the foure ridges are bounded on with Coxes hadlea East West with the towne, a Land of Thomas Wheelers North and with a peece of Thomas Hixes South.

Item at Botcleyden gate six ridges areable bound west with land of Roger Warners now in the occupation of Henry Knap Botcleyden feilde on the East and South; North a highway.

Item 5 Acres or thereabouts at Botcleyden gate parsonage grounde lately inclosed Bounded South with the highway North with a grounde called the Warren partly and partly on a common Lea therein incloased East with Botcleyden feild west it poyntes to Botcleyden gate which ground is in Sir Edmund Verney his hands for which they say the parsonage hath 5 Acres layed in a cloase about a mile from the parsonage house which the present incumbent thinkes noe good chainge. This 5 Acres makes the parsonage up a cloase of ten taken out of the common now in the possession of the present incumbent which cloase Butts upon a way called ridg way south on the East a Lane to Winslow on the North a cloase called Hintons cloase on the East a cloase of Widdow Simons.

Item a cloase at whithard at the Least eight Acres bounded West with a Lane East with the Lower end of endlands North with the nether end of fullmer in the occupation of Thomas Twinane South with Bushy cloase.

Item Lotts in the nether end of Boorne meade two yeards lying by Roger warner now by Henry Knap who holds Warners land.

Item in Deane meade by Lot two yeards by Roger Warners land now in the had of Knap.

Item in harepit meade two yeards by warners now in the hands of Knap.

Item 2 yeards Lott in the nether end of Riffam by warners now in the hands of Knap.

Item Tyyth in kinde of hey in these lott meades where those yeards lye.

Item for all the hade ground in the feild they pay 4d. a yeard land which hath beene a custome in the common feild in the new incloasure in the Lawne woods and grounds corn hey and all manner of tythes in Kinde.

The Demeanes payes a rate time out of minde of 4 l. 13s.4d. *per Annum.*

John Aris   Rector

William Rugdes

(D/A/Gt/3/11/1)

90. LITTLE MISSENDEN 1639

A Terrier of all the lands and buildinges belonging to the Vicaredge of Little Missenden as it was made by the Minister and Churchwardens there September the 30th 1639.

Inprimis We finde one Mansion howse commonly called the Vicaridg house consisting of seaven bayes of building having a Moate about it and a court before it and on the right hand of the court as one commeth forth a barne consisting of four Bayes, and on the left syde of the court one stable consisting of one baye, and a cowhouse consisting of one baye.

Item we finde one the right syde of the gate going out into the Towne two houses or Tenements, consisting of three bayes of building either of them.

Item We finde on the left syde of the sayd gate two other Tenements contayning either of them two bayes a peece.

Item we finde of glebeland belonging to the sayd Vicaridg besydes the Church yard First one Meddow with Orchard and gardens belonging to the sayd Vicaridge house, and the Tenements before Mentioned about two acres.

Item We finde one close of arable grounde lying on the West syde of the sayd Meddow contayning by estimation about two acres.

Item We finde at the east end of the Towne three closes commonly called the Vicaridg platts, contayning by estimation three acres, wherof one to witt the first, butts upon a lane that goes to Beaman-end The second butts upon a land as you goe to Amersham, and the third which is the uppermost, butts upon a feild commonly called great Brach.

Item We finde one acre more of arable ground lying on the west syde of the Towne in a feild call Imer-feild Now in the tenure and occupation of one John Child having on the North syde of it a Meddow commonly called Imer-Meade, and butting at the west end uppon a lane commonly called Kinges-street lane.

Item we finde one little garden adjoyning on the south syde to the house of one John Childe and now in the tenure and occupation of the sayd John Child which garden contayneth by estimation about four poles of ground.

Ita testor   Johannes Dunton   *ibidem* Vicar'

William Lovet   Churchwardens
The mark of William Stal[...]

(D/A/Gt/7/5/1)

91. MURSLEY 1625

A terrier of the Glebe Lands beelonginge to the Parsonage of Mursley in the County of Bucks.

Inprimis One Acre above Nashway.
Item one land beeing halfe an Acre in Longe stone Furlonge.
Item one halfe Acre at preists hedge.
Item one Acre in Dibnill Furlonge.
Item one halfe Acre on the west side of the Grove.
Item one yerde on pisthill Furlonge.
Item one yerd of Meddow in the Smeeth.
In all fower steres.

Item a Parsonage house a Kitching a Milk-house and a barne consisting of fower Bayes.

John Knowles   Churchwardens
John Maynard his marke

Concordat cum original' in Registro Eccle' Epico' Lincolne apud Lincoln emanent fact' examin'. per nos Jo. Proctor Not' Pub', Bath. Willcocke Not' Pub'

A coppie of this terrier was brought from Lincoln by Doct. Kinge of Aylesbury, who payd 6s. 8d. for it.

(D/A/Gt/7/7/1)

92. NEWPORT PAGNELL 1601

A Terrare of the Glibe land and Meadow ground and other the Apurtences belonging to the Viccaridge of Newport Pagnell in the County of Bucks made the twentieth day of July *Anno Domini* 1601.

Imprimis A Close wherein sometime did stand a Viccaridge house lyeing in Tickford in the parish of Newport aforesaid between the ground late the Queens Maiesties Doctor Atkins on the East And the ground of Thomas Stokys Edward Nurse thelder Doctor Atkins and John Styles on the west And extendeth from the High Street called Priory Street on the South unto the Meadow called Castle Meadow on the North and now is in the Severall Tenures of William Fisher Thomas Phillipps and Thomas Clethero.

Hayfield of Chichyley.

One Acre lyeing together upon the furlong Called Neither Hay furlong between the lands of Anthony Chester Esq on both sides.

Two Roods together on the same Furlong between the land of the said Anthony Chester on both sides.

Midle Feild of Tickford.

One Halfe Acre upon the Furlong shooteing on the Leys att Moulsoe Cross between the land of Thomas Withers on the East And the Land of the Queenes Majestie on the west.

The Feild of Caldecot lyeing next to the Pake.

One Halfe Acre upon the Furlong Shooteing on the hadland which shooteth on the Green of Caldecott aforesaid and the said halfe Acre lyeth between the land of the heir of Lawrence White on both sides.

West Meadow.

One Acre of Meadow between the Sallage Meadow and the Sallage Hook on the East And the Meadow of Andrew Knight on the West And Extended freom the Hedge of the pasture Called the Sallage on the South unto the River next to Gayhurst Feild on the North.

This is A true copy and all the particulars are in my present Possession this 19th day of September 1693.

Thomas Bankes   *Vicarius*

William [...]
Anthony Goodridge   Churchwardens

per me Thomas Yarrold   *Viccarium de Newport*
Thomas Barnes   Churchwardens
Thomas Ileing
(D/A/Gt/7/9/1)

93. NEWPORT PAGNELL 1640

A Terrier of all the possessions belonging to the vicarage of Newport Pagnell in the Countie of Bucks taken upn the Last Day of January AD 1639.

Inprimis Homestall or vicarage house there is None.

Item there is one Close belonginge to the said vicarage Conteyneing by Estymacon three roods of ground lieing in Tickford in the parishe of Newport aforesaid betwene the grounds belonginge to the Late Dissolved Priorie of Tickford aforesaid one the East and the ground of Thomas Stile gent and John Harley one the West and Extendeth from the street Called the Priorie street one the south unto the Meadowe Called the Castell Meadowe on the North.

Item one acre of Meadowe lieinge in the West Meadowe of Newport aforesaid betwene the Meadowe of John Knight gent one the west and the hallage Meade and West Meade hooke on the East, and abuteth uppon the hallage on the south and the river of Ouze on the North.

Item two halfe acres of arrable lande lieing together in the parishe of Chichely uppon a furlonge Called the Nether Haye betwene the landes of Sir Anthony Chester Baronett one both sides being the Eleaventh and Twelveth ridges from lake bridge lane one the North west and abutting uppon the land of the sayd Sir Anthonye Chester on the North east and upon the brooke Called Lake brook on the south west.

Item two roodes lieing together on the same furlonge betwene the landes of the said Sir Anthony Chester on both sides beinge the fiveteenth and sixteenth ridges from the said Lake bridge lane abutting as before.

Item one halfe acre in the Midle feilld of Tickford one the furlonge shootinge towardes Moulsoe Crosse betwene the lands of the Kings Majestie in the tennor of Mary Kurtland widow late wife of John Kurtland gent deceased, on the west and the land of Thomas Kilpin on the East and abutteth uppon the land of Sir Henery Atkins Kt one the Northe and on a greene slade shooteinge Neere the Parke hedge one the south.

Item one halfe acre in the feild of Calldecott in the parishe of Newport aforesaid uppon A furlonge Called Weekes furlonge betwene the landes of William White gent one both sides and buttinge uppon the upper hedland towardes Caldecott greene one the south East, and one the slade Called Caldecott Brooke one the North west lieinge next the Midel headland but one land betwene one the East side.

Item there is a stipend of ten pounds yearely payd out of the impropriation to the Vicar of Newport aforesaid.

In wittnes
Samuel Hustin   *Vicarius Ecclesiae de Newport*

Richard Come   Churchwardens
Phillip Lambert
James Marshall
Henry Knight
(D/A/Gt/7/9/3)

94. NEWTON BLOSSOMVILLE 1605

A true Terrier of the Glebe lands belonging to the Rectory of Newton Blossomvile in the County of Bucks.

In Belland brooke being the first feild of Arrable.

Imprimis in the Furlong called Littelley one Roode Rein Lowe one the east and Edward Boddington on the west.

Item one Roode under the Short how Anthony Smith one the east and John Lawton on the west.

Item half an Acker one the same Furlong Anthony Smith one the East and William Lawton on the west.

Item two Roodes one west Stonnyland Anthony Smith one either side.

Item two Roodes one Belland John Hoddle one the west and a balke of the Lords on the East.

Item half an Aker one the same furlong Thomas Lowe one the east and Edward Boddington one the west.

Item half an Acker one the same furlonge Skevington one the East and Dudlie one the West.

Item one Acker being a haddlande and another land Joining to it at the upper ende of Belland Edward Boddington one the East.

Item one Roode in the same Furlonge Edward Boddington one either side.

Item 2 Roodes one Little Whiteland the Lord on the North East part and Thomas Low on the south-west.

Item half an Acker one great Whiteland Skevington one the west and Hessy one the East.

Item half an Acker one the same furlong Thomas Law one either side.

Item one half Acker one the same furlong Thomas Law one the west and William Lawton one the East.

The Sum of ackers are 6 and roodse.

The Seconde Feild Called Coster Feeld.

Inprimis 2 roods one Bellanbrooke Forlongne the Rector of Clifton one the west and William Lawton one the East.

Item one half acker one Clifton Rinehill William Lawton one the East and the lord one the West.

Item half an acker one that furlong John Harding on the Easte and William Parsone one the west.

Item half an acker one the same furlong Dudlie one the East and Thomas Low one the West.

Item half an Acker one the same Furlong Thomas Lowe one either side.

Item one acker on the same furlong Dudley east and Low West.

Item half an Acker one Eastland the lord on the south Thomas Lowe one the North.

Item half an Acker one Ridgway Furlong Anthony Smith one the East and Dudley one the west.

Item half an Acker one hanging Furlonge the lord one the East and Thomas Lowe one the West.

Item half an acker one the same furlong Raynes Lowe one the east and the lord one the west.

Item half an acker under hanging Furlong [...] one the East and Raynes Lowe one the west.

The sum Acker 5 i half.

The 3rd. Feild called Meadfeeld.

Imprimis half an Acker one [...] the Lord one the south and Thomas Lowe on the North.

Item half an Acker in Cobwell John Hoddle one the east and William Lawton on the west.

Item one hadlande next to Cobwell Lying in eastlande John Lawton one the south.

Item one Acker one the same Furlonge Duddley one the North and Richard Harberd one the south.

Item one rood at Leyhedges Richard Harberd one the east and Anthony Smith one the west.

Item half an Acker next to Lang Furlong the lord one the south.

Item Half an Acker one Newton Reyne hill Skevington one the East and Dudlie one the West.

Item 3 roodes one the same Furlong Duddlie one the East and Thomas Low on the West.

Item a Haddland Lyeing an acker going through 2 Furlonges E Boddington and John Hoddle one [...].

Item 2 Roods one the furlonge under the Church hadland the lord one the west and Skevington one the east.

Item one acker on the same furlong Skevington one the East and William Lawton on the west.

Item 2 roods butting to the Lake ditch Anthony Smith one the west William Lawton one the East.

Item half an acker at the Meadside the Lord one the North and Thomas Lowe one the South.

Item 2 Roodes one Sladewell brooke furlong Skevington one the South and R: Harb: North.

Item 2 Roodes one the same furlong Skevington on the South and the Lord North.

Item 2 Roods one Reedbed furlong Skevington on the west and Thomas Lowe on the east.

Item half an acker one the same furlonge Thomas Lowe one the west and Richard Harberd one the east.

Item half an acker one the same furlong Jo. Lawton on the east and Anthony Smith West.

Item Half an acker one the [...] Land William Lawton one the North and Thomas Low on the south.

The Sum is 10 Acker and an half.

Of Swerd grounde.

Imprimis in Belland brook furlong one half acker Thomas Low.

Item one half acker in the Quedd Thomas Low one the East and the lord one the west.

Item half an acker one burch Furlong butting one [...] Harrison east and R:Harb: west.

Item half an acker in the Ham Skevington one either side.

Item of Meddow grounde Lyinge in the Lake and in the Meddow by lott as it Faleth 3 acre one Roode 4 Foot.

The homestedd Close garden and yard esteemed at 2 ackers.

This a a true coppie of a terriar of the Glibe of the said Newton which was made in the year of our Lord 1605 And ys found to be Just by us whose names are underwritten.

John Barton   Rector

Hugh Clifton
Edward Smithe
John Skevington   Sidsman

(D/A/Gt/7/10/1)

95. NEWTON BLOSSOMVILLE 1607

October 4 Anno Domini 1607 Annoque Regni Domini Regis Jacobi dei gratia quinto et quadragesimo primo.

A Survey or Terror of all the possessions...

Homestall.

Inprimis the Homestall or scyte of the parsonage scytuat and lyinge between the Waye on the east and South side and the land of the Right honorable Lord Mordaunt on the North and west side and contaynes by estymacon [...].

Item the parsonage howse consistynge of 6 Baies buylt all with Stone and covered with tyles Slatt beinge Chambred over and boarded and one other [...] Chambred with boards over yt one Kytchin or Mault howse cont[...] four bayes beinge thacked one stable and haybarne conteyninge 3 lytle [...] one other lytle barne conteyninge 2 baies thacked one other great thacked barne of 5 bayes and two lytle bays of hogstyes.

Meadow.

Item 10 Roods and four foote of Meadow in the Meadow of Newton [...] and in the Lake 3 Roods as yt lyeth by Lott.

Summa pratorum 3 acres 1 Rode.

Arable.

Item in everye yeardes Land one halfe acre in Readebed furlonge the land of Richard Lawton on the east and the Land of Antonye Smyth on the West.

Item one other halfe acre more lyinge on the same Furlonge the land of Richard Herbert on the east side and the land of Thomas Lowe on the west.

Item [...] on the same Furlonge the land of Thomas Lowe on the east side and the land of Thomas Skevington on the north side.

Item halfe an acre lyinge on east Stonyland the land of William Lawton lying on the north and the land of Thomas Lowe on the south.

Item one halfe acre lyinge on long Furlonge with the path on the north the Land of the lord on the South.

Item two Roods on Sladewolbrooke Furlonge the land of the Lord [...] the land of Thomas Skevington on the South.

Item two Roods lyinge on Meade Furlonge betwene the land of Richard [...] the north side and the land of Thomas Skevington on the south.

Item halfe an acre neare the Mead side betwene the land of the lord on the north and the land of Thomas Lowe on the South.

Item one acre under Ware hedge lyinge betwene the land of Thomas Skevington on the east and the land of William Lawton butteth on the west.

Item two Roods lying on the same Furlonge betwene the land of the Lord on the west and the land of Thomas Skevington on the east.

Item one Hadland more lyinge betwene the land of Edward Boddington and John Hoddle West and Sladewelbrooke Furlonge on the east.

Item 3 Roods lyinge on Rynell betwene the land of Edward Dudley on the east and the land of Thomas Lowe on the West.

Item halfe an acre on the same Furlonge lyinge betwene the land [...] Edward Dudley on the west and Thomas Skevington on the east.

Item two Roods buttynge to lakes Foord the land of William Lawton on the [...] and the land of Anthony Smith on the West.

Item one halfe acre in bone acre the land of the lord on the South Thomas Lowe North.

Item one halfe acre in Cobwell the land of William Lawton on the West John Haddell on the east.

Item halfe an acre on Eastland hadland to Cobwell on the North and the land of John Lawton on the South.

Item one acre on the same Furlonge betwene the land of Richard [...] South and the land of Edward Dudley on the North.

Item one Rood in the Claye betwene the Land of Anthony Smyth [...] and the land of Richard Harbert on the east.

Item halfe an acre on hanginge Furlong lyinge betwene the land of [...] the east and the land of Thomas Lowe on the west.

Item half an acre in the same furlonge the land of Reynes Lowe on the [...] and the lord on the West.

Item half an acre under hanging Furlonge lyinge betwene the land of [...] Joyner on the east and the land of Reynes Lowe on the west.

Item halfe an acre on Ridgewaie Furlong lyinge betwene the land of [...] Smyth on the east and the land of Edward Dudley on the west.

Item halfe an acre on eastland lyinge betwene the land of the lord South and the land of Thomas Lowe on the north.

Item halfe an acre on Clyfton Rynell lyinge betwene the land of [...] on both sides.

Item one acre on the same Furlonge betwene the land of Thomas Lowe and Edward Dudley on the east.

Item halfe an acre on the same Furlong betwene the land of William [...] West and John Norman on the east.

Item halfe an acre on the same Furlonge betwene the land of William [...] east and the lord on the West.

Item two Roods on bellam Brooke Furlonge the land of William Lawton [...] and the parsonage land of Clyfton on the west.

Item 2 Roods on blackland the land of Anthonie Smyth on both [...].

Item halfe an acre on Whiteland the land of William Lawton on the [...] And of Thomas Lowe on the West.

Item halfe an acre on the same Furlonge the land of Thomas [...].

Item halfe an acre on the same Furlonge the land of Thomas [...] and the land of Thomas Vessey on the east.

Item 2 Roods on lytle Whiteland the lord on the north and [...] Thomas Lowe on the South.

Item one acre on Reynes Gate hadland to Belland and the land of [...] Skevington on the east.

Item one Roode in the same Furlonge the land of Edward Boddington [...].

Item halfe an acre on bellam the land of Edward Dudley on the north and the land of Edward Dudley on the south.

Item halfe an acre on the same Furlonge the land of Edward Boddington on the South and the land of Thomas Lowe on the north.

Item two Roods on the same Furlonge the land of John Hoddell on the west and a balke on the east.

Item one Rood under the How the land of Anthonye Smyth on the east and the land of John Lawton on the West.

Item halfe an acre of the same Furlonge the land of Anthonye Smyth on the east and the land of William Lawton on the west.

Item one Roode in betwen the land of Reynes Lowe on the east and the land of Edward Boddington on the west.

Pasture.

Item one halfe acre on bellam brook Furlong the ground of Thomas Lowe on both sides.

Item halfe an acre in the quedd the lord on the West and Thomas Lowe on the east.

Item halfe an acre in Butts Furlonge Leyes betwene the leyes of Richard Harbert on the West and John Harryson on the east.

Item halfe an acre in the ham the leyes of Thomas Skevington on both sides.

Anthonye Smyth   Churchwardens
William Cockman
John Lowe   mark
John Norman   mark   Sidesman
John Whitebread   mark
(D/A/Gt/7/10/2)

96. NEWTON LONGVILLE 1607

The vjth daye of October Anno Domini 1607 Anno Regni Domini Regis Jacobi dei gratia quinto et Scorie quadragesimo.
A terror of all the possessions...

Imprimis the whome stale or site of the parsonage scituate and lyinge one the southe side and Contayneth by estimacon one halfe acre.

Item within the said bounds is Contayned A litle garden impaled by estymacion one pole.

Item the parsonage howse Consistyng iiij bayes buylt all of tymber and Coveried with tyle the said four bayes being loftyd and bordid and the whole buyldinge contryved to twoo storris and disposed into iiij Romes besid the hawle and the parlore.

Item one fayre barne consistinge iiij bayes and A Kyllis buylt over.

Item one haye barne and A stable consisting four bayes standing estwarde and one other house of four bayes Standing north ward.

There is noe close nor medowe nor laies belonginge to this Rectorie.

Item half A yarde Lande in the three fylds in the South fylde one acre nexte unto hewghe Kyng one the est and henry tomkyns one the west.

Item one acre one Lange Waste next Mathewe Rutlidge one the southe side and Mr Kyng one the northe side.

Item one acre at the gravell pittes next William tomkyns one the est and thomas bennet one the west side.

Item ij acres one the Downe next Richard Coles one the est side and henry Tomkynes one the weste.

Item in the West fyld one acre at litle broke next William Waldoke one the southe side and Septimus Cooke one the northe side.

Item in the Northe Fylde one acre in botts close next Jeffery Cooke one both sides est and west.

Item nyne yards shotting above steares dole furlong John Hawkens one the Estward and stears dole west ward.

Item one acre at the brydge next Richard Willis one the southe and William Waldoke one the north sid.

Item one acre and a yeard at the crabe tree nexte William frinkelowe one the est and Jo. Hawkins on the west.

Item one halfe acre one the same furlonge next William Kinge one the este sid and Jeffrey Hawkins one the west.

Item one half acre next Hewghe Kyngs on the est and William Cook one the weste side.

Item ij acres at the hill next William Tomckyns one the southe and Henry Tomkyns one the northe.

Item ij yard Lands in the hands of Roberte Willison And Thomas benet that paye noe tythe but for Compossicion paye Rente to the Newe Colledge Oxford.

Item Standen in the parsonage one benche in the hawle and one bedd stedd in the Lofte.

For stokes tenements or any other thinge inquyrable by the Canon and not hearein before nomynated and expressed their is Nothinge belonging to this Rectorie as Far as we knowe or can hear.

Ita est Sextus [...]   Minister

John Edwyn   Churche Wardens
Ambrose Rutlande
Robert Willis   SidesMen
William Grise
Item Habytants their William brinklow
Jeffery Cooke and William Tomkyns

(D/A/Gt/7/11/1)

97. OAKLEY 1639

November 22de Anno Domini 1639.

A Terrier of all the possessions belonging to the Vikridge and Church of Ockley *alias* Brill made and taken by the Minister and Churchwardens whose names are subscribed.

Homstall.

Imprimis The Homstall of the Vickeridge scituate and lying between one Close commonly called the Parsonage Close on the north and the Churchyard on the East The Streate on the south and the Orchard and Garden thereunto belonging on the west which Orchard and Garden contayneth by Estimation one Rood.

Edifices.

Item the Vickeredge House consisteth of Five bayes built with timber and thatched in the which are contained Eight Roomes *Vizt.* Hawle Parlour Dayhouse Three Chambers or Lofts boarded and three other Out Roomes.

Pasture.

Item One Close abutting on the Orchard aforesaid on the North and the Close aforesaid called the Parsonage Close on the East and a Lane called Birdbolts Lane and West the Close contayning by estimation Half an Acre.

Tythes and Offerings.

Item the Tythes belonging to the sayd Vickeridge (according unto what is now and for many years past hath been paid) are the tenth of milke the Ods of Calfe wool and lamb the tythe of feeding Cattle and of all such Cattill as are not or cannot be Tythed otherwise, than monies.

Item the tythe of Woode of flaxe of hempe bees fruits and all maner of Garden Commodities.

Item all the accustomed Offerings of the Communicants at Easter.

Item the accustomed dues that are payd at weddings churchings and burials.

Monies.

Item the monies payd out of the Parsonage of Ockley Brill and Borstall to the sayd Vicar thereof per annum are Foure Pounds.

Item from Brill two shillings and allso from Borstall two shillings per annum.

Item to the Mother Church of Ockley *alias* Brill the same two shillings per annum.

Church Land.

Imprimis The Land belonging to the Church of Ockley lyeth in a ground called Mile furlonge abuting upon Wormall field on the west and a Ground called Tipes Hill on the south and part of the foresayd Mile furlonge on the East and another ground called Ridwell abutting upon the Northend thereof which sayd Land Contayneth by Estimation Five acres and a half.

Item One Acre more (being an alotment alowed upon the disforestation out of the Kings ground to the said Church) the totall Conteyneth Six acres and a half.

Examined with the Original   Thomas Coxen   Vicar *ibidem*

JW   N Public
Francis Johnson   Churchwardens
Richard Bunts
(D/A/Gt/7/14/1)

98. PADBURY 1607

Octobris 4th Anno Domini 1607 Annoque Regni Regis Domini nostri Jacobi dei gratia Anglie Frauncie et Hibernie Regis etc fidei defensor quinto et Scotia Quadragesimo primo.

A true Survaye or Terrour of all the possessions ...

Homestall.

The homstall or Scite of the Vicaridge scituate and being betwene, the Tenements of Alsoles Colledg in Oxon on both sides abuteing upon the Street south and upon the field north and containes by estymacon halfe an acarr.

Edifices.

Item the Vicaridge house consistinge of three bayes built all of Tymber and covered with thatche two bayes chambred over and boarded.

Item one barne of two bayes built all of Tymber and covered over with thatche.

Meadow.

Item two acars of meadow whereof one acar lyeth in a mead called Shernold mead and the other acar lyeth in a Meade called Broddmoremead towards the keeping of a horse.

For pasture ground Arable land Stockes Implements Tenements or any other thing inquirable by the Canon and not herin before intymated and expressed there is nothing belonging to this Vicaridge as farr as we know or can learne.

Thomas Harris *alias* Smithe   Minister

Thomas Harris
Mathius East   Church wardens
Thomas Career
William Wreet
John Bunce
(D/A/Gt/7/17/1)

99. PADBURY 1639

A True description of the Vicaridge of Padbury in the County of Bucks exhibited the xiiijth of October 1639.

The Vicaridge house consisteth of three little Roomes that is a haule a kittchinn and a Chamber (all covered with Thatch) and also a little barne of two bayes and also a little Stable. It hath a little Backside Containing halfe a acar of ground, the Tenements belonging to Alsoules Colledge in Oxon lying on both sides. Also it hath belonging to it Three poles of meadow ground lying in a meadow called Shurnall meade betwene the Towne mead and the Tythe doles. Also It hath three poles of medow ground more lying in a mead called Brodmore mead betwene the towne mead and the Tythe Doles.

Thomas Smyth   Vicar

Thomas Hilsdon   mark   Churchwardens
John Kinge   mark
(D/A/Gt/7/17/2)

100. PENN 1635

A true terrier of all the glebe lands with the appurtenances belonging unto the vicarage of Penn in the County of Bucks made Veiwed and estimated the 13th day of January *Anno Domini* 1634 by William Alday and Thomas Dossit Churchwardens and Richard Lucas in habitants of the [...] parish of Penn aforesaid in the presence of William [...] Vicar there and nowe againe coppied out *Anno Domini* 1639.

Inprimis the Vicarage house consisting of fower bays of buildi[...] an entry and cut ende, being all in good repaire.

Item a barne consisting of three litle bays adioyning to the Church [...] being also in good repaire.

Item the yard and backside adioyning unto the said house and barne being by estimation halfe an acre.

Item a little Meddowe plott adioyning to the Churchyard on the south side thereof being by estimation a rood of grounde.

Item the upper vicars feild neere Penn Church adioyning to the land of Sir Gregory Norton Baronet on the West and North and to the highway leading unto Penn Church on the south contayning by estimation in arrable lande with the hedge rowes 8 acres.

Item the lower vicars feild ioyning to the same butting on the high way leading unto Penn on the Easte and south and the land of the said Sir Gregory Norton on the North contayning by estimation in arable land and hedge rowes 9 acres.

Item the further Vicars close at Winsmore hill abutting on the said Winsmore hill on the East and on the high way leading unto Beconsfeild on the west and lying betwene the land of John Playter the elder on the North and of John Playter the younger on the south contayning by estimation in arable lande and hedge rowes 4 acres.

Item the hither vicars close neare Winsmore hill and Horsmore feild abutting upon the land of John Playter the elder on the East and of John Playter iun' on the North and ioyning to the highway leading unto Beconsfeild on the south and west contayning by estimation in arable and Wood ground three acres.

Item seven peices of arrable land in the common feild called Horsmore bounded out by Merebankes contayning by estimation eight acres and a halfe.

Item one acre in Westfeild halfe arrable and halfe woodground lying within the land of John Penn Esquier and abutting upon the high way leading unto Beconsfeild on the East.

By me   William Linke   Vicar there

Edmond Grove   Churchwardens
John Browne
(D/A/Gt/7/18/1)

101. PITCHCOTT 1635

A true copy of a terrier taken of the parsonage house of Pitchcott within the County of Bucks and of all the arrable lands Ley ground meadowe ground and common, belonging to the same veiwed, bounded and sett forth by Henry Walkaden Rector and parson there Joseph

Hartwell and William Ollyffe Church Wardens, John Olliffe and William Hilton neighbours the first of Aprill *Anno Domini* 1635 as followeth:

Imprimis the parsonage house thatched 3 baies.

Item there, on hall seiled and a chamber over it seeled both newly done.

Item One parlour seiled and a chamber over it and 2 Cock lofts.

Item One Kitchin and a loft over it.

Item ioyning to the parlor and haule one the North side, one lyttle buttrey on lytle woole house and a milke house.

Item ioyning to the Kitchin one the South side, on lytle lowe roome.

Item ioyning to the Kitchin one the North side 2 lytle roomes.

Item one the North side the house, on yard about 6 poles in breadth and as much in length.

Item one the West side of the house, on lytle garden plott at the end of the parlor newly made.

Item One the West side of the house, One lytle yarde, betweene the lytle barne and the orchard being one with the former yarde.

Item there one bigger barne ioyning to the streate of 4 bayes On bay whereof at the North end is a stable.

Item Hogsties at the North end of that barne.

Item westward one lesser barne ioyning to the streate, of 3 bayes.

Item one the South side on lytle courtyard, a long the house side.

Item one the South side on garden and orchard together about 4 pole in breadth and 5 in length, where toe is added a slipp of ground from the streat, given by John Saunders esquire lorde of the mannor.

Item common of pasture for 40 shipp in the feild and six horses at Lammas (if the parson will) and by an olde custome cowes may be put for horses.

Item note that the cocke loft being newe sett up by the present incumbant may be taken away at his libertie.

Item note also that the lesser barne was sett up by the last incumbant because he occupied a farme besides the parsonage and that there is but one ancyent barne.

In the hill feilde.

Item One lande one windmill hill furlong the free land of John Ollyffe lying one the South parte and the farme land of the said John Olliffe lying on the North parte.

Item One other land in the same furlong the free land of the said

John Ollyffe lying one the South parte, and the land of the lord lying one the North parte.

Item On land in [...] slad the free land of the said John Olliffe lying one the west parte and the land of the lord one the East parte.

Item in bush furlong on head land the free land of the said John Ollyffe lying one the South parte.

Item On land in Grethorne furlong the land of the lord lying on the North Parte and the land of the said Joseph Hartwell lying on the South parte.

Item On other land in the same furlong the land of the said Joseph Hartwell lying on the North parte and a yard of ley ground of the farme land of the said John Olliffe lying one the South parte.

Item On land lying under the Lintes the land of the lorde lying one the East parte and the free land of the said John Olliffe lying on the west parte.

In the Hill feilde.

Item On other land in the same furlong the farme land of the said John Ollife lying one the East parte and the land of the said Joseph Hartwell lying one the west parte.

Item On other land in the same furlong the land of the lord lying one both sides.

Item On land lying in Leare end furlonge the free land of the said John Ollyffe lying one the East parte, and the land of the said Joseph Hartwell lying one the west, and an hade of grasse ground at the ende below.

Item On land in myddle furlong the free land of the said John Olliffe lying one the west parte, and the land of the lorde lying one the East parte.

Item On other land on the same furlong the free land of the said John Olliffe, lying one the East parte, and the land of the said Joseph Hartwell lying on the west parte.

Item On land in Colliars gate furlong, the free land of the said John Olliffe lying one both sides.

Item On land in the neither furlong, the land of the said Joseph Hartwell lying one the East parte, and the land of William Hilton lying one the West parte.

Item on other land in the same furlong the land of the lord lying on the East parte and the land of the said Joseph Hartwell lying one the west parte.

Item one head land lying between the neather and middle furlongs.

Item On land in Longway furlong the free land of the said John

Olliffe lying one the North parte and the land of the lord lying one the South parte.

Item on other land in the same furlong the farme land of the said John Ollyffe lying one the South parte, and the land of the said Joseph Hartwell lying one the North parte.

Item On other land in the same furlong, the land of the lord lying one the South parte and the land of the said Joseph Hartwell lying on the North parte.

Item On ley lying in Shothill furlong the leyes of the lord on both sides.

Item On ley lying uppon Shothill, next to the horse common and the ley of the lord lying one the South parte.

Item On ley lying at Leare end, the ley of the lord lying one the East parte and the ley of the said Joseph Hartwell lying one the west parte.

Item One plott of ley ground lying next to Carters close, containing halfe an acre be it more or lesse the ley of the lord South and East.

Item On ley in longway furlong, the free ley of the said John Olliffe lying one the South parte and the ley of the said Joseph Hartwell lying one the North parte.

Item On other ley in the same furlong, the ley of John Hearne one the South parte and the land of the said Joseph Hartwell lying one the North parte.

In the nether feild.

Item On land lying in a furlong called Broady land neer unto Frauncis Frytwell his house the free land of the said John Olliffe lying one the west parte and the land of the lord lying one the Easte parte.

Item On other land in the same furlong, the land of Joseph Hartwell lying on the West parte, and the free land of the said John Olliffe lying on the East parte.

Item On other land in the same furlong, the free land of the said John Olliffe lying one both sides.

Item On land one Sandyhill furlong the land of the lord lying one the East parte and the free land of the said John Olliffe lying one the west parte.

Item On land in the bottom of the slad, the land of the said Joseph Hartwell lying one the South parte and the land of the Lord lying one the North parte.

Item On land one Sandy hill the free land of the said John Olliffe lying one the west parte and a peice of ley ground belonging to the Rectory of Pitchcott called the parsons capp lying one the East parte.

Item On land lying in blackbord lane the land of the lord lying one the west parte and the free land of the said John Olliffe lying one the East parte.

Item On land one white leyes furlonge the land of the lord lying one the East parte and the land of the said Joseph Hartwell lying one the West parte.

Item On land one Hickmanbutts the farme land of the said John Olliffe lying one the South parte and the land of the said Joseph Hartwell lying one the North parte.

Item On land lying uppon Smale haydon, the land of John White lying on the west parte and the free land of the said John Olliffe Lying on the East parte.

Item On land lying in Crosse Waules the farme land of the said John Olliffe lying one the West parte.

Item On other land in the same furlong the free land of the said John Olliffe lying one the East parte.

Item On land lying in westall furlong the farme land of the said John Olliffe lying one the South parte and the land of the said Joseph Hartwell lying one the North parte with the slade by it.

Item On land lying in brooke furlong the land of the lord lying one the East parte and the freeland of the said John Olliffe one the west parte.

Item One other land in the same furlong the land of the lord lying one the East parte and the freeland of the said John Olliffe lying one the west parte.

Item On other land in the same furlong the farme land of the said John Olliffe lying one the west parte and the said Joseph Hartwell lying one the East parte.

Item On other land in the same furlong the land of the said Joseph Hartwell lying on the East parte and the farme land of the said John Olliffe lying on the west parte.

Item On land in water furrowes the land of the lord lying one the west parte and the land of the said Joseph Hartwell lying one the East parte.

Item On land in Short furlong the free land of the said John Olliffe lying on the South parte and the land of John Hearne lying one the North parte.

Ley ground in the same feild.

Item On ley lying behind the Towne the free ley of the said John Olliffe lying one the North parte and the ley of the lord lying on the South parte.

On Lea uppon smale Hadon the land of William Robinson lying on the west parte and the ley of the said Joseph Hartwell on the East parte.

Item On ley lying one Shrendall the free yeard ley of the said John Olliffe lying on the South parte and the ley of Richard Coxe lying one the North parte.

Item in the same furlong on litle parcel of ground called three swathes lyinge as an head leye.

Item On ley lying in White leyes furlong the farme ley of the said John Olliffe lying one the west parte and the ley of the said Joseph Hartwell lying on the East parte.

Item On ley in the Ham the free ley of the said John Olliffe lying one the North parte, and the horse common lying one the South parte.

Item One plott of meadowe ground called the parsons Hooke, the ground of Sir Henry Lee Knight lying one the South.

Item in the fallowe mead 4 lytle Doells contayning 2 swathes a peece be it more or Lesse.

In the myddle feild.

Item On land in the pound furlong the free land of the said John Ollyffe lying on the west parte and the land of William Hilton lying one the East parte.

Item On land in Long way furlong the land of the said Joseph Hartwell lying on the North parte, and the land of the lorde lying one the South parte.

Item On other land in the same furlong the free land of the said John Olliffe lying one the North parte, and the land of the Lord lying one the South parte.

Item On land in Nether Read the free land of the said John Olliffe lying one the west parte.

Item One land in Myddle read the free land of the said John Olliffe lying one the west parte and the land of John Coxe lying one the East parte.

Item On other land in the same furlong the land of the said John Olife [Joseph Hartwell *deleted*] lying on the west parte and William Hilton lying one the East parte.

Item On other land in the same furlong the farme land of the said John Olliffe West and William Hilton East.

Item On land in ditchend furlong the free land of the said John Olliffe lying one the west parte and the land of the said Joseph Hartwell lying one the East parte.

Item On land in Bricknell furlong the land of the lord lying one the North parte and the land of the said Joseph Hartwell lying one the South parte.

Item On land in Rotten way, the free land of the said John Olliffe lying one the North parte and the farme land of the said John Olliffe lying one the South parte.

Item On other land in the same furlong the land of the lord lying one the North parte and the land of the said Joseph Hartwell lying one the South parte.

Item On other land in the same furlong the free land of the said John Olliffe lying one the North parte and the land of the lord lying one the South parte.

Item On in Smyth Headland furlong the free land of the said John Olliffe lying one the North parte and the land of the lorde lying one the South parte.

Item On other land in the same furlong the free land of the said John Olliffe lying one the North parte, and the farme land of the said John Olliffe lying one the South parte.

In the middle feild.

Item In Butt yarden furlong On land the land of the lord lying one the East parte and the free land of the said John Olliffe lying one the West parte.

Item On headland in Gorbroad the land of the said Joseph Hartwell lying one the North parte.

Item On land in the Slad furlong the farme land of the said John Olliffe lying one the East parte and the land of the said Joseph Hartwell on the west.

Item On other land in the same furlong the land of the lord lying one the East parte and the land of the said Joseph Hartwell lying one the west parte.

Item On ley in Quicksetts furlonge the ley of the said Joseph Hartwell lying one the North parte and the ley of the saad William Hilton one the South.

Item On ley in Blackgrove hedg furlong the ley of the lord lying one the west parte, and the ley of the said Joseph Hartwell lying one the East parte.

Item On other ley in the same furlong the free ley of the said John Olliffe lying one the East parte and the ley of the said William Hilton one the west parte.

Item On other ley in the same furlong the free ley of the said John Olliffe lying one the west parte, and the ley of the said William Hilton one the East parte.

Item On ley in nether Read furlong the land of the lord lying one the East parte and the ley of Joseph Hartwell lying one the west parte.

Item On other ley in the same furlong, the free ley of the said John Ollyffe lying one the west parte and the farme ground of the said John Olliffe lying on the East parte.

Item On ley in Rotten way furlong, the leyes of the said Joseph Hartwell lying one both sides.

Item On ley at Smiths Headland the ley of the lord lying one the South parte, and the ley of the said Joseph Hartwell lying one the North parte.

Item On ley in seaven Acres furlong the ley of John Hearne lying one the South parte and the ley of the said Joseph Hartwell lying one the North parte.

Item On ley in Slad leyes furlong the free ley of the said John Ollyffe lying one the west parte, and the ley of the lord one the East parte.

Henry Walkeden   Rector *ibidem*

John Hearne his marke   Churchwardens
William Bobenden his marke

(D/A/Gt/7/19/1)

102. PRESTON BISSETT 1639

A Terrior of the Glebe belonging to the Parsonage of Preston Bissett Com' Bucks and Diocese of Lincolne, made the 20th day of October 1639.

Imprimis the Dwelling house consisting of 4 bayes of building the Barnes stables and other out houses about 5 bayes more with one ground a Garden Pasture adioyning containing about 4 acres together with a plot of ground called the [...] and a Hemplot wherein stands a [...] bounded Eastward by the land of Thomas [...] north ward [...] and Christopher Ellard Westward and part South by [...] field the other part south by the Churchyard.

Item 3 yards land of arable meadow and pasture lying dispersedly in the comon fields of Preston as followeth:

In the far field.

Two yards at the outside of Twenty acre butting northward on Roger Webs hadlay the land of Mr Butterfield East West and South.

Two yards more in that furlong butting Southward on The [...] Roger Web [...] field east the [...] west.

[...] in the same furlong butting west on the far mead east on the [...] Mr Butterfield North and South.

Two yards More in the same furlong Widdow George South Henry Mercer North.

Two lands at Weaving Hedges butting West on the Mead east on the Parsons hadland Mr Butterfield South Ed Maior North. That hadland and its fellow Weaving hedge furlong west Ed Maior East.

Two yards at Blackpitt Butting East on William Dudley west on Roger Web Mr Butterfield North Christopher Ellard South.

Two Lands at Padducke in hole Mr Butterfield North and south.

Two yards shooting into the west mead Thomas Trent South Roger Web North.

Three Yards at Burtland butting South on the Mead North Henry Mercer Mr Butterfield East the Highway Weast.

Two Lands at Milditch shooting west on Chetwood East on the High way John King South Ed Maior North.

Four Yards at Long Casemore Mr Butterfield north John Coxe south.

Two Lands at Long Casemore shooting West on John Gaters forshooter Mr Butterfield North Thomas Waddop South.

Two Yards at Short Casemore Ed Maior South John Coxe North.

Two lands at Weedbed butting East on Cowley wood Roger Web South Mr Dudley North.

Two buts at Weedbed butting East on Widow Scots hadland Thomas Weddop South Roger Web North.

Two Lands in the same furlong butting East on Thomas Tetlers Hadland Mr Butterfield North John King South.

In the East Field.

Six Buts and a Ley at Parsons Bottle shooting North into Hobrook Slade Ed Maior East, the High way west and south.

One Land more at Highway hedge Mr Butterfield East glebe Land North and South.

Three yards at Chacwell Balke Shooting South into the brook George Rooms East Thomas Trent West.

Two Lands at Crabtree shooting likewise into Howbrooke Mr Butterfield East Ed Maior West.

Two Lands at Longland shooting Southward into Parsons furs Richard Ellard West Mr Butterfield East.

Two buts shotting south on Cowley wood Widow George West Mr Butterfield North and East.

Two buts more in the same furlong shooting North into Thre brooke south on Cowley wood Thomas Waddop west Ed Maior East.

Two more little buts in the same furlong Mr Butterfield East and West.

Two buts more in the same furlong shooting into Three brooke Thomas Waddop East John Gates West.

Two lands shooting North into Three brooke South Mr Butterfield Thomas Trent East John Coxe West.

Two Lands more about the Middle of Three brooke Slade Widow Scot East Mr Butterfield South and West.

Two lands at Cowley Planks Mr Butterfield East Mr Dudley West.

Two Buts on the Hill butting North [...] South Ed. Maior Roger Web East Richard Ellard West.

Three Lands on the hill butting South on Mr Butterfield North on Widow Scot Thomas Tetlor East John Coxe West.

One Land more on the Hill butting South on John Coxe North on Widow Archer Mr Butterfield East the Highway West.

[...] at Townsend shooting North on [...] Willowes Roger Web East and West.

[...] leas at Parsons furs Ed. Maior North [...] East and South.

Two leas in Howbrooke the Slade North Roger Web South.

In the West feild.

Three yards at Herestret Henry Mercer East John Gater West.

Two Lands at Herestret Gab. Robins East Thomas Titloe West.

Two more Lands in the same furlong on the other side of the Slade butting northward on Ed. Maior Roger Web East Thomas Trent West.

Two Lands in the same furlong butting Northward on Thomas Tetlers Mr Butterfield East John Coxe West.

Two lands more in the same furlong butting Northward on John Coxe Christopher Ellard East Thomas Tetlar West.

Two yerds and a Picked lea shooting into Clatterford way Mr Butterfield East Thomas Trent West.

Two little yerds shooting on Clatterford Mr Butterfield East John Gater west.

Two lands at Absons Bower butting Northward on Richard North southward on Thomas Tetler Richard Ellard East Ed. Maior West.

Two Lands shooting southward on Clatterford Northward on John Gater Thomas Trent East Widow George West.

Foure Buts at Horsepoole Hedge butting West on Chetwode East on the Parsons foreshooter Ed. Maior South John Gater North.

Two Lands more in the same furlong butting East on Gab. Robins Hadland Richard Ellard South John Coxe North.

Two yerds in the same furlong Mr Butterfield South Thomas Waddap North.

Two Lands in Chetwode Brooke furlong butting Southward on John Coxes foreshooter Thomas Waddop South Thomas Trent North.

Two Lands more in the same furlong butting East on John Gaters Hadland Thomas Trent South Thomas Tetloe North.

Three little Butts in the same furlong Thomas Tetloe South John Gater North.

Two Lands in Smallmead furlong Henry Mercer West Christopher Ellard East.

Three yerds in the same furlong Thomas Tetloe East Christopher Ellard West.

Two more lands in the same furlong John Coxe East Thomas Tetloe West.

Two Lands more in the same furlong Mr Butterfield East Thomas Moores West.

Two Lands more in the same furlong at the Stone William Kirby East Mr Butterfield West.

One Land upon the Hill next the Highway East John Coxe West.

Two Lands More on the same furlong Mr Butterfield East Thomas Trent west.

Five yerds in the same furlong John Coxe East Thomas Waddop west.

A great peice of Land called the Stocking Lillies Furlong south Chetwode ground west Chetwode Common North Midsommer ground East.

Meadow Ground in the far Meads 6 acres 5 gores.

1. The first Acre buts East ward on Roger Webs buts Westward on the River Mr Butterfield South John Coxe North.

2. The second acre buts Eastward on Thomas Tetloes hades West on the River, Mr Butterfield South Thomas Waddop North.

3. The third acre buts Eastward on Weaving hedges West on Goddington Railes, Mr Butterfield South Thomas Tetloe North.

The thre other acres and the five gores shoot from Twenty acre North, on Twyford Meadow South.

4. The fourth Acre lyeth betweene Mr Butterfield west, widow Scot East.

5. The fift Acre lyeth betwixt Mr Butterfield West John Coxe East.

6. The sixt Acre lyeth betwixt Mr Butterfield west and Thomas Tetloe East.

The five Gores lye betwixt Thomas Waddop West, Widdow George East.

Item Cowley a Hamlet belonging to Preston the Parson hath for his Glebe One Close of Pasture containing by estimation ten acres the land of Sir Alexander Denton East, Mr Maior West North and South.

Five yerds more in Perycroft called Chappell close or Holtons Cloose the Land of Mr Maior on all sydes.

Waleden Wood   Minister

James Hurst   Churchwardens
Richard How
(D/A/Gt/7/21/1)

103. PRINCES RISBOROUGH 1639

A terrier of the Land belonging to the parish church of Risborough aforesaid made July 17 1639.

Item of arrable land i acre and a Roode.

Francis Herne   Minister

Thomas Dwite   Churchwardens
John Cooseley   Senior
(D/A/Gt/8/5/1)

104. RADCLIVE 1639

The Copye of A Terrior of the Glebe Land Howsing and other Rightes beside the tithe belonging to the said Rectorye and Parsonage of Radcliffe cum Cheackmore aforesayde. *Anno Domini* 1639.

Imprimis The Parsonage dwelling house Consistinge of Eight Baye, Built all of Stone, whereof Five Baye are covered with slatts one Tile, 3 Thetched, all Lofted The whole disposed into Fourteene Roomes: Six Belowe, *viz.* One at the entrance, which serveth for A Hall, within A Parlour and two cellars: On the other side A Kitchin and A Dayery house: Above there are Eight Chambers whereof A Studie Over against it in the yard there are two Baye with A Cullis Latelye Built of Tymber, wherein there is an Outkitchin an Oven A Kill, and A Maulting Floore.

Item in the yard ther are two Barnes, the One towards the Street conteyning six Baye, which the present Incumbent hath Built new, the one end of Stone, the other of Tymber, with A little Stable and Cowe house at the farther end. The other Barne containeth Three baye and A Cullis and is wholly Built of Tymber, The Homestall round about with the garden and Orcharde Containeth by estimacon one Acre and A Roode be it more or lesse.

Parsonage Glebe.

Imprimis at the Churchyarde Stile A plote of arable by estimacon two Acres be it more or lesse Shooting Downe from the Parsonage homestall [...] the Ferme of arden west, the footway to the Mill Eastwards.

Item Belowe that A parcell of meadow called the Millholmes composed round about with Water conteining One Acre and A Rood by estimacon be it more or lesse, The towne commoning in it after Lammas.

Item on Hasely side beyond the River there belong to the Parsonage the Commoning for Five Beasts, and also Fifteen Lands or Leas by estimacon Five Acres heretofore Arable, Whereof Nine Lands lye together in one parcell, and 3 in another on the farr side of the highwaye from Tingewicke to Buckingham: The Nine shooting east and West, the other three North and South in the middle most and greatest of the three grounds as they are now divided) belonginge to the Farme of Radcliffe on that side the Waye: the other three lands lye togeather on the side the waye nearer Radcliffe Betwixt Asheclosse and the river, not farre from A little plott of meadowe ground which belongeth alsoe to the sayde Parsonage and Lieth betwixt the river and the footwaye from Radcliffe to Buckingham having A fine spring running into the river at the end thereof next to Buckingham. For and in consideracon of all which land, meadow and Commoning on that side the river, the Farmer alloweth the present Incumbent A closse on this side commonly called Elme Peece Conteyning by estimaton Five Acres be they more or lesse, and about an Acre of meadow ground adioining thereunto, at the hither end of Highmeadow neare the Bridge.

Item in the common feilds of Radcliffe and Cheackmore there belongeth to the Parsonage A yard land with the commons and rights belonging thereunto:

Imprimis in the little feild by Cheackmore it hath by estimacon One Acre inclosed upon the Moores betwixt John Astons freehold now purchased to the Colleadge use on the one side and the coppy holde Land Late in the tenure of John Lucas on thother side.

Item in the same feild Foure lands Arable, whereof 3 shoote East and Weast, the first hath the moory closses North, and Seman south having A Balke on both sides: the second Widow Ayres, now Mr Moores Freehold South and Hill North: the third Mr Moore North, Cleeve south. The Fourth shooteth North and South, Saman West, Reignold West on the est.

In the North feild.

Imprimis it hath one halfe Acre on the Downes shooting in to Stow Weye Hills, now Henry Kings Land North, and Mr Moore South.

Item in Balland furlong 4 londs shooting North and South the first hath Saman Est and Mr Moore West. The second Hill Est Mr Moore west Third Berlowe Est The Lords Lease land West: the Fourth Hill Est Mr Moore West.

Item one land by Sworne Leas Hill West Mr Moore Est.

Item in Hatched hedge furlong One Land Hill North Mr Moore South.

Item two lands shooting into Ditching Waye, the one betweene Saman and Wests towne lands: the other betwixt Barlow and Astons now the Colledge freehold in the Parsonage tenure.

Item in peaseland moor furlong One Land betwixt Mr Moore and Samon.

Item on Long Sands One Land betwixt Cleeves Coppyhold and Arnetts towne land.

Item on the upper Sands Furlong Two Lands, One betwixt Barlow and the Colledge Land, in the Parsonage tenure: the other neere Bradimore betwixt West and Barlow.

In these 2 feilds 17 Ridges besides the Moory closse.

In the West feilde 18 Ridges Arable.

Imprimis in Stonwell furlong 2 Lands, One betwixt Burnons towne land, and Mr Moore: thother betwixt Hills, now Henry Kings, and Barlow.

Item on CuttleMill hill One land betwixt Hill and Barlow.

Item on Longland furlong One land betwixt Hill and Mr Moore.

Item in Pipewell One Land betwixt Mr Moore and Barlow.

Item One Land Shooting into Rushmoore meade betwixte the common Balke and Mr Moore.

Item one Lond in Rushmore furlong betwixt Mr Moore and Hill.

Item in Hayfurlong 3 Lands, One betwixt Mr Moore and Barlow the second betwixt Henry King and Mr Moore The third betwixt Mr Moore and John Turvye.

Item in Pittfurlong one Hadland that headeth Hayfurlong Eastward: Mr Moore West.

Item on Wayting Hill One Lond betwixt Henry King and Burnam.

Item one Land shooting into the Cowpasture betwixt Hill and Burnam.

Item in Hedgway furlong 3 Londs: the first hath Lucas now Boughton Est Armott West. The second Mr Moore Est Samon west: the third Mr Moore Est Hill now Henry King west.

Item two Butts shooting into Brockly Waye betwixt West and Demaines left in common.

Item 5 Leas betwixt West and the Cowpasture in the same feild.

Item A lott of Furse, as elsewhere of Bushes and meadowes proportionable for A yard land.

In the Est feild.

Imprimis 5 Lands shooting into Buckingham Brook: the first betweene Cleeve and West the second A hadland having Goldwell furlong North and Cleeve South. the third betweene West on the North and Saman South: the fourth hath Saman South and the Colledge freehold in the Parsonage tenure North: the fift hath another of Samans South and West North.

Item one Lond on Michcroft Cleeve South, the Colledge Land in the Parsonage tenure North.

Item in the furlong called Reddittch 4 Londs, the first betweene Barlow and the Colledge land in the Parsonage tenure, the second betweene Saman and West the third hath Cleeve on the North And the Colledge in the Parsonage tenure South. The Fourth West South and Saman North.

One Lond shooting upon Blackwater betwixt Cleeve on the South and the Colledge freehold in the parsonage tenure North.

Item One Lond in Small brooke furlong Cleeve South West North.

Item one Land in Rowslade Betweene West and Saman.

Item in Nowman Furlong One Lond betwixt West and Cleeve.

Item in the same feild 4 Leas of grasse ground shooting into Buckingham waye at the entrance into the lane, One on the left hand haveing Samans Sideling betwixt it and Buckingham Brook: thother 3 on the right hand shooting downe to the river by Argushall. There belong also to the sayd Parsonage two parcells of meadow ground in the same feild, the one usually called Preistslade or apple slade, because as they saye it hath bene anciently allowed for tithe apples which [...] of Cheackemore have payd in the memory of men butt such only as have had noe Common in the feild. As Mr Moores Cottage in Normans tenure etc. Thother parcell is knowne by the name of the Parsons sidelong which was Anciently allowed for the tithe of theyr hades meadowes and Balkes. There belong also to the Parsonage of Radcliffe all the tithes of 5 Ridges in Stow feild closse by Cheakmore *viz.* of the 5 next Ridges within the hedge by the waye from Cheackmore to Stow.

Per me Ambrosium Sacheverell   Rector *ibidem*

Thomas Locke   Churchwardens
William West
Henry Kinge
Thomas Arniat
Edward King
John Burnam
(D/A/Gt/8/2/1)

105. RADNAGE 1639

A Terryer of the howses and glebe land belonging to thc Parsonage of Radnedge in County of Bucks exhibited the first day of August 1639.

There are belonging to the said Parsonage One Mansion howse Conteyneing in particular roomes One Hall one Parlour one Studdy one Buttry and one other little roome belowe And also two upper Chambers And two Barnes Contayneing each of them three bayes of Building a peece.

And also Seven acres of Glebeland bee it more or lesse thereunto belonging lying about the said Parsonage howse next to a Lane highway on the west the land of Robert Gibons on the North The land of Thomas Wyen on the Est and the land of Thomas Wheeler on the Sowth.

John Hartt   Churchwardens
the marke of Thomas Newell
(D/A/Gt/8/3/1)

106. SAUNDERTON 1639

A true and perfect terror of all the gleabes possessions and Lands belonging to the Rectory of Sanderton in the County of Bucks and deanery of Wicombe made and taken by the minister and Churchwardens there the 12 th day of September *anno domini* 1639.

The homestaule or parsonage scituat and being betweene a feild in Horsenden parish called Woodfield on the East and an high way called the Parsonage way on the west and butting upon part of the said Wood feild on the south and a close in the tenure of Thomas Wilcocke on the north. Within which bounds are contayned a close and backside contayning in all by estimation two acres.

Item the parsonage house consisting of V bayes and an halfe and disposed into severall roomes *viz.* an hall a Kitchin a parlor and buttery and over them these roomes a loft over the hall two chambers and a study over the parlor and the buttry and lofts over them all covered with tile.

Item one barne consisting of 3 bayes and a cutt end and a porch new built one other barne of 3 bayes One other house consisting of a bay and an halfe used for a stable and cowhouse all thatched.

In Devon field or parsonage deane.

Item 3 yards along with the parsonage house East Henry Meads land west butting Acnel way North and a land belonging to the parsonage south.

Item one Land bounding upon the parsonage close East and high way and on a yard of Henry Meads west butting on the highway south and upon the lands of Henry Mead and Daniel Wingrove north.

Item 3 yards bounding upon an acre of Richard Bentons the yonger east and on an acre of George Butts west and butting upon Acnel way north and a land of Daniel Wingrove south.

In Crookash feild.

Item 3 lands ioyning on a close called Hayes close south and bounding on a whole furlong north butting upon Rewes way west and a land of Edward Dorrells east.

Item in a furlong called gouldens bush furlong 2 lands bounding upon 2 lands of Henry Meads west and 2 lands of William Parslowe east butting on Steven Dorrells hedland south and Steven Dorrells lands north.

Item 2 lands next the said 2 lands of William Parslow west and 2 lands late in the tenure of Frauncis Hitchcock east butting on the aforesaid hedland of Steven Dorrell south and Henry Meads 3 lands north.

Item 2 Lands bounding on a land of Daniel Wingrove west and a land of Daniel Wingrove east butting on a hedland of George Butts south and an hedland of Daniel Wingrove north.

Item 2 lands bounding on the high way east and 2 lands late Frauncis Hitchcocks west butting upon Acnel way north.

In Fox hill feild.

Item in a furlong that heddeth white peece and goeth with Bledlow way 2 lands bounding on Bledlow Way west and Daniel Wingroves land east butting upon Acnel way north.

Item in Horseley hill picks among the balks 2 Lands bounding on a land of Steven Dorrells west and a Land of Steven Dorrell east butting on a hedland late Frauncis Hitchcocks north and a land of William Parslowes south.

Item in a furlong that shooteth to Crooked ditch 2 Lands bounding on 2 lands late Edmund Meads west and 2 lands late Frauncis Hitchcocks east butting on the warren south.

In Court feild.

Item in welhead pond furlong 3 lands bounding on the parsonage Close east and the balke on the west and butting upon Acnel way south and welhead pond north.

Item in grove furlong 4 lands betweene 2 balks bounding upon 4 lands of William Lanes west and a land late widow Coryes east butting on grove close north and an headland late John Baldwines south.

In East feild.

Item in a furlong called the parsonage peece that shooteth on Wicombe way 6 butts contayning 2 acres bounding upon Horsenden parish north and a whole furlong south butting on Wicombe way East.

Item in the Millway furlong 2 lands bounding on 4 lands late John Baldwines east and 2 lands late John Baldwines west butting on a butt late John Baldwines north and a headland belonging to the parsonage south.

Item 2 lands next Wicombe highway east and a land of Edward Dorrells west butting on one of the parsonage butts north and an headacre of Steven Dorrells south.

Item in Stony deane furlong one headland bounding on 4 lands of Georg Butts south and upon a whole furlong north butting on 2 lands of Edward Dorrels west and a land of Steven Dorrells east.

Item 4 lands bounding upon 4 lands of Georg Butts north and an acre Late Thomas Bennets south butting on a land of Steven Dorrells and 3 lands belonging to the parsonage east and an hedland of Edward Dorrels west.

Item in a furlong called Hemley hill 3 yards bounding on 2 yards of George Butts east and 2 lands of George Butts west butting on an hedland of Richard Bensons the younger north and Horsenden ground south.

Item one land in the same furlong bounding on an acre of Edward Dorrels east and George Butts land on the west butting on an hedland of Richard Bensons the yonger north and Horsenden ground south.

Item in a furlong that shooteth into Wicombe Way 3 lands bounding on 2 lands of Richard Bensons the yonger north and 4 lands of Steven Dorrels south butting on Wicombe high way east and upon the parsonage ground west.

In North feild.

Item in a furlong that heddeth brach-furlong one land being one hedland bounded on 3 yards of Richard Bensons the yonger south and brach furlong north and butting on a close of Richard Bensons the yonger west and a close late Edmund Meads east.

Item in a furlong against new close 2 lands bounding on 2 lands late John Baldwines west and 2 lands late John Baldwines next new close east and butteth on the lands late John Baldwines north and south.

Item in Rushley furlong one holeyard acre bounded on a land late Widow Coryes and a land late John Baldwines west and the land late John Baldwines east butting on Rushley close north and a land late John Baldwines south.

Item in the same furlong 2 Lands bounding on 2 lands of William Lanes east and 2 lands of Richard Bensons the yonger west butting on an hedland late Edmund Meads south and upon Rushley close north.

Item 2 lands bounding on 2 lands of Edward Dorrel east and 7 lands late Edmund Meads west butting on Edmund Meads hedland south and upon Rushley close north.

Item in new close furlong one land bounding on 7 lands late John Baldwines east and butting on a land late John Baldwines north and a close late Edmund Meads south.

Item 3 yards of Leas lying at the Lake Richard Bensons the younger his 3 yards on the north some wast ground and a close of Richard Bensons the yonger on the south and butting on Edward Dorrels home closse west and a close late Edmund Meads east.

Item ij acres of pasture inclosed at Lokendon bounding on Edward Dorrels close north and a close late Thomas Bowkers south butting on Bledlow feild west and upon Risborow feild east.

Item one close with a smal cottage contayning by estimation one acre whereon the parsonage of St. Nicholas sometime stood bounding upon a close late Widow Coryes east and the highway west butting upon Acnel way south and upon welhead pond peece north.

Richard Benson   Rector of Sanderton

(D/A/Gt/8/6/1)

107. SHALSTONE 1639

A Terrier of the Glebelands and possessions belonging to the Rectory of Shaldeston made the 1st of November 1639 and delivered into the Registry at Alisburry.

Edifices.

Imprimis the Parsonage house built partly with Stone and partly with Timber and thatched hath in it foure lower roomes, a Hall, a parlor and twoe buttries and hath five chambers boarded.

Item one Kitchen consisting of twoe nether roomes and one loft of earth, A Dayrie house with a little roome adioyning to it built the most of them with stone and thatched.

Item one barne consisting of severall small bayes built with stone one stable one cowhouse one hovell one hogsty.

Item one garden and twoe orchardes contayneing by estimation one acre.

Pasture.

Item one cloase ioyning to the Orchardes contayneing by estimation one acre.

Meadowe.

Item four plattes of Meadowe in lue of tithe of the fallow meades of the Lordes ground, Twoe of them in the drie feild butting upon Stratforde feilde Southeastwarde, the third in the Neather corne feild peace unto the gate goeing into Stratforde feild on the right hand, the 4th will not bee fownde.

Item twoe grasse Leas under the Moores and one at the Purles.

Arable.

Item of Arable ground on both sides Blinde well Slade sixteene ridges Tenn Northward and Six Southward.

Item betweene the Moores twoe landes.

Item three landes butting upon Atkins hadland.

Item three more shoting into Homerslade.

Item twoe Landes shooting into the Fallow Leas.

Item one throughout Lande at the Purles.

Item in Bartons peece three Landes together and one by itselfe.

Item one Land alone, a land of from [*sic*] Bartons peece hadland.

Item shooting into Woodway on the West side six landes and a butte.

Item foure landes and three butts on Safforne Hill.

Item five landes shooting on Safforne Hill.

Item one Land more next Woodway save one shooting into the cowpasture hedge.

Item twoe landes shooting into the little slade Eastwarde.

Item one land on the same furlong shooting over the Hamme.

Item certaine short Butts called Parsons Hill.

Item twoe hadlands one an hadland to the short Butts, and the other shooting into Evance Meade.

Item one other Land on the same furlong shooting into Evance Meade.

Item three landes in the long furlong shooting into great slade.

Item one land on long Evershawe.

Item three Butts lying on the Westside of the great Slade.

Item twoe Landes of the toppe of Costway.

Item one land by nomans Greene.

Item foure yeardes putting butting upon Abbots furrs.

Item twoe landes of Hanging furlong.

Item five Leas of furrs one in the Tenn lands, one after oldwicke Hedge and three on the Homerside Diggin Hedge.

Item Commons in the Woodes of Shaldeston Westbury and Biddelsden Without stint.

For stock Implements Tenements or any other thing inquirable by the canon and not herin expressed there is nothing belonging to the Rectory as farr as wee know or cann yet learne.

Ralph Purefey   Rector de Shaldeston

John Danyell   Churchwardens
Edward Nabrooke

(D/A/Gt/8/8/1)

108. STEEPLE CLAYDON 1607

September 23 Anno Domini 1607 Annoque Regni Domini Regis Jacobi Dei gratia 3 et 39.

A Survey or Terrour of all the possessions...

Homestall.

Imprimis [...] Homestall or Scite of the vicaridg scituate and lying between the dwelling house of William Snow on the south side on the freehold of Bennett Kybble on the north side and lying neare the higheway west ward and having on the east side there of a close.

Item within the sayd is conteyned on little garden and a yard by estimacon halfe a roode both which are hedged about.

Item the Vicaridge house consisting of two bayes and a cut and covered with thatch having on of the bayes chambred over and boarded.

Item on Barne consisting of two bayes with a leane to ioyned to the same for a cow house and on hay barne consisting of three bay likewise thatched.

Item [...] side of the house conteyning [...].

Item on woodyard in pudde lying on the [...] to the woodyard of Jeffery Arnatt and on the North side next to the yard of William Snow and fower hades in bourne hades two whereof are next to the hades of William Richardson on the west side and to the hades of Edward Wootton on the east syde and the other two are next to the hades of Jeffery Arnott on the east side and the parsonage hades on the west side which foure hades and and meadyard are by estimacon two acres.

Item in the bourne mead, in brook mead, in Lanes waie in puddle in west slade, in foxholes and in litlemarsh in all and every of these meadowes so much lot mead as in lotted to every two yard land being by estymacon seaven acres.

Summa pratorum 9 acres.

Item at black more hill fowre lands two lay next the lands of William Richardson on the Eastside and the land of Robert Kibble on the west side, the other two betwene the land of Edward Kybble on the east side and the land of Walter Taylor on the west at King mead way on acre betwene the land of the wydow Carter on the East side, and the land of the parsonage on the west at Hayes croft on Land between Thomas Newman his land and Robert Kibbles land on the North and Robert Kybbles Land on the south side at Wooburne way on acre betwene the land of Mathew Hazell on the north and the Land of the parsonage on the south, in the furlong shooting to marse brooke on acre betwene the land of Bennet Kibble on the north and the land of William Richardson on the south side.

In the furlong shooting downe to the heards way on acre between the land of the parsonage on the north side and the land of Richard Thorpe on the south side, at [...] land on acre betwene the parsonage land on the north and the Land of Edmund Hall on the south side, at foxholes on acre betwene Thomas Snows land on the north and Thomas Woltons land on the south, in the furlong on this side [...]hill on acre which lyeth betwene the parsonage land on the south and the land of John Stanly on the north. at Berryhill on acre betwene the land of Edmund Hall on the south side and the land of Christopher Carter on the north, at fouer pit leas on land betwene Bennet Kibble on the north syde and William Richardson on the southside. in the furlong shooting on Bassets hadland on acre betwene the land of Edward Kibble on the west side and the land of Edmund Hall on the east syde at Strithill on acre betwene the land of Jeffery Arnott on the north and the Land of Edward Kybble on the south, at Hogburye on acre betwene the land of William Richardson both on the east and west, two butts next to the hcards pasture on the south and William Snows on the north.

Item there are [...] lots so much as come to two yard land at Robert Kibble close and 4 butts betwene William Richardson on the south and Jeffery Arnott on the north, at Ramclose end on acre betwene the parsonage on the east and Mathew Hazells Land on the west, at no mans plot on acre being the hadland and lying next the land of Jeffery Arnott on the south. At Nyndmilk way on acre betwene William Snow on the east and William Barton on the west, at Claypits on acre betwene William Snow on the east side and Walter Tayler on the west on acre next to the way on the [...] at Whitfeild on acre betwene the land of Walter Taylor on the north and the Land of Henry Chamberlayne on the south [...] betwene the land of Henry Chamberlayne [...] on the west [...] on the east side and the land of [...] on the west and betwene the land [...] on the north on the south [...] the [...] between the land of Walter Taylor on the north and the land of Henry Chamberlayne [...] on the east and the land of [...] on the west foure butts shooting downe to the pasture [...] which lye betweene the land of Thomas Newman on the east and William Richardson on the west side.

Item for the sayd two yard gleab land belonging to the Vicaredge [...] may be kept in the fields [...] so many horse sheepe and beast as are alowed to be kept for any two yard lands.

Item we do esteme the [...] of the arrable [...] furrowes thereto belonging to be 26 acres.

For Stocks, Implements, Tenements or any other thing inquirable by the canon and not before here intymated and expressed there is nothing belonging to this vicaradge as for as we know or can learne.

Adryan Baylie   *Vicarius ibidem*

Walter Taylor   his mark
Mathew H[...]   his mark
Robert Kibble   his marke
Anthonye Kinge
Thomas Newman   his marke

(D/A/Gt/3/12/1)

109. STOKE GOLDINGTON 1607

October the 3 1607

A Terre of all the gleebe landes boothe landes leyese medowes and Closses within the towne and Parishe of Stooke gouldington made the thirde Daye of October in the yeare of our Lord 1607 by William Yeamans parson Francis Warrin Robart Wrighte Belcher Houton Robart Abraham Churchewardens and Sidesmen hosse hands are under written

Wyllyam Yemans   Parson of Stocke goldington

Frauncis Warrin   Churchwardens
Robert Abraham
Frauncis Warrin

Robarte Wrighte   (mark)   Sides man
Belcher Hooton
Belcher Hooton

These are free houlders and inhabitants in the parish above said.

1. *Imprimis* for Pasture grounde: first one Closse contayninge 2 Acres more or lesse, buttinge upon the streete over againste the parsonage housse the grounde of the Ladye Digby lyinge on booth sides.

2. Item Twelve leyes which are called the parsons Closse lyinge in the northe feilde the grounde of the Lady Digby on the southe side; and Coopers grenne on the northe side nere unto the Kinges highe waye.

The Northe feilde.

3. Item in the northe feild one Aker of land lyinge on woode furelonge; Robart Willobye gentleman lyinge on the west side, and the above sayde Belcher Hootton on the East.

4. Item one Roode of Lande lyinge on the sayde wood furlonge; the lande of John Abraham on the west syde and the lande of Francis Warrin on the East.

5. Item one haulfe aker of Land on the sayde wood furlonge the land of the Lady Digbye on boothe sides.

6. Item one Haulfe Roode lyinge on Hadsmore hill; with one Ley; the Land of the Ladye Digbye lyinge on boothe sides.

7. Item one Roode of Lande lyinge under Hodsmore Hill; the aforesayde Lady Digbey lyinge on boothe sides.

8. Item one Roode of Lande lyinge one Hodsmore arme furlonge; the Lande of Belcher Houton lyinge on the west syde; and the lande of the Lady Digbey on the Est side.

9. Item one Roode lyinge on Longe Roodes the Lady Digbey on boothe sides.

10. Item one haulfe aker of Lande with a short butt sharpe at the south ende and the haulfe aker sharpe at the southe ende; the fourlonge called the sharpe haulfe aker.

11. Item one halfe aker shootinge Downe to Churche land ende; the land of the Lady Digbey lyinge on the Este syde and John Haselbey on the weste.

12. Item one aker of Land lyinge on a furlonge that is called Lime Butes; the lande of Francis Orpin on the west side; and the lande of Thomas Birche more on the Est side.

13. Item on haulfe aker of Land Lyinge on a furlonge caled slauter house the land of John Hasellbey beinge on the west syde and the land of the Lady Digbey on the Est syde.

14. Item on Roode on the sayd slauter house furlonge the Lady Digbey on the west syde and the land of William Warrin on the Est syde.

15. Item one haulfe aker of Land of a furlonge called Waspe Hill, the land of Francis Warrin on the west syde; and the lande of the Ladye Digbey on the Est.

16. Item on Roode upon a furlonge called Litell-well furlonge; the Ladye Digbeyes landes leyinge on boothe sydes.

17. Item one aker of Lande lyinge on a furlonge nere unto sharpe haulfe akers and shootethe Downe to Ravenston brooke the Ladye Digbey lyinge on the on side west and Francis Warrins land on the other syde Este. [*this paragraph is cancelled in the document*].

The Mydell feilde.

18. Item one haulfe aker of lande of a furlonge called litell well furlonge the Ladey Digbyes land leyinge on bothe sydes.

19. Item Two Roodes lyinge on morter pites furlonge the Landes of the Ladye Digbey leyinge on bothe sides.

20. Item fower litell landes with on of them sharpe at the southe ende shotinge upon sharpe halfe akers Francis Warrins lande on the west side; and the Lady Digbey on the Este syde.

21. Item one haulfe Roode of lande upon a furlonge shootinge downe to Ravenston brooke the Ladye Digbeys lande on boothe sydes.

22. Item Two akers of lande lyinge on a furlonge called liver landes Francis Warrins lande on the west syde and William Dicons land on the Este.

23. Item one haulfe aker of lande lyinge on a furlonge shootinge

downe to Turlers meade Francis Warrins lande lyinge on the west syde and the Ladye Digbeys on the Est.

24. Item one Rood of lande on a furlonge called Thicke thorne Hill the Lady Digbeys land lyinge on booth sydes.

25. Item one Roode of lande of a furlonge called wood Roodes the Lady Digbeyes land on booth sides.

26. Item an other Roode on the sayde furlonge called Wood Roodes, the Lady Digbey lyinge on the west syde; and Francis Warrins lande on the Este.

27. Item two leyes lyinge on a furlonge beneath Liver landes, betwixt the leye of Robert Willobye gentleman on the west syde and the hadens of William Warren of the Est syde.

28. Item one ley of a furlonge called under holme furlong the lady Digbeys ley beinge on the north syde and the ley of Thomas Birchmore on the southe syde.

29. Item on haulfe aker of lande of the sayde underholme furlonge the Ladye Digbeis lande lyinge on the southe syde; and Francis Warrins on the northe syde.

30. Item Three haulfe akers of land of the sayde underholme furlonge; the Ladye Digbeys land lyinge on the northe syde; and the lande of Thomas Birchemore lyinge on the southe syde.

The mill feilde.

31. Item one ley at Whitemore the lady Digbey on the Est syde and the ley of Thomas Birchmores on the west syde.

32. Item one ley shootinge upon Otecrofte betwixte the Close of Francis Warrin on the weste syde and the land of the sayd Francis on the Est. Allso one lande called counte Roodes the Ladyes Digbeyes land on booth sydes.

33. Item one litle lande lyinge on a furlonge called by the name of bame lande the Lady Digbeyes lande on the Est; and Belcher Houtons on the west.

34. Item one Rood of land lyinge on Moule Butes the Ladye Digbeyes lande leyinge on boothe sides.

35. Item Two landes beinge a litle aker shootinge to litle meade brooke the ladyes Digbeyes landes leyinge on boothe sides.

36. Item one litle haulf acker shootinge upon the saide litle meade brooke John Hasellbeyes lande on the west and the land of the lady Digbey on the Est.

37. Item one litle aker of land called Shorte aker betwixte Lady Digbyes lande on booth sydes.

38. Item one haulfe acker of a furlonge shootinge downe to Lamcotes

meade; the Ladye Digbey lyinge on the west syde and the land of Belcher Houton on the Est syde.

39. Item one acker of lande of a furlonge called mutton lambes havinge a lande of Thomas Burchmores of the Est syde; and the Ladye Digbeys on the west syde.

40. Item one haulfe aker of land lyinge on the sayde mutton furlonge or mutton landes the Ladye Digbey lyinge on the Est; and the land of John Haselbey on the West.

41. Item one Roode of land lyinge at Hogges Bushe furlonge the Ladye Digbey lyinge on booth sides.

42. Item one aker of land lyinge on a furlonge shootinge Downe to Ravenston brooke nere unto Aley burge the lady Digbeyes land on bothe sideis.

43. Item one aker of lande of the aforesayd furlonge nere unto heywardes brake; Francis Warrins landes on the northe side and the Lady Digbeys on the southe.

44. Item one litle ley shootinge Downe to Aley burge fourthe; the Lady Digbeys lande on boothe sydes.

The Southe feilde.

45. Item one haulfe aker of lande lyinge on holme furlonge the Ladye Digbeys lande on the northe syde and the lande of Johne Hasellbey one the southe syde, allso an other aker of lande on the sayd holmefurlong the Ladye Digbeys land on booth sydes.

46. Item on haulfe aker of lande on mydell furlonge John Hasellbey on the northe syde and Belcher Houton on the southe syde.

47. Item on haulfe aker more in the seyde mydell furlonge the Lady Digbes landes lyinge on boothe sydes.

48. Item on haulfe aker of lande lyinge on a furlonge betwixt Tumbre and Stanwell; the Ladye Digbes landes lyinge on boothe sydes.

49. Item one haulfe Roode beinge a ley lyinge in Tumbre the Ladye Digbeyes lande on boothe sydes.

50. Item one haulfe aker at Delves furlonge John Hasellbey on the west syde and the Ladye Digbye on the Este.

51. Item on lande shootinge downe to the parsons pitt the Ladye Digbey on the weste syde; and Belcher Houton on the Est syde.

52. Item one haulfe aker of Lande shootinge upon a furlonge called Harle landes the Ladye Digbeyes lands lyinge on booth sydes.

53. Item one haulf aker lying of a furlonge called longe Harley the Ladye Digbeyes land on boothe sydes.

54. Item on haulfe aker of Leys beinge a stoone pitt on yt; of Delves furlonge; the land of John Haselby lyinge on the west syde.

55. Item one ley one a furlonge called gore brode; the land of Belcher Houton lyinge on the Est, and the lande of the heyers of Mr Cave lyinge on the southe and west sydes.

56. Item one Roode of ley; leyinge on a furlonge which shoothe downe in Toumbre; the Ladye Digbey lyinge on boothe sydes.

57. Item on Rood of lande lyinge upon a furlonge is called oulde Dewles; the lande of the Lady Digbey on the northe syde; and Francis Warrin of the southe syde.

58. Item 7 landes lyinge of the fourlonge called 7 land Thre of them go thoroughe and ley upon dead man butes the 7 landes ley betwixt the land of the Lady Digbey on the Est syde; and the land of Thomas Birchmore on the west syde. and 5 buts upon the Ladye Digbey on the west; and the sayd Birchemore on the Est syde.

59. Item one haulfe acker of ley leyinge on a furlonge called Fenneill furlonge, betwixte the Lady Digby on the west; and Francis Warrins lande on the Est.

Item on Roode on a furlonge called ould crosse the lady Dygbies land lyinge on eyther sydes.

Item one litle peece of lande shootinge downe to parsons closse; commonly called 2 Akers (more or lesse) the land of the ladye Digbey lyinge on boothe sydes.

Item one other litle peece of land and leyes; conteyninge 2 akers more or lesse betwixt the ground of the ladye Digbey on the southe syde and the ground of Francis Warrin on the northe syde.

For the meadowe groundes.

63. *Inprimis* one Roode of meadow in holme mead in the first 12 beinge the 17 Roode betwene the meadowe of the lady Digbey on the northe syde; and the meade of Belcher Houton on the southe syde.

64. Item one swathe belonginge to the sayde Rood being the 7 swathe; betwixt the Lady Digbey on the northe syde; and Belcher Houton on the southe syde.

65. Item 4 leyes in standewell hoole belonginge to the gleabe in like manner.

66. Item on Roode in the second 12 Roodes, beinge the 7 Roode Mr Nevilles mead on boothe sydes which nowe is in the lady Digbyes hande.

67. Item one swathe beinge the 7 swathe; the Lady Digbey being on boothe sydes.

68. Item one pole bredthe called the flat Man; beeing the 7 the sayde Ladye Digbye on boothe sydes.

69. Item one Roode in the first 12 beinge the seventh Roode the Lady Digeby being on booth sydes.

70. Item one swathe beinge the seaventhe: the Lady Digebeyes lyinge on boothe sydes.

71. Item one Rood in the seconde 12 Roodes being the seaventhe; shootinge out in the southe ende with a picken.

Litell meade from the Meere stonne Downeward.

72. Item one Roode of medowe beinge the seaventhe Roode; the ladye Digbey beinge on boothe sides.

73. Item Three polle in the nether ende of the sayde litle meade, the Lady Digbey one boothe sydes.

74. Item one swathe beinge the seaventhe the Lady Digbey one boothe sydes.

75. Item one Roode in the sayde litell meade from the meare stonne upwarde being the 7 Roode The Lady Digbey on boothe sides.

76. Item one Rood beinge the 7 Roode in the next twelve Roodes the Ladey Digbeies meade on the Est syde.

77. Item one Roode in the third twelve beinge the 7 Roode the Lady Digbeies mede on the Est syde.

78. Item Sixe poole in the ende of the meade the Ladye Digbey on the Est syde; and olney fee aker of the west syde.

79. Lastly Two Roodes in Tumbre meade beinge the seaventhe Roode in every twelve.

Item thre Roodes beinge ommitted lyinge in the northe feilde; buttinge upon a lande of Belcher Houtons lying on Waspe hill furlonge the Lady Digbeys lande lyinge on bothe sydes.

(D/A/Gt/8/16/1)

110. STOKE HAMMOND 1640

A true Terrier of all the houses and lands belonging to the Rectory of Stokehamond in the county of Bucks (taken and made by the Parson Church wardensand the parishioners of the same parishe January 10 1639.

Imprimis a Parsonage house withe barnes stables and other edifices there unto belonginge.

Item 2 litle orchards.

Item 1 close called the parsons holines lyinge by the river there.

Item 1 parcell of medowe thereto adioyninge, called Docky hooke.

In the Common medowes *viz.* in

Leade meade   5 acres.
Fenne Meade   2 poles.
Neates medow   3 poles.
Northe meade   5 poles.
litle Northe meade   2 poles.
wede bed medowe   2 poles.
Banke medowe   2 poles.
Litle banke medow   2 poles.
Fullwell necke   2 poles.
upper Smethe medowe   2 poles.
wilowe bridge medowe   2 poles.
longe Smethe meade   1 pole.
1 pole adioyninge to dene acre.
Shipcote foorde medowe   3 pole.
Clay poole medowe   3 poles.
Chibbwell medowe   2 poles.
South medowe   5 poles.
Smallbrooke medowe   2 poles.
Clacke brooke   1 pole.

In the Common fields *viz.* in Northe felde halfe acres 37 roodes 20 and a plott of pasture ground about 2 acres, common betwene the parson and the lord of the Towne. West field half acres 29 roods 20. South field half acres 30 roods 17.

William Hickes   Parson

William   [...]   Churchwardens
Francis   [...]
Peter Woodward
John   [...]
Francis   [...]
John   [...]
(D/A/Gt/8/17/1)

111. STOKE POGES 1607

Octobris 6 Anno Domini 1607 Regni Domini Regis Jacobi dei gratia 5 et 41.

A Survaye or terrour of all the possessions...

Inprimis The homestall or scite of the vicarage Scituate and lyinge betwene the bordes by Hell more on the este and the lordes Cops on the weste and a buttinge on the kings hie waye on the northe and appon the lords greate ponde on the southe and contayns by estimacon twoe acres and within the said boundes are contayned on lyttell garden hedged about contayning by estimacon fower poles 2 acres 4 poles.

Item the vicarege howse concistinge of three roomes built all with tymber and Covered with tyle being chambred over borded and newlye repayred and disposed into fyve roomes.

Item one closse cauled the vicareg close butting upon the lords great more on the northe and on the kings high waye on the southe lying betwene the bromefeilde and the more conteining by estimacon 3 acres.

Item on mead and a spring conteyning by estimaton three acres butting on oke grove on the west and the kings high waye on the est lying by pie grove 3 acres.

Item seven acres of errable land in a feild cauled sowe crofte, where of fower acres lying together buttinge on the lordes ground one the north and uppon James Weldens ground one the southe. 7 acres.

Item twoe acres butting one the lane one the west and uppon the lords ground on the este.

Item an other acre butting one the lane one the southe and upon the lords ground one the north.

Item in the leefeild in a shott caulled the Layne three acres and one roode buttinge uppon lee hawse on the este and uppon west mors one the west.

Item more one acre and three roodes in a shott cauled seven acres butting one stoke lane on the west and under frime lee hedge on the southe.

Item mor one whole acre in lee feild butting uppon north crofte and lying next the parish acre. 6 acres.

Item one acre in Canon downe butting one Smytherlonnge one the southe and uppon the Ward one the northe 1 acre.

Item the Churchyeard with a picle anexed butting on the warren conteyning by estimacon twoe acres 2 acres.

Summa totalis 24 acres 4 poles.

per me Johannem Duffeild   Vicar

The marke of Clement Sturte   Churche wardens
The marke of Tristram Cranwell
Thomas French
The marke of Nycholas Mychell   Sidman
The marke of William Grome Senior
The marke of Edward Frenche

(D/A/Gt/8/18/1)

112. STOKE POGES 1639

A Terrer of the Glebe Lands and other possessions belonging to the vicarage of Stoke Poges in the Countye of Bucks.

Imprimis the vicarage inset house Consisting of 7 Roomes above and belowe.

Item a Barne of 2 bayes and a leaneto for a stable.

Item the homestal yard and gardein plott about one Acre.

Item a little meadow Joyned to the homstall eastward di. acre.

Item one other meadow Conteyning by estimacon 4 Acres. thus abbutoled The land Leading from Stoke to Farnham on the East and south The parsonage woods North and west.

Item a little pasture Close Called the Broome close Conteyneing about 2 Acres Thus Abbutoled The sayd Land Leading to Farnham on the South The Lords Broome feild on the East a medow of the Lords Called the Moore North and West.

Item 7 Acres of Arrable Land in a feild Called Souithecrofte 4 of them Abbuting upon a headland of the Lords of the Manner on the North and of an Acre of Edward French on the South.

One acre Lyeing next to the widow Chenies close on the East and butting on the Little Land on the South the other 2 Acres in the same feild Lyeing betwen the Lords Lands and butting on the West upon the Little Lane in all Acres 7.

Item in a feild Called Cannons Downe.

One Acre Lyeing Amongst the parsonage Lands East and West and abbutteth upon the park and prime waye on the North and on a mede of the Lords Called Smitherlandmede on the South.

Item in the feild Called Leefeild 6 Acres. thus abbutolled 3 Acres and a Roode parcell of the sayd 6 acres butting on a close Called Westmarsh on the west betwen the parsonage Lands South and North on the East abbutting upon a close Called Lee hawes.

One Acre and 3 Roodes parcell of the sayd 6 acres in a shott Called 7 Acres abbutting on Stoke lane Leading to Winesor on the West on a close Called Frimeleyes on the South Mr Winsors Land on the North and on a water course on the East.

One other Acre parcell of the said 6 Acres butting upon a headland of Mr Winsors on the North Lyeing betwen the Church Acre on the west and Mr Winsors Land on the East.

Nicholas Lovell   Vicar

Thomas Salmon   Churchwardens
John Stanton
(D/A/Gt/8/18/2)

113. STOWE 1607

Octobris 12 Anno Domini 1607 Annoque Regni Domini Regis Jacobi Dei gratia 5 et 41.

A Survey or Terreur of all the possessions...

Homestall.

Inprimis The homstall or Scite of the vicarage scituate and lying betweene the streete on the East and the feild on the West a butting uppon Chinalles close on the North and upon the Churchyarde on the South and conteines by estimation 1 acre 1 roode.

Item within the sayde boundes are conteined one garden walled by estimation 2 poles and one Orchard hedged about and well replenished 11 poles.

Edifices.

Item the vicarage house consisting of 8 bayes built of stonne the one halfe covered with tile and the other with thache 6 baies beeing chambred over and boarded etc. and the whole building contrived in 2 stories, and disposed in to 15 roomes *vizt.* the halle two parlours 7 chambers a kitchen etc.

Item one Barne consisting of 6 baies built all of timber.

For pasture meadow arable out tithes Stockes Implements Tenements or any other thing inquirable by the cannon and not herein before intimated and expressed there is nothing belonging to this Vicarage as farr as we knowe or can learne.

John Marshe   Minister

John Dunny   Churchwardens
Thomas [...]
John [...]
[...] North   Inhabitants
Thomas Grove
Roger Nicolls

(D/A/Gt/8/22/1)

114. SWANBOURNE 1607

Octobris 7 Anno Domini 1607 annoque Regni Regis Jacobi dei gratia etc quadragessimo primo.

A survie or terrour of all the possessions....

Homestall.

Inprimis The homestall or scite of the vicaridge scituate and Lying betweene the street on the west Mathewe Deverell on the east the Churchyard on the south Mathewe Deverell on the north and contaynes by estimation 3 roodes.

Item within the said bounds are contained one Little garden And one orchard by estimation [*blank*].

Edifices.

Item the Vicaridge howse consisting of v baies built all of wood and earth And covered over Wyth tyle And strawe iiij Baies, being chambered over and boarded and the whoall building contryved And Disposed into xj roomes.

Item one Kitchin with A little howse and A stable adjoyning contayning iij baies covered wyth strawe.

Item one Barne consisting of iij baies built as aforsaid And covered with strawe.

Arable.

Item in the south field of tillage xxiij Lands Little and great and containes by estimation 8 acres.

Item in the west Field of tillage 30 Lands Little and great And containes by estimation 10 acres.

Item in the north Field of tillage 32 Lands Lyttle and great and containes by estimation 10 acres.

Laie ground.

Item of Laie ground in the south field by estimation 3 roodes.

Item of Lay ground in the west Field vij And containes by estimation 3 Acres.

Item of Laie ground in the north Field A plott and iij Laies by estimation 2 Acres.

Meadowe.

Item in the south meade one acar togather And v single yards by estimation 2 Acres 1 Roode.

Item in the west mead ij single yards by estimation 2 roods.

Item in Alling mead ij single yard by estimation 2 roods.

Item for out tythes not Anie. And for stookes Implements or anye other thing Inquirable by the Cannon (and not before hear Intymated And expressed, theare is nothing belonginge to this Vicaridge as farre as we knowe or can Learne.

Thomas Low[...]   Minister

Mathew Deverell   Gardianes
Robart Adams   mark
Edmond Beckley
Adam [...]   mark
Ambrose Sheppard
Jereme [...]   mark
Robart Lane

(D/A/Gt/8/23/1)

115. SWANBOURNE 1639

A Terrier of the Arrable and grasse grounde belonging to the Vicarige of Swanbourne in the County of Bucks.

The North feilde.

Inprimis one yerd above Mead [...] on the East Mr Mayne on the west.

Item one Land in short foxton Mr William Mayne on the west Mathew Deverell on the east.

Item [...] yardes above Meade Mr William Mayne Lyinge on both sides.

Item A rode at Varnam John Henly on the South John Fryer on the north.

Item one land at Debdin John Henly Lyinge on both sides.

Item one hedland in Rowland the furlonge south Mathew Deverell North.

Item a lande in Welland John Henly on the south Ambrose Curle north [...] Rowland Ambrose Curle lyinge on both sides [...] to the west Mathew Deverell east.

Item one land [...] Mathew Deverell on the west John Carpenter on the east.

Item one Land att Loggs John Henly on the East John Addams on the west.

[...] on the west John Henly on the east.

Item a yerde in [...]hill Nicholas Loughton on the North John Henly on the Sowth.

Item A Roode in Leeke slad Ambrose Curle on the North Mathew Deverell on the south.

Item A Roode in Streetland slade Ambrose Curle on the East Mr Mayne on the west.

Item two Roodes in Streetland slade [...] Mayne on the west Churchill furlonge on the East.

Item three Acres Lyinge together in Marbrooke William Deverell East Mr Mayne West.

The Tillage of the West feilde.

Inprimis A Lande at Langmeade John Addams on the west John Henly on the East.

Item A Lande in Dunslade Mr William Mayne on both sides.

Item two yerdes att West [...] Mathew Deverell on the west Mr Mayne on the East.

Item one Land at Crowton slade Mr Mayne one the west John Henly on the East.

Item one Land att Hocomb John Henly on the West Mathew Deverell on the East.

Item two yerdes at Bondes leyes Mr William Mayne on the East the Furlonge on the East.

Item [...] Lands and a yerd at Dunstead Hill John Henly on the East John Addams west.

Item one Lande att Roach John Henly lyinge on both sides.

Item A Roode att Foote bridg Mr Mayne on the North Thomas Deverell on the south.

Item another Roode att Footbridg John Henly on the South Mathew Deverell on the North.

Item one Lande in the Riddy Richard Colls on the south John Henly on the North.

Item A Lande in dead furlonge Mathew Deverell on the east John Henly on the West.

Item A Yerd at Hollow lane Thomas Askew on the south Thomas Curle on the North.

Item A Butt on this side the Riddy John Henly on the South John Addams North.

Item two Landes under Moore Thomas Deverell on the South John Henly on the North.

Item one Lande on the same Furlonge John Henly on the South Mathew Deverell North.

Item one Peece under Moore of three Acres Richard Bonde on the west William Deverell East.

The Tillage of the South feild.

Imprimis a lande at Ridgway Robert Carter on the West Mr Mayne on the East.

Item A Lande at Hungerhill Thomas Askew on the East John Parrett on the West.

Item A Lande at Outland William Deverell on the North Thomas Askew on the South.

Item one Lande att Stepitt John Carpenter on the East John Henly on the West.

Item one yerde att Allfeeilde Robert Lane on the East Mr Mayne on the west.

Item one Lande att Windemill Hill Edmond Thorne East John Henly west.

Item one yerde at Washpoole Ambrose Curle on the west John Henly on the East.

Item one Lande at Steepmeade John Henly lyinge on both sides.

Item one Acre at Charland Thomas Askew west John Henly on the East.

Item one Lande at Charland John Henly on the East John Addams on the west.

Item A Lande above Kemsmead Thomas Gylbert on the west John Henly west.

Item A Lande att Buckslow John Addames lyinge on both sides.

Item A Lande at Reade Richard Pottes on the west John Henly on the East.

Item An Acre att Rush Mathew Deverell on the west John Henly on the East.

Item A yerde under Preis Mathew Deverell on the west Thomas Askew East.

Item A Lande in the Meithe John Kinge on the East Mathew Deverell on the West.

The Grass Grownd of the South Feild.

Imprimis A Ley Land at [...] the pasture of Mr William Mayne North.

Item One Acre in sowmead John Addams on the North John Goddin on the South.

Item A Roode in the same Meade Beniamin Hunter on the East Walter Webb West.

Item one yerd in the same Meade John Henly on the East John Godwin on the west.

Item one Roode in the same Meade John Henly North Walter Webb south.

Item one halfe Acre in the same Meade William Deverell East John Henly East.

Item one Leye [...] Henly on the North William Deverell South.
Item A Roode at [...] Meade John Henly lyinge on both sides.

The Grass grownde of the North feilde.

Inprimis one Ley att Dodly Hill [...] on the North the furlonge south.
Item a platt shootinge from [...] Nicholas Laughton west John Henly east.
Item two leyes at Clack lane End John Addams on the east Ambrose Curle west.
Item A Plott in Narbrooke Thomas Deverell on the south the vicarige North.

The Grass grownde of the West feild.

Imprimis one Headley betweene the Dunslades Mr Mayne North the furlonge South.
Item a Headley att the upper end of Dunslade Mr Mayne East the furlonge West.
Item one Headley next little [...] west Ambrose Curle East.
Item one Headley [...] Richard [...] South the Furlonge North.
Item a little Rood Platt in Smale brooke John Avery North Mathew Deverell South.
Item a yerde at Footebridge John Goddin North mathew Deverell on the South.
Item a yerde in Allen Meade Beniamin Anstey North John Goddin on the South.
Item an Head Roode in Willow greene Richard Bonde East Mathew Deverell West.
Item two Leyes att Chalkehill forde, Mr Mayne East Robert Carter West.
Item a yerde in longe Doles John Henly lyinge on both sides.

Vicarige Howse Contayninge fower Bayes and an halfe [...] Roomes and six other roomes, two Chymies: The howse halfe Tyled [...].
A Cowhouse adioyninge to the ende of it.
A Barne contayninge three Bayes a leanetoo A Kitchin Gatehowse, wood house and stable of three Bayes [...] orcharde with a little Platt adioyninge. All which by Estimation [...] there abouts and thus butted and bounded : The streete west : William Deverell East The Churchyard South George Deverell North.

Ita est Robertus Lowndes   *Vicarius*

Robert Carter   Churchwardens
Robert Lane
(D/A/Gt/8/23/2)

116. TAPLOW 1639

A Terrior of the Glebe lands and Church duties belonginge To the Parsonage of Taplowe in the County of Bucks and in the Dioces of Lincolne Delivered upp the Fourth Day of October *Anno Domini* 1639.

1. *Inprimis* iiij Acres on the backside of the Parsonage, lying in Roake Furlonge.

2. Item halfe an acre in Towne Furlonge on the North side next to Richard Kings one Acre.

3. Item iij halfe acres in Bradley on the north side next to the Meare waie.

4. Item halfe an Acre more in Bradley next to Mr Hampsons iij halfe Acres on the North side.

5. Item halfe an Acre more in Bradley next to iij halfe Acres of Mr Thomas Hampson Esq. on the South side.

6. Item halfe an acre upp and downe hill bounding on Towne Furlonge betweene half an Acre of Mr Henry Manfield Esq and halfe an Acre of Andrewe Todd.

7. Item halfe an Acre in Leadmore Veire lying betweene a half Acre of Sir Arthur Mainwaring on the North, and iij halfe Acres of Richard King on the South.

8. Item a yeard over Windsor waie on the North side of John Chilburies yeard.

9. Item halfe an Acre by Small meade: being headland to viij Acres of Mr Hampson Esq.

10. Item halfe an Acre in Marsh Veire shooteing on the East on Hitcham Marshes.

11, 12. Item two halfe Acres over Cockeine thorne Waie Andrew Todd haveing a halfe acre lying betweene them.

13. Item half an Acre on Beedwell hill on the West side of Mr Hampsons 5 Acres.

14. Item halfe an Acre more in the same Veire on the East side of Mr Hampsons iij halfe acres.

15. Item halfe an Acre in Fernie Furlonge, on the west side of Mr Hampsons Acre called Fulmer Acre.

16. Item an acre shooting on the longe Elmes, Mr Manfields land lying on both sides thereof.

17. Item halfe An acre shooting upon a Butt of Richard Clarkes that boundeth on Winmemy Feild waie.

18. Item half an Acre in Bovetowne on the North side of water plaish Close, betweene Twoe Acres of Mr Mansfields.

19. Item an Acre more in Bove towne shootinge on John Phipps Close, westward and on the high waie Eastward.

20. Item halfe an Acre lyinge upp and downe hill, on the Towne lane westward, next to the Ellmes.

21. Item halfe an Acre in Foxholes betweene Richard Kinge and Thomas Golds land bounding on Lee Chequer Mead westward.

22. Item a yard in Stone Veire lying betweene Mr Manfields land on both sides shooting on the Thames banke.

23. Item a halfe Acre lying in the same Veire betweene Mr Hampsons land on both sides.

24. Item a yeard ioyninge to the Meare banke on the South side of the 10 Acres of Mr Hampson bounding on the Thames.

25. Item an halfe Acre in Thames Veire lying on the South side of Mr Hampsons Acre and bounding on the Thames.

26. Item halfe an Acre in Crowch Veire bownding on the Meads on the West, and lying by Mr Hampsons halfe Acre Northward.

27. Item halfe an Acre on Stanthill, lying betweene Richard Kings iiij acres on the South side, and Mr Manfields land on the North.

28. Item halfe an Acre at Lockmead lying betweene the land of Mr Hampson on the North and Mr Manfield on the South.

29. Item halfe an Acre in Witley bedds toward Cowlees gate; betweene the land of John Earle on the North and Mr Manfield on the South.

30. Item a yeard neere long Iudas shooting on Cockine Thorne, by the Marsh hedge betweene Richard Kinges and Sir Arthur Mainwarings land.

31. Item iij yeards abutting on the iiij Acres of meadow of the Parsons, adioyninge to Mr Manfields land on the North side.

32. Item iiij acres togeather of meadow grownd, adioyning to vij acres of Mr Manfielde on the south side.

33. Item iij halfe Acres more in three severall places in the meads, ij in lon[...] and one in Taplow Marshe meade. The Parson of Hitcham have [...] but the Parson of Taplow lyeth next to Taplow in all of them [...].

34. Item hee hath halfe an acre more in lott meade of meadowe.

35. Item halfe an acre in Small meade which usually hath been by lott [...].

36. Item halfe an Acre in Stile meade adioyninge to Richard Kings la[...].

Item a little Close called Brewins, bounding on Bovetowne North.

[...] on the Streete South valued ij Acres.

Item a Parsonage howse a great Barne, a lesser thatched Barne, a stable at the end of it an out howse and hovell, all in good repaire, a great Orchyard, and a little orchyard behinde the great Barne, with two gardens and a little Court yard, the ground that conteyneth all these, with the great yard is two acres more or lesse.

Church Dues   for a marriage   ijs. vjd.
                   a Burriall   js. vjd.
                   a Churchinge   vjd.
                   a Buriall in the Chancell   xiijs. iiijd.
                   a Buriall in Mr Hampsons vault by Composicon
with the fownder thereof, as in the Chancell, And xijd. per Annum for the place digged out of the Churchyard, besides the duties at any Burialls.

The parishoners paye Tithe milke to the Parson, from the 2 of Maye to Lammas Day every 10th day; morning and eveninge for all their Kyne that give milke vizt 10 mornings and 10 evenings.

They pay also Tith Calfe *vizt.* the 10th when it falleth or the 10th parte if it be sold if killed the shoulder.

Tithe Fishe for that parte of the River of Thames that is in the parishe of Taplowe and Tith Oziers is paid to the Parson yearly and Tithes of Wood and Conies And all other Tithes that by the lawes of the land are payable and dewe.

In Witnes where of wee have hereunto putt our handes the date and yeare written.

William Edmondes   Rector *ibidem*

John Chilbey junior   mark   Churchwardens
Mathew Grove
Andrew Todd his marke

(D/A/Gt/9/1/1)

117. THORNBOROUGH 1639

A Terrior of all the house ground and gleblands belonging to the vicaridge of Thornborough 1639.

Inprimis the vicaridge house which containeth three bayes of buildinge and a barne containeing three bayes of building the backside on the north about a rood of ground.

Item two leyes in the middle croft about three roods of ground.

Item in the piltchfeeild, one land on mickledon Colleddg land on both sides.

Item one land att piltch towne leyes on the north free land on the south.

Item one land on worship a moore, Colledge land on both sides.

Item one land on blakenell Colledge land on the west luffeild land on the East.

Item one butt by the parsonage meade, Colledge land on the south parsonage north.

In the Egbororowe feeild one land on Ausdon, luffeild land on the south free land on the north.

Item two butts shootting into mill slade, luffeild land on the north free land on the south.

In the mill feeild two lands shootting into Stoundill waye Colledge land on the south free land on the north.

To these pertaine a yardland meddow and halfe yardland Commons in the vicars tenure that now is, tenne peeces.

Testified by James Carey   Vicar

Rallfe Pollard   Churchwardens
Thomas Grace
(D/A/Gt/9/2/1)

118. THORNTON 1639

A Terrier of the Parsonage house and Gleabe Landes nowe belonging to the Rectory of Thornton in the County of Bucks And diocese of Lincolne October the xxvth *anno domini* 1639.

Imprimis the Parsonage house nowe in the tenure of Robert Rud Rector of the Church there, Contayning five bayes of building with the yard, and one small close abuttinge on the Kings highe way towards the North and upon the pasture of Sir Edward Tyrrell kt. and Barronett called Jennings towards the Sowthe and lieth betwixt the park of the said Sir Edward to the East and the lands of the said Sir Edward in the tenure of John Hudson John Skinner and William Palmer towards the West And Containeth by estimation one acre three Roods.

Item two Peeces of Meadoe ground called the quabbes lyinge together betwixt the River of Owse towards the North: and the Lands of the said Sir Edward Tyrrell towards the south And abutteth one the ground of the said Sir Edward called the Longe Meadoe towards the West, And the Hogge yards of the said Sir Edward towards the East And they containe by estimacon two Acres.

This part of Meadoe doth not belonge to the gleabe, nor is not gleabe: for it is in an other parish But the Parsone of Thornton hath formerly heald it: Item one Meadoe containing by estimacon one acre three Roods Lying betwixt the highway towards the West, and Wickhammon Meadoe towards the East and abutteth uppon the Close of the said Sir Edward Tyrrell towards the North and upon the River of Owse towards the South.

Robert Rudd   Rector *ibidem*

Thomas Hobes   *signum*

(D/A/Gt/9/3/1)

119. TINGEWICK 1639

A Terrier of the Glebe etc of the Parsonage of Tingeweecke *Anno Domini* 1639 October 23.

Imprimis the Parsonage house the Barnes, Stables, Cowhouses, Gardens Dove-house Orchards and yard All of them butting to the North ward upon the Colledge Close and Church yard to the South upon John Holdings Messuage and Orchard and William Perkins his Close to the South and to the East upon the Church Lane, and to the West upon William Perkins his Close.

Item foure Tenements lying to the East upon Thomas Grove his close and Orchard to the West upon the Crosse Lane to the North upon the Rode to the South upon the wood-streate.

Item in the East feild in Ridgway furlong one yeard Richard Waddup to the west and Waddup to the East, one land Richard Clark to the west and Thomas Whitmell to the East one Land Edward Tutchin to the west, and Mary Hale to the East, one land Richard Waddup laying to the west, and Georg Cowley to the East and all the lands in this furlong abutting upon Danstrey Ash way to the South and upon Ridg-way to the North.

In Hares-Ash-furlong one land laying along Brastow hedg way to the South, Georg Cowley to the North one land Richard Clarke to the South George Cowley to the North and these two lands shute upon Edmund Durrants hadeland to the West, and uppon Fasam-Way to the East.

In Stallage furlong one land Richard Waddup to the west and John Perkins to the East in the North upon Stallag and to the South upon Richard Wadings Hadeland two yards Shoting toward Clock-more Spring, Edward Tutchin on the west, John Whitmell Junior on the East, butting John Tutchin on the South and to the North butting upon two Butts of William Perkins his and one of John Bruces and upon another of John Waddups.

Item one land in Litle-well furlong Georg Cowley to the west and Erasmus Grove to the East One land Browne to the West and Alice Jackson to the East and these two lands land on the South Richard Clarks Hade land and John Jefferey had-land on the North.

Item one land Richard Waddup to the West Henry Whitmell to the East John Jefferies had-land to the North Edmund Durrants Land to the South.

Item one Land under Clock-moore John Jefferies hadland to the West and Henry Marcam Senior to the East Richard Clarke to the North and Henry Marcam Junior to the South.

Item, one thoroughout land Shooting in Fasam way to the West and William Brownes had-land to the East. Robert Fosket to the South and William Browne to the North.

Item in Ratliffe pond furlong two yeards John Tutchins had-land on the South East, Edmund Buckinghams had-land North West Southwest George Cowley and Northwest Mary Hale.

Item two yeards at Dudley-Bridg William Browne to the West, Erasmus Grove to the east, Edward Jeffery to the North and Buckingham way to the South.

Item a land in Thick-ferne William Perkins senior to the North John Perkins to the South Henry Marcam senior on the west, and John Perkins on the East.

Item one land upon Grove-hill Buckingham way to the South, William Perkins Junior to the South, William Browne to the West and John Whitmell Junior to the East.

Item a But at Gaffard-gate, Buckingham-way to the North William Perkins Junior to the South. Richard Waddup both on East and West.

Item one Land in Church-had-land furlong Dunstrey-Ash-way to the North and the Church-had-land to the South. Georg Cowley to the West and Henry Marcam Junior to the East.

Item one land more in the same furlong John Whitmell Junior on the west, and Edmund Durrant on the East the Church hadland on the South and Dunstry-Ash-way on the North.

Item one yard abutting on Erasmus Groves yard on the North and the Church hadland on the South Henry Marcam Junior on the East, Richard Clarke on the West.

Item in the Middle field one land abutting on the Colledge Close end to the South William Perkins senior to the North John Whitmell Junior to the west and John Perkins to the East.

Item one yard on the same furlong abutting upon John Tutchin to the North The Demeanes on the South Richard Clarke on the west and Henry Marcam Junior on the East.

Item one land in the upper Plash, Georg Cowley on the north William Perkins senior on the East, the Upper Plash on the North and Shooting Southward into John Perkins his Land.

Item one yeard in Catehangers hedg-furlong Richard Clark on the South and William Browne on the North Eastward Richard Clarkes had-land, and West ward Catehangers-hedg.

Item one land in the same furlong William Perkins Junior on the North and John Bedford on the South, and the same hadland and hedg East and West abutting it.

Item one land shooting into Groves Close on the North and into Henry Marcam Junior his hadland on the South, on the West Richard Clarke, and on the East Georg Burtons land.

Item one land in Wooland Georg Cowley on the west, on the North Fulwell-way John Tutchins had-land on the South, and Erasmus Grove on the East.

Item one land at Dredens Crosse Edmund Buckingham laying Southward and John Perkins Northward, Shooting Westward into Dredens Crosse and Eastward into Richard Clarks Piece.

Item one ley at Stratford stile Richard Waddup both on North and South and shooting into John Perkins his had-land Eastward, Westward into John Holdens hadland.

Item Nine leyes lying by Egersham on the North, and by Edmund Durrants leyes on the South, Shooting into the way of Stratford-foord on the West and on the East into Henry Marcam Junior his hadland.

Item one Land shooting North ward to Egersham hedg Southward into John Whitmell senior his land William Browne one the west and William Perkins Junior in the East.

Item on Land shooting into Fullwell way South ward and North ward into William Browns land William Perkins Junior on the West and John Whitmell Senior on the East.

Item one Land in the same furlong Shoting on the South into Fulwell way on the North into Georg Cowley his lands on the West Richard Clarke on the East Mary Hale.

Item one land shooting upon Bul-hoock-Spring in the North Southward into William Perkins Junior his land and lying by Georg Cowley westward and by Edmund Durrant Junior Eastward.

Item one Land shooting Northward into Bul-hoock, and into William Perkins his land South ward, William Browne on the west and Georg Cowley on the East.

Item on land Shooting into Mill-greene-way Southward John Whitmells land on the North and Georg Cowley both on East and west.

Item one Land Shooting into the Lower Plash Southward

Northward into Mill-greene-way. John Fosket on·the East, William Browne on the west.

Item one land in Northam Shooting Westward into Stone-pit ford and Eastward into Thomas Groves hadland Richard Waddup on the North and William Perkins Junior on the South.

Item one Land Shooting Northward into Northam Meddow, Southward into Thomas Groves Peice, Richard Waddup on the East, William Perkins Junior on the West.

Item one Ley Shooting North ward into John Perkins his ley John Jeffery on the west Thomas Groves ley on the South William Tutchin on the East.

Item another Ley in Northam shooting into Henry Marcam Junior his ley Northward and Shooting into a land earable of the same Henry Marcam on the South Richard Waddup on the East. Georg Cowley on the West.

Item one Land in Northam William Browne on the West John Perkins on the East Shooting into Thomas Groves ley on the North and Millgreene Way on the South.

Item one Butte Shooting upon the Mill on the North and Henry Paxtons Land on the South Georg Cowley on the West and John Jeffery on the East.

Item one land at Mill-leyes Shooting Westward into Robbert Folkes had-land, and Eastward into Richard Waddups hadland in the East field and in the North Richard Waddup, Thomas Whitmell on the South.

Item one land in Chackmans Deane Shooting Northward into Henry Marcams hadley and southwards into Fulwell way William Browne on the West, Richard Waddup on the East.

Item one land in Ridgway furlong, Shooting into Ridgway on the South and Fulwell way on the North Richard Waddup on the west William Tutchin on the East.

Item another land on Ridgway furlong Shooting into Ridgway on the South and Northward into Henery Whitmells Balkes George Burton on the East John Perkins on the West.

Item four lands at Millway Ridgway furlong on the South, Henry Paxton on the North Fulwell Way on the east and Henry Marcam junior his hadland on the West.

Item one hadland at Ridnell furlong Shooting into One-oke-way on the West and Thomas Groves Land on the East John Perkins on the North Bowling-Alley-furlong on the south.

Item one Land more in Bowling-Alley furlong Shooting into Ridgway on the South and the Glebe hadland on the North Georg Burton on the East Richard Waddup on the West.

Item one land in Northam Downe furlong Shooting into Mill Mores on the North, and Fulwell way on the South, Edward Tutchin on the West and William Perkins Junior on the East.

Item one Ley in the upper Plash William Tutchin on the East George Cowley on the West Fulwell way on the North John Waddup on the South.

Item in Westfield at Sand pit hill one Land, Butting into Finmere way on the South into Henry Whitmells hadland on the North and William Brown on the East Georg Cowley one the West.

Item one land in Gorbroad furlong Shooting into Edward Tutchins land East ward into Edmund Buckinghams in the west Mary Hale on the South, John Perkins on the North.

Item another land Shooting into Erasmus Groves hadland on the East and into John Waddups in the West Richard Waddup in the North side Mary Hale on the South.

Item one Land in Buckingham hadland furlong Richard Clarke on the South, Edward Buckingham on the North John Whitmell on the East, and Richard Clarke on the West.

Item one Land in Elderdon furlong Shooting upon John Whitmell Senior his hadland on the West William Tutchin on the East Georg Cowley on the North Richard Clark on the South.

Item another Land in the same furlong Shooting into William Perkins Junior his hadland on the East, and on Henry Marcam Junior on the West, Richard Clarke on the North, Thomas Grove on the South.

Item one Land at Stonepits Henry Paxton on the North Richard Waddup on the South, Georg Cowley on the West Richard Waddup on the East.

Item one Land in Langford furlong Shooting upon Langford Meddow on the East Richard Waddups hadland on the west, William Browne on the South, William Perkins Junior on the North.

Item one Land in High moore furlong Shooting into Finmere highway on the North and Henry Marcam Senior on the South John Perkins on the West Richard Waddup on the East.

Item one Land at Cutloe hill Shooting into Finmere way on the West and Edmund Durrant senior on the East, Richard Clarke on the North, William Perkins Junior on the South.

Item one land more at Cutloe hill, William Marcam on the West, Edmund Buckingham on the East Georg Cowley on the North Richard Waddup on the South.

Item one Land at Halkwell-hill-furlong Thomas Whitmell on the East, Finmere way on the west Georg Cowley on the North William Browne on the South.

Item one land more in the same furlong Shooting into Henry Marcam senior his hadland Eastward, into Edmund Durrant Senior his hadley on the west Edward Jeffery on the North, William Perkins Junior on the South.

Item two Butts more in the same Furlong Shooting into Edmund Durrant Senior his had-ley on the West, Edmund Buckinghams hadland on the East William Perkins Junior on the South Georg Cowley on the North.

Item one land at Bow-back-randome Shooting into Erasmus Groves had-ley on the North, into Richard Waddups yeard on the South Edward Durrant Junior on the East Richard Waddup on the West.

Item one lay more in the same furlong Shooting into Finmere way on the North, and Henry Marcam Junior on the South Richard Waddup on the East and West.

Item one land in Finmere Way furlong Shooting into Finmere Way on the South, into Edward Buckinghams hadlay on the North Richard Waddup on the East William Browne on the West.

Item a Butt in the Same furlong Shooting into William Cowleys land on the North, into the hieway on the South Richard Waddup on the West William Perkins Junior on the East.

Item another land in the same furlong Shooting into Thomas Groves hadland on the North into Finmere way on the South and Richard Clarke on the West Mary Hale on the East.

Item one land more in the same furlong Shooting into Finmere Way on the South, into William Brownes land on the North George Barton on the East Georg Cowley on the west.

Item one land at Smalepath Shooting into Edward Jefferyes fore shooter on the North, and Smale Path on the South.

Item one ley at Cutloe Shooting upon Edmund Durrant senior on the East and Mary Hale on the West John Perkins on both sides.

Item one land in Brook furlong Shooting into Finmere Way on the North Mary Hales had-land on the South Georg Cowley on the West, and William Perkins Junior on the East.

Item another land on the same furlong William Browne on the West John Fosket on the East.

Item another land in the same furlong John Perkins on the East Richard Clarke on the West.

Item another land in the same furlong Richard Clarke on the West, John Fosket on the East.

Item another land in the same furlong Richard Waddup on the West, Frenches land on the east.

Item one ley [...] on the West, Erasmus Grove on the East all these lands of this furlong Shoot into Finmere Way on the North and into West brook ditch on the South.

Item in Wood furlong one land John Perkins on the East, Georg Cowley on the West.

Item another land in the same furlong Richard Waddup on the East William Perkins Junior on the West.

Item another land in the same furlong Edward Jeffery on the East William Perkins Junior on the West.

Item another land there Georg Cowley on the East William Browne on the West.

Item another there William Perkins Junior on the East and Georg Cowley on the West.

Item another land there William Tutchin on the East, Georg Cowley on the West.

Item one ley in the same furlong Georg Cowley on the West Edward Tutchin on the East, and all the lands of this furlong Shoot into West-brooke Ditch on the North and into Wood hedg on the South.

Memorandum that the Dwelling house conteineth about six Bay the Kitchin two Bay the two Barnes nine Bay the Stables and Gate-house three Bay the orchard Gardens and yeard Conteine half an Acre of grownd and Some what more.

John Urrey   Rector *ibidem*

Francis Bushell   Curatus
Thomas Grove   Churchwardens
Henry Whitmell

(D/A/Gt/9/4/1)

120. TURWESTON 1634

A Tarrier of the dwelling house oute houses Barnes stables homestall gleabe land both earable and pasture belonging to the parsonage of Turweston in the County of Bucks as now they are in occupation of Thomas Phillpott Rector *Anno Domini* 1634.

Inprimis the dwelling house 3 baye, one Leaneto butting estward on the highway west [...].

Item one barne 4 baye and one Leaneto one stable 2 baye one Cowhouse 2 bay butting east on the greene and west on the barne, butting south on the Church yard north on the Lane.

Item one malting house 4 bay butting south on the Churchyard north on the way to the Lane.

Item one hay barne 3 baye, butting south on the grene north on the way to the Waie Lane.

Item one Close on the North side of the barne one orchard adioyning unto it conteyning one acer, buttinge south on the Churchyard and farme house north on Thomas Yats his close.

In the North feilde Ridges 62.

Inprimis at Portway 18 ridges buttinge south on the highway north on Thomas Maves land.

Item at short seven acres 12 ridges butting East on sommer fallow west on John Yats his land.

Item at longe seven acers 5 ridges butting west on the Cowpasture East on Robert Wells land.

Item at Knot yards end 3 ridges butting north on the farme land south on Robert Wells his land.

Item shoting downe on these Lands 2 ridges butting East on Thomas Yats Land West on the parsons wife.

Item at the Carrion-pitts 4 ridges butting North on William Knight south on the former Land.

Item at Hawe-hedge 1 ridge buttinge North on Mr Haynes his land south on Hawe hedge.

Item at the Breach 2 ridges butting North on Widow Wollom south on Robert Webb.

Item shotinge on the Breach 11 ridges buttinge North on widow Wollom south on Robert Webb.

In the Midle Feilde Ridges 54.

Inprimis at litle hill 10 ridges buttinge North on Portway south on Woofurlonge.

Item next to Hawhedge 3 ridges butting East on the parsons Hedge west on Thomas Yats land.

Item at Stone-pitts 3 ridges butting on the pitte north, south on Widow Wollams Land.

Item at the Water sladd 2 ridges buttinge East on Robert Webbs Lea West on the parsons Land.

Item on the other side of the sladd 2 ridges butting North on the highway south on the sladd.

Item by the same water sladd 9 ridges buttinge south on Thomas Barrett north on the sladd.

Item on the other side of the sladd 8 ridges butting allso south on Thomas Barret North on the sladd.

Item at Wosted hedge 11 ridges butting south on Brakeley way North on William Harris Land.

Item beyond Wosted hedge 2 ridges butting west on Mrs Wriglesworth East on Thomas Yates Land.

Item by old windmill hill 3 ridges butting West on Roger Knights East Thomas Yates Land.

Item by Bromers house 1 ridge buttinge East on John Yates west on Bromers house.

In the Farre Fielde Riges 32.

Inprimis at Williams Crosse 12 ridges butting North on the highway south on the Cross.

Item at the hanging of the hill 8 ridges butting south on John Yates North on Mrs Wriglesworth.

Item at the grove hill 6 ridges butting East on Thomas Yates West on John Yates Land.

Item at grove lease 2 ridges butting North on the highway south on William Harris Land.

Item shooting on the grove 2 ridges butting to the North and South on Thomas Yates his land.

Item on the other side of hill hanging 2 ridges butting North on Thomas Yates south on John Yates his land.

In the North feild of Medow 2 Akers dimid'.

Inprimis one platt of medow 2 akers butting south on the shire brooke north on the ferme Lands.

Item at seven Akers 12 hades butting allso uppon the saide brooke and ferme Lands.

In the Middell Feilde.

Inprimis at Woo furlonge on aker dimid: butting south on Westbury north on Robert Webbs Land.

Item at Water sladd hades and pleck one Aker butting south on William Harris north and the parsons Land.

In the Fardest Feilde.

Inprimis [...] 2 akers butting south on the shire brooke north on the farme grove.

Item at [...] 2 long sidelings buting south on the ferme lande North on Cowpasture.

The totall of erable Landes Ridges 148 in all Akers 58.
The totall of Medow Akers 8

Ita testor Thomas Phillpott   Rector

Thomas Yates   Churchwardens
William Harris

(D/A/Gt/9/6/1)

121. TURWESTON 1639

A trew Tarrier of the Dwelling house Outhowses Barnes Stables homestall Gleabe both of Earable and Pasture beinge three yard lande in all belonginge to the parsonage of Turueston in the County of Bucks as they are now in use and Occupation of Thomas Phillpott Rector September 27 AD 1639.

Inprimis the dwellinge howse 3 bays one leane to.

Item one new built Study with A buttrie underneath and A wolloft above.

Item the out howses 2 bay.

Item the Barne 4 bay one leanto.

Item the hay barne 3 bay.

Item 2 Stables 3 bay.

Item the homestall one close buttinge on Mrs Haynes close: one Orchard bounded with the Church yard and the farme closes.

Item one close cauled the horse close bounded with the Churchyard on the west side and the towne greene on the East side. in all 2 Akers.

In the North feild.

Imprimis at portway Ridges: 18: Buttinge South on the highway North on Thomas Yeats his hadland and the cowpastor.

Item at short Seven Akers: Ridges: 12 Buttinge East on sumer fallow West on John Yeats his Hadlande.

Item at longe seven Akers ridges: 5: Buttinge West on Cowpasture, East on Robert Webs his Hadlande.

Item at Knots yards ende ridges: 3: Buttinge North on the farme grounde South on Robert Webbs hadland.

Item Shooting downe on those lands Ridges: 2: Buttinge East on Thomas Yeats and west on William Knights hadlande.

Item at the Carrion pitts Ridges: 4: Buttinge North on William Knights and South on the farme lands.

Item at haw hedge Ridge: 1: Buttinge North on Mr Heynes towne on Hawe hedge.

Item at the Breach Ridges: 2: Buttinge East and west on John Yeates his Lands.

Item more Shouting upon the Breach: 11: Buttinge North on Widow Williams South on Robert Webbs. Ridges 62 Akers 20.

In the Middell feilde.

Imprimis at littell hill Ridges: 10: Buttinge North on portway South on Woofurlonge.

Item on the other side of hawe hedge cauled the South side: 3: Ridges Buttinge East on the Common west Thomas Yeats.

Item at the stone pitts: 3: Ridges Buttinge North upon the stone pitts South on Widow Wollams lands.

Item at the Water slade Ridges: 2: Buttinge East on Robert Webbs land West on the parsons plott.

Item on the other side of the Sladde Ridges: 2: Buttinge North on the highway South on the slade.

Item more by the same slade Ridges: 9: Buttinge North on the farme land South on the water slade.

Item at the other side of the slade Ridges: 8: Butting South on Thomas Baret North on the slade.

Item at Wosted hedge Ridges: 11: Buttinge south on Buckingham way North on the salde.

Item on the west side of Wosted headge Ridges: 1: Buttinge South on Bucksway North on widow Wollams.

Item by olde Wimmell hill Ridges: 3: Buttinge East on Thomas Yeats West on the Winemill hill.

Item at the tounes End, 1 Ridge: Buttinge East on Mrs Riddelsworth West on Bremers house. Ridges 54 Akers [...].

In the Far most feilde.

Imprimis at Wollams Cross Ridges: 12: Buttinge North on the highway South on the Cross.

Item at the hangings Ridges: 8: Buttinge South on John Yeats North on Wriglesworth.

Item at the grove hill Ridges: 6: Buttinge East on Thomas Yeats West on John Yeats.

Item at grove lease: Ridges: 2: Buttinge North on highway South on William Haris.

Item Shooting on the grove Ridges: 2: Buttinge North and South on Thomas Yeats.

Item at the other side of hanging: Ridges: 2: Buttinge North on Thomas Yeats South on John Yeats. Ridges 32 Akers 16.

In all of Earable Ridges 148 Akers 54.

The Medow Ground.

In the North feild 3 plots containinge 3 Akers in all Buttinge west on the shire brook East on brake.

Item in the same feild 12 hades by short seven Akers Buttinge East on the ploude lands west on the Brake 1 Aker.

In the middell feild at Wooefurlonge i Plot of 3 Akers Butting North on the farme land South on the parsonage Land.

Item at Wooe furlong of hads and Placks nere Water slad 1 Aker Buttinge North and South on the parsonage land.

In the ferthest feild one plack by the grove contayninge 3 Akers Buttinge South on the brooke North on the grove.

Item at Curlock 2 Placks caled sidelongs contayning 1 Aker both Buttinge North on the farme South on the Cow pastor. Akers 12.

The Totale of Homestall, Erable and Medow = Akers 68.

Thomas Phillpott   Rector

John Turne   mark   Churchwardens
Thomas Barret   mark

(D/A/Gt/9/6/2)

122. UPTON 1607

Septembris xx 1607 Annoque Regni Domini Regis Jacobi Dei gratia Anglie etc. Quinto et Scotie xlj.

A Survey or Terriour of all the possessions...

Homestale.

Inprimis the homestale or Scite of the vicaredg with certeine pitles of land to the same adioyning bounding uppon a feilde belonging to Upton Corte called Titchforde feild, on the est and a lane leading from Upton Church towards London highwaye on the west and a close belonging to Upton Corte called the Vicaredge close on the North and the common greene on the South. Within which bounds are conteyned one litle dwelling howse tiled and built with tymber consisting of iiij smale Baies being converted into viij Roomes *vizt.* A hall a Kytchen, a milke house, ij lowe Chambers a butterie, and ij high Chambers.

Item a Barne of ij Bayes half tiled and the rest thatched, A litle yerde or corte a garden an orcharde replenished with some olde trees and three litle pitles of meadowe or pasture, called longe pitle middle pitle and Rownde pitle all conteyning by estimacon ij acres.

Pasture.

Item one Close of pasture called Arberhill lying betwene the Kinges highwaye leading from Windsor towards Slowe on the West, Upton lane North, Wymble feild est, and a Meadowe of Thomas Davies South conteyning by estimacon iiij acres.

Medowe.

Item one pitle of Meadowe, adioyning to the said Thomas Davies meade north and est, and a meadowe of Andrewe Windesor esquire South the Kinges higwaye aforesaid Weste conteyning by estimacon dimid.ac'.

Item in Upton meade in the seconde caste by Lott being the ferme dimid.ac'.

Arrable.

Item in Stonebridge feild betwene the lands of John Pitt North and South and the high waye este   dimid' ac'.

Item in Gasson feilde, betwene John Pitt est and John Atlee west dimid'ac'.

Item in Upton West feild, betwene John Pitt North and Widowe Cogram South dimid'ac'.

Item in the same feilde called Longe shott acre betwene Mr Woodwarde est, and George Bartlett John Pitt and Morrishe Fysher West 1 acre.

Item in the same feild called the Rye acre lying betwene Widowe Cogram est and Thomas Duck esquire west 1 acre.

Item in the same feild betwene Widowe Cogram est John Pitt west shooting uppon the kings high waie South dimid'ac'.

Item in the same feild betwene Thomas Reade est and George Bartlett weste dimid'ac'.

vij ac' dim'.

Item in Upton Estfeild one acre called the greate Acre betwene Thomas Reade South and North i acre.

Item in the same feilde in a fere called Canlandes fere betwene George Bartlett South and the kings Lande North dimid'ac'.

Item in the same feilde and fere betwene Edward Woodward esquire South and John Urlian North dimid'ac'.

Item in the same feilde in the Watrie fere betwene Edward Woodward North and George Bartlett South dimid'ac'.

Item in the same feilde and feere betwene John Urlian North and Richard Newington South dimid'ac'.

Suma arrable vij acres dimi'.

Summa totalis xiiij acres and a halfe.

For Stockes, implements, Tenements or anie other thinge inquirable by the Canon (and not herein before intimated and expressed) there is nothing belonging to the Vicaredg, as farr as we knowe or can learne.

Per me Owenn Johannes   *Vicarium ibidem*

Thomas Davie   Churchwardens
Jasper, Wheler   mark
William Montayne   mark   Sidman
George Bartlett   mark
George Newington   Inhabitants there
Thomas Byshop
(D/A/Gt/9/8/1)

123. UPTON 1639

Anno Domini 1639.

A Terryer of all the vicaridge land of Upton in the County of Buck and of all the howsing and barnes belonging theretoo.

Imprimis three Chambers above Staires and three roomes below.
Item a barne Consisting of 3 bayes and a Cutting for a Stable.
Item a message belonging to the house devided into 3 picles.

Land more belonging there too.

In Chalnir feild neare spittle crosse feild one halfe acre of arrable ground.
In Gasens one halfe acre of arrable.
Amber hill close and a picle called ten acre of pasture ground by estimation three acres and a halfe.
In Upton meade halfe an acre.
In slow feild 3 acres and a halfe of arrable ground.
In Windmill feild 3 acres of Arrable ground.

Abraham Man   Vicar

Roger Pitt   Churchwardens of Upton
Daved Periman
(D/A/Gt/9/8/2)

124. WALTON 1640

A tarrier of all and singuler the Glebe Lands and howse Belonging to the Parsonage of Walton made the 20th day of January *Anno Domini* 1639.

Inprimis on dwelling howse Contayning three bay with A Barne of fower bays and a stable of On bay.

Item On Close of pasture adioyning to the [...] howse Contayning eight Acres or thereabouts by estimacon Bartlemew Beale gent. on the west and Thomas Kilpin on the East and the Streete Way North.

Item on other Close of pasture caled by the name of Abels Contayning by estimacon 2 Acres Bartlemew Beale gent' both North and South.

Item in Norden a plot of Meddow Containing halfe an Acre or there abouts the River on the west and Bartlemew Beale gent on the east.

Item two Acres more in Norden by estimacon on acre the towne grownd sowth and Bartlemew Beale gent north.

Item on halfe acre of land in the same furlong Bartlemew Beale gent North and South.

Item one other land in the same furlonge Bartlemew Beale gent North and Thomas Kilpin sowth.

Item three halfe acres more by estimacon within Norden gapp Bartlemew Beale gent East and West.

Item in the slade feild on peece of land caled the parsons peece by estimacon tenn acres or there abouts A furlong caled the cross furlong lying sowth and the highway west and Thomas Kilpin East.

Item an Acre in Gable thorne Bartlemew Beale gent west and Thomas Kilpin East.

Item on Acre more shooting into the slade Bartlemew Beale gent East and Thomas Kilpin west.

Item on land in gravilpit furlong Thomas Kilpin East and Bartlemew Beale gent west.

Item two Roods on the same furlong Thomas Kilpin East and Bartho: Beale gent East.

Item on Acre more in the same furlonge Barth; Beale gent East and Thomas Kilpin west.

Item on acre more in a furlong Caled the slade furlong Barth: Beale gent East and Thomas Kilpin west and the slade North.

Item on acre more in the same furlong Barth; Beale gent East and west.

Item on acre more butting sowth upon the Common way Thomas Kilpin west and Barth; Beale gent East.

Item on acre more in [...] furlong Bartlemew Beale gent east and west.

Item two Roodes more One being a had Roode at the Upper end of the slade Thomas Kilpin North.

Item In Goslinghole furlonge On acre Thomas Kilpin west and Barth; Beale gent East.

Item in shortland furlong one acre more Barth: Beale gent Est and Thomas Kilpin west.

Item three half acres more in A furlong Caled long sands Bartlemew Beale gent East and Thomas Kilpin west.

In the Willow Feild.

Item In Rowe Bush furlong One acre Bartlemew Beale gent East and West.

Item two Roods lying in a furlong Caled under the hill the Land of Thomas Kilpin in Portway feild west and butteth South upon the great March.

Item 4 Roods more on the same furlonge Thomas Kilpin lying East and west.

Item on acre more in the same furlong Thomas Kilpin west and Bartlemew Beale gent East.

Item on Land more in the same furlong Bartlemew Beale gent East and West.

Item on acre more in Little Fursons Thomas Kilpin west and Bartlemew Beale gent East.

Item in great Fursons on halfe acre Bartlemew Beale gent East and west.

Item In Minggle hedge furlong On land Thomas Kilpin south and Bartlemew Beale North.

Item at Broad Banks one Acre Bartlemew Beale gent East and West.

Item on acre more in the same furlong Thomas Kilpin East and West.

Item on Acre more in Fidnum Thomas Kilpin west.

Item two more in the same furlonge Bartlemew Beale gent west and Thomas Kilpin East.

Item in Willow Close furlong two acres or thereabouts Thomas Kilpin East and Bartlemew Beale gent west.

Item on acre more in the same furlong Thomas Kilpin East and west.

Item one Acre more in Fidnum Thomas Kilpin west.

Item two more in the same furlong Bartlemew Beale gent west and Thomas Kilpin East.

Item in Willow Close furlong two acres or thereabouts Thomas Kilpin East and Bartlemew Beale gent west.

Item fower Roodes more in the same furlong Bartlemew Beale gent East and Thomas Kilpin West.

Item in the nether Smellins on Land Thomas Kilpin East and west.

Item in the same furlong one Land more Thomas Kilpin east and Bartlemew Beale gent west.

In further Smellins fower Roods Thomas Kilpin East and West.

Item one Acre more in Hether Smellins Thomas Kilpin East the town ground west.

Item in the March furlong one Acre Thomas Kilpin North and South.

Item a Acre more in the same furlong Thomas Kilpin North and South.

Item A parcell of Meadow lying at Yardon Bridge Caled the little Hooke Bartlemew Beale North and the towne ground Sowth.

Item one hooke more Caled the great Hooke Bartlemew Beale west.

Item lott Meadow iij Little March In the first twenty pole on Roode out of six Acre and halfe A Roode out of three pole.

Item in the second twelve pole One Roode out of Six acre and halfe a Roode out of three pole.

Item In the third twentie pole One Roode out of Six Acre and halfe A Roode out of three pole.

Item of Glebe Meadow in Mr Beale his plot in the North March one Roode thirtey seven pole of statute measure or thereabouts.

Item Glebe Meadow in Thomas Kilpin his part in the North March One Roode twenty eight poles or thereabouts.

Item In the Sowth March In Mr Beale his plot twenty five poles of statute Measure or there abouts of Glibe Meadow.

Item in the Sowth March, of Glebe meadow In Thomas Kilpin his parte there twenty six poles of statute Measure or thereabouts.

In Portway Feild.

Item in New Heetch on Acre Thomas Kilpin East and west.

Item in Greene End furlong One acre Bartlemew Beale gent. East and west.

Item in Marewell furlong One Acre Bartlemew Beale gent East and West.

Item One Land more in the same furlonge Bartlemew Beale East and Thomas Kilpin west.

Item in the same furlonge three Lands Thomas Kilpin East and West.

Item in Brooke hades two Roodes Thomas Kilpin East and west.

Item in the same furlong One Acre Butting Uppon Brick hill Brook sowth and nere to Masons Close.

William Roberd   Rector

Thomas Kilpin   Churchwardens
William Chapman

(D/A/Gt/9/9/1-2)

125. WATER STRATFORD 1639

A survey or terrier revived and Compared with the antient terriers of the Glebe lands and meadowes as allso the mantion houses barnes and stables with other Edifices belongeinge to the rectory of Water Stratford in the County of Bucks made and taken by the Minister Churchwardens and other inhabitants in the sayd toune this presente twentith day of October *Anno Domini* 1639.

Imprimis one parler borded with a seller adioyninge unto yt Contayning twoe bayes.

Item the hall Contayninge three bayes and the Kitchinge Containinge Twoe bayes.

Item 4 Chambers Contayninge twoe bayes a peece with Cocke lofts all these beinge newly builded by Mr Samuel Marshall Rector *ibidem*.

Item a Milke house woodhouse study one stable one pounde all newly builded.

Item one barne Contayninge seven bayes and allso an other new one of two bayes.

Item an ould orchard before the Dore beinge payled South and North.

Item allso a younge orchard upon the Est newly planted with a garden payled.

Item one Close about 3 akers of ground beinge the backside Mr Frankyshe on the south and Richard Webe on the north which by the former parsons hath bene divided into two parts.

Item the parsonage hath two yarde lands of Glebe with all manner of Common and grasse ground.

Meadow ground belongeinge unto yt as other yarde lands in the toune have.

Item Mr Frankysh for lands doe butte on all sides of them Est West North and South.

The Est feilde.

Inprimis in the lonnge sands 2 halfe acres.

Item upon Whatland way furlonge one halfe acre.

Item in Gore brode furlonge one halfe acre.

Item [...] furlonge 3 halfe acres.

Item in Boycott wridges one halfe acre.

Item in Wolland furlonge one hafe acre.

Item in Hutchings path furlonge one halfe acre.

Item in Morewell furlonge one halfe acre.

Item in Stockewell one acre.

Item in Sharp-sands 2 halfe acres.
Item in Worthart peece one halfe acre.
Item in Cuttle brooke 2 hafe akers.
Item in the Sterte 2 halfe akers.

The Middle fielde.

Item in Whaw furlonge 4 halfe acres.
Item in Longe Fryday halfe an aker.
Item in Shorte Fryday halfe an aker.
Item Cruty furlonge one aker and a halfe.
Item in Witland way one aker.
Item in Grove furlonge 2 yards.
Item in Sandwith furlonge one acre and a Chickon.
Item in hangeing furlonge one halfe aker with a butt at the end.
Item in Short Bursome one halfe aker.

The West feild.

Item in pagefurse furlonge 2 halfe akers and one aker.
Item in Shalstone Brooke Lees one halfe aker.
Item in Mamewell one aker and a halfe aker.
Item in Bitter sweete tree furlonge 2 halfe akers.
Item in Coxwell more one aker.
Item Hollowe more one halfe aker.
Item in Middle furlonge one halfe aker.
Item in Grimlowe furlonge one halfe aker.
Item in Bandland waye five halfe akers and a yard.

Layes at Newbottle hill or the Cow pasture.

Item in Crow halfe akere one aker of fursleyes.
Item New bottle hill 2 Layes.
Item in ashmore hole one aker of leyes.

The parcells of Meadow belongeinge to the Glebe.

Imprimis halfe an aker of meadow in shorte meadow [...] foure lots.

Item an sideling or plot of grounde next to the vicar beginning at the forde at Stanton gape and reachethe to a gutter allmost at the parsons paddocke beinge about 4 yardes distant.

Item an other parcell of Meadow Called the parsons Paddock usually in bull hooke compassed with the river.

Item a parcell of meadow Lyinge in Bearshams the river on the Est side the hades on the west and goeth a little beyond the turning of the river.

Item a middow lyinge in Cunniberry middow moarnd about beinge about 2 akers and a halfe upon the Est it reacheth from the farthest springe in [...] field and so Close to a grate willow on the west.

Item one aker of Meadowe lyinge in a meadow next Phinmore Mill betwixt Richard Webb and the ten akers beinge 4 poles in bredth and every pole Containinge eightene foote to the pole.

Item a plotte of Meadowe in todnam meade caled the triangle plot moarnd aboute.

Item a plot of Meadow in todnam meadow Commonly Called Mixbury Meade nexte to the Mille homes.

Item a swath of Meadow betwixt horsenam and Cockenam as much as the best mower can mowe at one stroke.

Item a sidelinge on the west side of Huntmill knole furlonge betwixt Mr Frankishe and the drie gutter towards Shalston. It was ditched by the rector Mr Samuel Marshall and reacythen south downe to the farthest ende of the grate bushes unto a little gate in the drie gutter carriinge about a lode of hay or butter.

This terrior was reviuud and Compared with the antient terriers of Mr Richard Maior John Poller Thomas Patsall Robert Sybthorpe Dr of Divinity Roger Bird George Sale.

And now allso exhibited and Confirmed by us.

Samuel Marshall   Rector de Water Stratford

Thomas *signum* Aris   Churchwardens
John Pollerd   *signum*
Edward Whitton   *signum*
Richard Collins   *signum*
Richard Mathews   *signum*

(D/A/Gt/9/10/2)

126. WAVENDON 1640

A Terrier of the glebe lands belonginge to the Parsonage of Wavendon made the 23 th of March *Anno Domini* 1639.

Imprimis the Parsonage house conteyninge a seller a Parlour, with a little withdrawinge roome or study a buttery An hall a milhouse a boultinge house a Kitchin a brewhouse with six chambers above whereof two have chimneys and two cocklofts all which roomes are contiguous and tiled.

Item two bayes separated from the dwellinge house conteyninge a milke house and a wood house both thatched.

Item a coale house tyled.

Item two orchards on the East side of the house.

Item a garden plotte on the south side with an orchard on the west side conteyninge about a rood and a half.

Item a barne commonly called the Tythe barne conteyninge five bayes with a leane to att the west end thereof.

Item another barne called the glebe barne conteyninge three bayes.

Item a stable with a chaffe house and hay house contayninge in all fower bayes.

Item a lime house next the glebe barne conteyninge one baye.

Item a haye barne conteyninge three litle bayes.

Item a ricke yard adioyninge to the North side of the Tythe barne.

Item a close lyinge on the North side of the orchard and ricke yard conteyninge about six acres with free boarde on the North side and on the west.

Item a Tenement conteyning two bayes standinge in a pightell abuttinge on the North and East side upon a close of Mr William Sanders Commonly called Berry orchard Close, and uppon the South and west side uppon the street in which pightell standeth att the south end a Smiths shed for the standing whereof uppon the Parsonage ground the smith pays rent to the Parson att the Parsons will.

Item a half acre of ley ground lyinge in the East end inclosed North South and west and some part of south end inclosed East, the other adioyninge to a ley of Bernard Gregories East upon a close of Sir John Thomsons west and abutting uppon the East feild South and uppon the street North.

Item another ley inclosed lyinge next to Robert Fitzough East and West and abuttinge upon the Common feild North.

Item another ley lyinge on the outside of gravell pits furlonge West and abuttinge south uppon the streete and adioyninge unto a ley of Mr William Sanders East, now in the occupation of Robert Francis and uppon a close of John Collins West now commonly called Moore close.

In Portway feild.

Inprimis two Roodes beneath five acres the towne land west Hoppers East.

Item one halfe acre beneath five acres Norman west Bernard Gregory East.

Item two roods there and a land Thomas Norman East and west.

Item one throughout acre on the same the heire of Thomas Dewberry lyinge East and west.

Item another acre on the same the heire of Thomas Dewberry East and west.

Item another acre on the same Thomas Norman west Mr Cranwell East.

Item one land and a roode on the same the high way East Mr Cranwell West.

Item one land in Portway furlong Edwins North and south.

Item one halfe acre on the same Sir John Thomson North Quaint South.

Item one halfe acre att new dickins furlong Mr Hopper North Parret South.

Item one halfe acre on Langland furlong Mr Bernard Gregory East Day West.

Item one halfe acre one small meade furlong Edwin North Kilpin South.

Item one halfe acre on the same Mr Sanders North Mr Wells South.

Item one halfe acre more there Mr Cranwell North Kilpin South.

Item one halfe acre more there Goodman south.

Item one halfe acre more there Mr Cranwell North Edwin South.

ᵢ Item one halfe acre more there shootinge toward Walton way west John Collins North Day South.   ᵢ

In Ortenden feild *alias* Broad mead feild.

Imprimis One halfe acre in small meade furlong Mr Cranwell North Mr Wells South.

Item One halfe acre more there Edwins North Kilpin south.

Item two Roodes more there Sir John Thomson North Kilpin South.

Item one halfe acre more there Edwin North Sir John Thomson South.

Item One halfe acre more there Milton hedge North Mr Cranwell South.

Item on Fenne furlong one acre Gregory East Edwine West.

Item Two Roodes on the same Norman East Day West.

Item one halfe acre buttinge on the south-head of Sir John Thomsons Mr Cranwell East and West.

Item one halfe acre more there Mr Hopper East and West.

Item one halfe acre on the said Fenne furlong Mr Cranwell East Mr Hopper West.

Item Two Roodes on Fen-hill Bernard Gregory East Mr Wells west.

Item one halfe acre on neather Duplax Parrat North Mr Hopper South.

Item one halfe acre more there Mr Cranwell North.

Item Two Roodes in over Duplax Mr Wells North Kilpin South.

Item one halfe acre on Nunninge heapes Edwins East Sir John Thompsons West.

Item one halfe acre shootinge on Broadstreet Mr Saunders East and West.

Item one halfe acre on Dove house furlong Mr Cranwell East and West.

Item one halfe acre att small Meade end Day East and West.

Item one halfe acre on litle Meade furlong Sir John Thompsons North Edwins South.

Item one halfe acre more in broade street way Gregory East Mr Thomson West.

Item one halfe acre buttinge on Tweene streete Edwin East Hopper West.

Item one halfe acre more there Gregory East Parrat West.

Item one halfe acre by Bacon Selands Mr Cranwell North.

Item one halfe acre on litle Meade furlonge Kilpin East Wells West.

Item on halfe acre on Northon pitte furlong Bernard Gregory East Mr Wells West.

Item one halfe acre on Wheatehill furlong Collins North Parret South.

Item Two Roodes Butting on the mill way Sir John Thomson East Day West.

Item one halfe acre more Gregory East Parret west.

Item one halfe acre more buttinge on Aspley way Mr Wells North Norman South.

Item Two Roodes on bryers bush furlong Parrets [...].

Item Two Roodes into Aspley way Mr Wells North Gregory South.

Item one halfe acre buttinge uppon the closes Gregory East and West.

Item Two Roodes on Gosse furlong Day East Parret West.

Item one land on gravell pitts Mr Sanders East.

Item one halfe acre on Anbred furlong abutting uppon Fitzhugh East and the brooke west and havinge Sir John Thomsons on both sides.

East Feild.

Inprimis Two Roodes on Barlingdons furlong Mr Wells North Norman South.

Item Two Roodes more there Norman North Kilpin South.

Item One Roode on Burgeam furlong Thomas Day East and West.

Item one halfe acre more Kilpin East Parret West.

Item two Roodes on Maggotts furlong Hopper East Mr Cranwell west.

Item One halfe acre Uppon East strongland Parret North Gregory South.

Item One halfe acre uppon the same furlong Mr Wells North Gregory South.

Item One halfe acre uppon Burgeam way Quaint North Day South.

Item one halfe acre Uppon Steppingden furlong Quaint East Mr Hopper west.

Item One halfe acre butting uppon Elstoe Mead Mr Cranwell East and West.

Item one halfe acre more lyinge on Bandland furlong Thomas Norman East Mr Cranwell West.

Item One halfe acre more Quaint East Sir John Thomson West.

Item one halfe acre on sallow furlong Collins North Parret South.

Item Two Roodes on Restborrough Sir John Thomson West.

Item halfe acre on the same Sir John Thomson West.

Item one halfe acre uppon Rieland furlong Kilpin North Hopper South.

Item one halfe acre on the same Gregory North and South.

Item one halfe acre more buttinge uppon Chadwell Sir John Thompson North and Day South.

Item one halfe acre more Sir John Thompson North Kilpin South.

Item one halfe acre at rieland hole buttinge uppon Sanders South Mr Cranwell west Collins East.

In the [...] feild.

Imprimis [...] in litle Deiths furlong Gregory [...] Mr Wells West.

[...] Elstowe Meade the Meade North

[...] Mr Hopper East Day West.

Item one halfe acre more John Collins West and William Kilpin East.

Item Two Roodes upon stonyland furlong Gregory [...] south.

[...] one greene ditch furlonge one of them [...] Parret South.

[...] buttinge uppon the same Kilpin East.

Item one halfe acre upon Green ditch furlong Sir John Thompson North Mr Hopper South.

Item one halfe acre more buttinge uppon Gregories [...] Mr Hopper East and West.

Item one halfe acre more on the same Edwin East and West.

Item one halfe acre upon waine close furlong Norman East Gregory West.

Item one halfe acre more Thomas Parret East.

Item one throughout acre upon the same furlong Bernard Gregory West.

Item one halfe acre buttinge uppon Medberries way [...] Thompson North William Kilpin South.

Item one halfe acre on great Deith Hadway Gregory East Sir John Thomson West.

Item one halfe acre buttinge on the Deith Mr Wells East Day West.

Item one halfe acre more Mr Cranwell East Mr Wells West.

Item one halfe acre upon Medberries furlong Kilpin [...] Mr Hopper West.

Item one halfe acre upon the March the heire of Thomas Dewberry South the heire of Robert Saunders North.

Item Two Roodes on the same furlong the Towne [...] North Norman South.

[...] fidnam furlong eight lands esteemed att [...] acres Quaint East Wavendon way West.

In the same Feild beyond the brooke.

Imprimis one land on brooke furlong Mr Hoppers East the Towne land West.

Item one halfe acre more Goodman East Norman west.

Item one halfe acre more Goodman East Dayes land west.

Item one Roode more Mr Hoppers East the highway West.

Item Two Roodes more Hopper East Norman West.

Item Two Roodes more Kilpin East Parret West.

Item sixe roodes on the bellow furlong Kilpin North Mr Wells South.

Item one halfe acre on the wood furlong being [...] hadland Mr Hoppers East.

Item one halfe acre more the highway East Mr Wells West.

Item One halfe acre on slademead furlong William Kilpin East Thomas Day West.

Of Meadow ground.

Inprimis one Meade called the Tythe Meade on the north side of the Towne esteemed at fower or five acres more or lesse lyinge by five leyes

South Hilly Meade North Sir John Thompsons Meade att the hedge East and part of Duplax West.

Item one acre of meadow ground called the tythe acre buttinge upon the brooke North upon hilly meade south and lyinge by throughlongs on the west side and by East longs on the East.

Item another Meade in the Woodfeild called alsoe the Tythe Meade esteemed at an acre and an halfe more or lesse adioyninge to the Rielands East to the Riddy West to Restborough North and shootinge upp into the hollow south.

In the lotted Meadowes.

The first halfe acre in the Crosse in every dole-leet that is to say;

In Anbred mead one halfe acre.

In Wheate hill one halfe acre.

In litle Meade one halfe acre.

In the two leets of Duplax in each on halfe acre.

In Hillymeade one halfe acre.

In Westlongs one halfe acre.

Of the two leets in throughlongs in each an halfe acre.

In the Preists hookes one halfe acre.

In the Goshookes two halfe acres *viz.* in every leet one.

Of the three leets in small meade in each an halfe acre.

Of the two leets in Burgeam in each halfe acre.

In litle deith an halfe acre.

Of the two leets in greate deith in each an halfe acre.

Of the three leets in slademeade in each an halfe acre.

In Eastlongs an halfe acre.

Of Ley ground.

One ley land lyinge in litle Water furrowes Parret North Kilpin South.

One Roode ley lyinge upon Fenn leyes Parret North Gregory South.

One ley on neather Brache Day East Kilpin West.

Two Rood leys on over Brache Day East Parret West.

One ley at Pyninge hookes Edwins hadland North Mr Wells south.

One ley upon five leyes Mr Thompson North.

One ley upon praskett leyes Edwins west.

One ley in litle deith Mr Wells East William Kilpin West.

Two leyes lyinge in lettice leye bush close and greate maggotts lyinge on the one side and Day on the other side.

In Wood Leyes.

Three leyes in the starres neast Bernard Gregory South William Kilpin North.

One ley [...] downe upon greate deith.

Two leyes butting upon the haywardes hookes Day East.

One ley in Chadwell neere unto Abrahams nappe Parret South.

Divers other leyes which cannot with any certainty be bounded.

One ley buttinge North wardes uppon rushie slade Gregory East Parret West.

Equal right of Commons with the rest of the free holders in all Commonable places of the parish time out of minde proportionably to the glebe land belonginge to the Parsonage.

William Norton Parson with protestation of addinge more if more be to be found belonginge to the Parsonage.

Edward [...]   mark
William Parratt

(D/A/Gt/9/11/1)

127. WENDOVER 1607

Octoberis 22 1607 Annoque Regni Domini Regis Jacobi Dei gratia 5 et 41.

A Survey or terriour of all the possessions...

Homestall.

Imprimis the homestall or scite of the Vicarege scituate and lyinge between the personage on the South east and the church on the Northwest and Conteyns by estimation 1a.

Item within the saide bounds are conteyned a Lytle Garden Ground Walled Two poles square, and Two Orchards, one having some eight oulde trees, And the other Within these eight yeares planted by the Minister presentt, by estimation one Roode.

Edifices.

Item the vicarege howse consistinge of 3 Baies built of studde worke and covered with Tyle the thre bayes beinge chambered over and boarded and the whole buildinge Disposed into 12 roomes *viz.* one hale, one parlor one Kychinge one studdie thre chambers, one boltinge howse one milkehowse one aple lofte.

Item one barne consisting of fower baies built of studde worke and covered with straw with one cow howsse Joyninge unto itt.

Pasture.

Item one closse called the vicares shaftes bounding upon the great shaftes on the west syde and hacmans streette on the north syde and conteynes by estimation thre Acres.

Item one acre of grownde Lyinge the claye called the Vicars Moore.

Summa pasturarum 4 acres.

Meadow.

Item 4 acres of Meadow Lyinge in the lott meades called Kings Mead and great shafts.

Summa pratorum 4 acres.

Arable.

Item one close conteyninge by estimation 9 acres called the hayle closse and lyinge under bottendon hill 9 acres.

Item in the clay 4 acres and one halfe 4 acres 2 poles.

Item upon Oxen hill thre acres abuttinge upon Acnell way on the west and Halton woode on the east 3 acres.

Item in the Feelde called the malme 6 acres Joyninge unto Dove howsse closse, one acre in Whople Deane, one acre shutting up to bottendon hill, one acre nere unto We'heade with green balkes on both sides one acre in ponde closse right against the church having a greate green balks [sic] on the North syde, Two lytle Picles called Well heade Pycles Joyninge unto the parsonage closse Called Barlye closse by estimation contayninge one acre and halfe acre.

11 acres 2 poles.

Item in South Feelde 3 acres and one halfe acre 3 acres 2 poles.

Item in Harleley 2 acres 2 acres.

Item att the North ende of the Feelde called the heath 5 acres London highwaye on the West 5 acres.

Item one acre in longte Deane 1 acre.

Item one halfe acre 2 poles.

Item one acre att the hayle Layne ende, Lyinge by meanecroft hedge 1 acre.

Item one half acre in blynde furlonge 2 poles.

Summa arabilis 41 acres and one halfe.

Totalis omnia 51 acres.

Out tythes.

Item the Messuage of Richard Baldwyne of Dunridge The farme of Thomas Grange of Thomas Baldwyne of Mr Larraunce of John

Gynger of Sct Leonards all of them within the parishe of Aston Clyntone, are lyable to the vicaredge of Wendover for ther Land Lyinge within the parish of Wendover as the incumbent and they Doe agre.

Item the parishoners of the Lee for there pasture in Kingswoods.

Item the farme of Alden for the Land in Wendover Parishe his farme beinge in the parish of Ellisborow.

Item Mr Babame of Weston Tyrvell for his Land.

Item The Tenants of Mr Elmes of great Missendnen.

Item the farme of Goodman Randell of Cublers of the hill of the parish of Great Hampden for his Lande in Wendover parish as the First is to paye.

For Stockes, Implements and tenements or other thinge inquirable by the Canon (and not herein before expressed) there is no thinge belonginge to this vicarrage as farr forthe as we knowe and can learne 1607.

William Kelly   Vicar of Wendover

William Harris   Churchwardens
William Gery
John Coller
Christofer Gybson   his Marke
Thomas Good   his Marke
Peter Wells   his Marke

(D/A/Gt/9/12/1)

128. WENDOVER 1639

Julij 25 Anno Domini 1639.

A Terrior of all the Glebelandes belonging to the Vicaredge of Wendover Com' Bucks made by the Minister and Churchwardens therof, whose names are subscribed.

Imprimis A Mansion house, with one little garden and a little yard and one orchard thereunto adioyning.

Item an outyard, one barne with a little stable and a little pightell therunto adioyning.

Item one other Pightell of arrable conteyning by estimacon one acre (more or lesse) the Land of the Parsonage on the West, and a Common Lane on the east parte.

Item one other Little Pightell of arrable land conteyning by estimacon about halfe an acre adioyning to the ground of Andrew Mattingley on the North parte and the Common feild called the South feild on the south parte.

Item a severall Close shooteing east and west Halton Lordshipp on the North, and east parte, The land of John Collett on the south and west parte conteyninge by estimacon Tenne Acres.

Item a Close of meadow ground shooteing upon Hackman streete conteyninge bye estimacon fower acres (more or lesse) being Lammas ground called the Vicars Shafte.

Item one acre of Lott Meade lyeing in the Common Shafte and Three acres more lying in kings meade knowne by the name of the Crowne.

In a Common feild called the Cleyfeild.

One acre neere unto Tanners Close Corner shooteing east and west the land of Henry Jewson on the South parte and the land of Thomas Ginger on the North parte.

Item one halfe acre in the same feild in a furlong called Hony Deane shooting east and west The land of Henry Benning on the North and the land of Francis Clarke on the South parte.

Item one other acre in the same feild in a furlong called Brooke Furlong, the land of John Machell gent on the south and North parte.

Item one other acre in the same furlong the land of Sir Richard Fermor Knight on the South parte and the land of John Machell gent on the North parte.

Item one other acre in the same feild in a furlong there called Hollow Well hill The land of John Machell gent on the North parte and the land of John Stace gent on the south parte.

Item a parcell of Mead ground in the same feild called the Vicars More the land of the Earle of Carnarvon on the West parte, and heading a furlong called Hollowell hill on the east parte.

Item in feild called Oxen hill one acre shooteing upon Eglon way att the west end and lyeing betwene the land of John Machell gent on the North and of Sir Richard Kt on the south.

Item one acre more upon the same hill in the Middle furlong there the land of John Kipping on the North and of John Machell gent' on the south.

Item one other acre on the same hill in a furlong shooteing upon the Middle furlong last before menconed the land of John Machell gent' on the North and John Collett on the south.

In a feild called the Malmefeild.

One peece of land conteyning by estimacon seven acres lying to-geither with a lynce on the south parte thereof a Close of Henry Welch called Paradise Close on the Westsyde therof and the land of Sir Richard Fermore on the east.

Item one acre in the same furlong, the land of the Earle of Carnarvon on the east and West parte.

Item another acre in the same feild in a furlong called Whipple Deane shooting North and south the land of John Stace on the East and West parte.

Item one halfe acre in the same feild in a furlong called Snayle hill the land of the Earle of Carnarvon on the east and of John Stace gent' on the west.

Item one other acre in the same feild shooting east and west the land of Fabian Clements on the North parte and of Mr Beake on the south.

Item other acre in the same feild beyond Pinnocke hedge shooting North and south the land of John Machell on the west parte and of the Earle of Carnarvon on the East.

Item one acre in a feild called Pond Close the land of John Stace gent' on the south and of the Lady Wolley on the North.

In a field called the South feild.

One acre in a furlong shooteing on the Parsonage Close att the west end the land of Thomas Benning on the south parte and of John Machell gent' on the North.

Item one halfe acre on Gravelly hill in the same field neere the High way on the west, and the land of John Machell gent' on the East.

Item one other halfe acre shooting upon London highway weste, betwene the land of the Lady Wolley on the North and of John Machell gent' on the south.

Item one acre in the same furlong the land of John Stace gent' on the North and of William Hakewill Esq. on the south.

Item one halfe acre in Middle furlong the land of Lady Wolley on the North and of William Hakewill Esq. on the south.

Item one acre shooting North and south adioyning to Tomsloe Way on the east and the land of Sir Richard Fermore on the west.

In the Heath.

Item in a feild called the Heath a peece of Fyve acres (more or lesse) lying together the land of Sir Richard Fermor on the south and of James Necton Esq. on the North.

In Hartley.

Item in a Feild called Hartley one head acre shooteing east and west the land of Sir Richard Fermor on the North and south parts.

Item one other acre in the same Feild shooting North and south the land of James Necton Esq. on the west parte and the way leading from Wendover Deane towards Barkhamsteede on the East parte.

Item neere unto the Hale.

Item in the Malmefeild neere the Hale one acre the land of William Hakewill Esq. called Mencrofte one the east and his land also on the west.

Item another acre lying in a furlong called Long Deane the land of Mr Hakewill on the North and the land of John Collett on the south and shooting upon Ship way on the west.

Item halfe an acre lying in Blind furlong the land of Mr Hakewill on the south and of John Collett on the North and shooteing upon Shipway on the East.

Item one other halfe lying in Hale hyll a severall Close of Mr Hakewill called Hammons south and west shooteing upon the lande of John Collett on the East and the land of Mr Hakewill on the North.

John Armitage   Minister

Richard Streame   Churchwardens
Silvester Saunders

(D/A/Gt/9/12/2)

129. WESTBURY 1607

Auguste 25 Anno Domini 1607 Annoque Regni Domini Regis Jacobi Dei gratia Quinto et 41.

A Surveye or Terrour of All the possesions...

Homestall.

The homestall or scite of the Vickerege situate And lyinge betweene the parsonage on the Sowthe side And Mr Mordants close caled gills close on the northe side buttinge esteward And contaynes by estimation An Acare and An halfe.

Edifices.

The Vickerege howse consistinge of 3 bayes And 3 loftes.
The Vickerege barne consistinge of 3 bayes And A colles.
the Kichinge consistinge of 2 bayes And A colles.

Medow.

Item one halfe of 3 Dowles with the parsone in Ame Dowe called the Fenn homs the Lott beinge Knowen by the crosse.

Item 4 halfe Dowells withe the parsone in Ame Dowe called the Dowle medowe called the crosse Dolles And one Wholle Dowle proper unto the Vicker called the Shillde Dolle.

Arible.

Item in Standills 2 landes
Item in Landmed 2 landes
and in everie feeld the parsons lande Lieth on the Sowthe side of the Vickers land.
Item A yeard in the forlonge called the Shorte standills in brooke furlonge 4 Landes 2 yeardes.
Item in pikfurlonge 3 Landes.
in the white cleye one yeard.
Item in Smalldole 2 yeardes.
in Ashefurlonge one Lande.
Item in brockerige one yeard.
in Shorte brockerige one yeard.
Item one Land butinge towards the fursons by the wood waye.
Item in cattes brayne 4 Landes.
in a Pease furlonge 2 Landes.
Item in litle short furlonge 2 landes.
in the on arshe 3 yeardes and A lee.
Item in greate oute furlonge 4 Landes.
in croftelande one lande.
Item in hinmore 3 yeardes.
in Somerland 2 landes.
Item in Wofurlonge 2 landes.
in Shallstone Slad furlonge 5 landes.
Item in longe five Acres one land.
in the grippe one land.
Item in shorte Samporte hill 2 yeardes.
in Longe Samporte hill 2 landes.
Item in Lange furlonge 3 yeardes.
in Blecham furlonge 4 Landes.
Item one yearde At fullwell brigge.
Item one Lee shoutinge in to feelld Slad.

Summa totalis 27 Acres And A halfe and A rood.

Richard Crocket   Vicker

Richard Jakeman	mark	John Parkins	mark
John Meder	mark	Thomas Sowtham	Gard'
Thomas Paynter	mark	Aphonsus Eaton	Gard'
		John Chambers	Sidesman
		Edward [...]	Sidesman

(D/A/Gt/9/13/1)

130. WESTBURY 1639

December 1639. A terroll of the viceridge house and yard land Appurtenances in Westburi in the Countie of Bucks made by Nicholas Jakeman and John Savidge Church Wardens as followeth.

Inprimis the said Viccaridg house and the edificies thereunto belonginge conteineth Tenn bay of buildinge haveing a Close and yard thereto adioyneinge and belonginge by the same Containeing in Measure by estimacion one Acre and a roode of ground.

1. One land in Lande Meade butting north and South the Personage land on the East and the Lord of the Mannor land on the West.

2. One land more in the same furlonge the Lord West the parson East.

3. Item One land in Standells butting east and west the Lord north the parson south.

4. One land more in the same furlonge the lord north the parson south.

Item One yeard in Short Standells butting East and west the Person south and Magdalen Colledge land north.

Item One land in Furbrooke furlonge shooteing north and south the Person on the East and the Lord West.

One land more in the same Furlonge Nicholas Jakeman West the parson east.

One land in the same Furlong the Lord west and the parson East.

One land in the same furlonge the parson est Nicholas Jakeman west.

10. One yeard in the same Furlong the Parson east: the Lord West.

Item One land in Pitt furlong butting north and south the Person east and Nicholas Jakeman on the west.

12. One land more in the same lying as aforesaid.

13. One land more in the same furlong the parson [*blank*] the lord.

14. Item One yeard in Whiteclay Butting est and west the parson on the south and Nicholas Jakeman on the North.

15. Item one Butt in the Marsh shooteing est and west the Personage land on the south and Sir Peter Temples land on the north.

16. Item One land in Pese furlong butting est and west the lord north and John Showler south.

17. One land in the same furlong the parson south the Lord North.

18. One headland in the same furlong the parson south Catsbraine north.

Item One land in Catts braine butting south and north the parson East and the Lords land west.

20. One land in the same the parson east and Mrs Sills free land west.

21. One hadland in the same the parsonage land east Broadway hedg west.

Item One yeard in Smalledoe butting north and South the lord west and the parson East.

23. One Yeard more in the same furlong the parson est and the lord West.

24. Item One land in Ash furlong shooteing north and south the Person East the Lord West.

25. Item One land over the Gripp butting east and West Mrs Sils on the North and the parsonage land on the south.

Item One land in Brooke furlong shooteing north and south the parsonage land East and Mrs Sills free land west.

27. Item One Butt shooteing as aforesaid lying in the Marshes the parson est and the Colledge land West.

Item One land in little Outfurlong butting east and west the Person south and the Lords land North.

29. One land more in the same furlong Richard Tanner north parson south.

Item One land in Catsbraine butting north and south the parsonage land East Mrs Sills land west.

31. Item one yeard in Shorte broade butting east and west the parson South and Sir Peter Temples land North.

32. Item One land at the upper end of short broade the parson east the Lords land west.

Item One Land in Great outfurlonge Shooteing east and west the parsonne South and Mrs Sills land North.

One land more in the same furlonge the parsonne south Thomas Nuyn North.

One Land in the same furlonge the parson south Mrs Sill north.

36. One land in the same furlonge the parson South the Lords land north.

Item One land in Craft land butting east and west the parson south the lord north.

Item One land in Lang furlong shooteing north and south the parson west and the Lords land east.

39. One land in the same furlonge the parson west and Mrs Sills land East.

Item One Yeard at Fullwell bridge butting east and west the parson south and the Colledge land North.

Item One thoro out land in Blechain furlonge shooteing east and west the parsonage land on the south and the Lords land north.

One land in the same furlong the lord south and Mrs Sills land north.

One land in the same furlonge Mrs Sill south and the lord north.

45. One land in the same furlonge the parson south Jesper Cowley north.

Item One land at stone pitts butting north and south Mrs Sill east the parson west.

Item One land in Shalston slade furlonge shooteing east and west the parsonne south and the Lords land east.

One land in the same furlonge the parson south and the lords land north.

One land in the same furlong the lord north and the parson south.

One land in the same furlonge the parson south and the lord North.

One land in the same furlonge the parson south and the lord north.

52. One land more in the same furlonge bounded as aforesaid.

Item One land in short samport well Butting East and West the parson south and the lord North.

55. Two Yeards lying togeather in the same furlong the parson south and the Lord north.

Item One land in long Samport well butting east and west the Personne south Mrs Sill North.

57. One land in the same furlong the parson south and the lord north.

Item One land in Sower land butting east and west the parson south and the lord north.

Item One land in the same furlong the parson south and Mrs Sill north.

One had butt at Sille well Butting north and south the parsonne West and Mrs Sill East.

61. One Butt more in the same the parson west the lord East.

Item One land in Wooe furlong butting east and west the parsonne south And Mrs Sill North.

63. One Ridg more in the same the parson south and the lord north.

Item One Yeard in Little Hinmore the parson south and the lord north.

One Yeard in the same furlong the parson south Mrs Sill north.

One Yeard in the same furlong the parson south and the lord North.

Item One Ridg in Shortlang furlonge Butting North and South the Lord est And the Personage West.

Item The One halfe of fower lotts lying with the Person in the Dole Meade.

Item One whole lott of meadow in Dole mead.

Item the One halfe of three lotts of meadowe lying with the parsonne in the Venyams.

Item Common of Pasture in all Commonable places within the parish of Westbury aforesaid for all manner of Cattell as far forth as all others the inhabitants there have.

Thomas Dane   Vicar, subscribed hereunto by us

Nicholas Jakeman and John Savidg   Churchwardens
(D/A/Gt/9/13/2)

131. WEST WYCOMBE 1607

October decimo Anno Domini 1607 Annoque [...] Regis Jacobi dei gratia quinto [...].

A survey of all the possessions...

Homestall.

Imprimis the homestall or scite of the vicarage scituate and lying[...] close called the home pease on the east side and a [...] on the north side and the church lane on the west side whiche [...] and lane belonge to Sir Robert Dormer knight and a messuage wherein [...] smithe now dwellethe on the southe side.

Item within the said mowndes are contayned.

Item the vicarage house consisting of vij baies and a leanto bylte of timber worke earthe walles and covered withe tile twoe baies [...] Lofted and five not lofted and the whole buildinge contrived in three stories and disposed into xj roomes *viz.* a hall a parlor a butterie lofte over the parlour ij letle chambers and a lofte over them a kitchin a well howse and ij other roomes, one quadrangle and a litle gardin withe a pentice covered with tile and a backside wherein are [...] tenn yonge fruit trees the grownde wherin the said vicarage howse quadrangle garden and backside is contayneth by estimation [...].

For stocks implements tenements or any other thinge inquirable by the Canon (and not before intimated and expressed) [...] belonginge to this Vicarage as far as we know or can[...].

per me Gulielmus Whit'   *Vicarium ibidem*

George Hutchinson
Robert Hunt
Thomas Saunders   Sidemen
William Keene
(D/A/Gt/16/1)

132. WEST WYCOMBE 1639

A terrior of the house, aedifices and gleebe land belonginge unto the viccaredge of Havingdowne *alias* Westwycombe in the county of Bucks and Dioces of Lincolne made the xxiiijth day of July *Anno Domini* 1639 by us whose names are here subscribed.

Imprimis one mansion house wherin Robert Evans vicar of the said parishe now dwelleth.

In the said house ther is a parlour a litle buttery a litle chamber and milke house lofted over. Ther is a halle and A Kitchin unlofted All the said buildinges contayne three bayes of housinge or therabouts and are all tiled or covered with tyles. To the said viccaredge house is adioyned A hayehouse and other outhouses which contayne two bayes of buildinge or therabouts and are tiled.

Item ther belongeth unto the said viccaredge half an acre of ground by anciente estimacon, which is booted and bounded on the Easte side and on the north End on a field called the Peece and the Churchefield now in the tenure or occupacon of Andrewe Hunte of the parish aforesaid husbandman And on the Weste side is booted and bounded in one parte on a lane called Church Lane and in the other parte on A hyll called Churche-hille And on the southe End is booted and bounded on parte of the foresaid buildings And some parte of the said half acre of ground is a garden adioyninge to the said viccaredge house.

Robert Evans   *Vicarius*

John Hunte   Churchwarden
(D/A/Gt/10/16/2)

133. WESTON TURVILLE 1639

A Terriour made in the yeere of our Lord god 1639 of the parsonadge house of Weston Turvile in the County of Bucks and of the Glebe Lands belonging to the same Rectorye as they are now Butted

and Bownded By Richard Badham Gent and Edward Cutler
Churchwardens and by some other of the inhabitants of Weston
aforesaide.

The Parsonage house An Entry on the lefte hand whereof is a Kitchin
and one other little roome Lofted over and a leane to all covered with
tyles On the righthand of the same entry is a Hall, a Parlour tow
Butteryes and a dayrie house all now lofted over and covered with
tyles. One the backside of the saide dwelling house is a woodhouse of
one Baye covered with strawe. On the Foresyde of the Dwelling howse
as a stable and a Cowehouse consisting of three small Bayes adioyning
to the Brooke and covered with strawe. One Hogstye and a Hen house
of two small bayes covered with strawe. One haye house lately sett up
by the present Incumbent consistinge of tow bayes and covered with
strawe, One large Barne consisting of seven Bayes with a leane too att
either end and on both sides and a Porche all covered with tyles.

To the same house ther is two yardes one to Laye wood in and an
other greater yard to Fodder cattle in and for other uses.

Item one garden and one orchard with two Fishe ponds,
contayninge one acre and a halfe of ground or ther abouts.

Item one close conteyning by estimacon one acre anciently held of
the Lord of the manor of Butlers under the rent of 3d. ob. by the yeere
by name of a plott of ground in which the barne of the Rectory is now
built but is now called the close or Pithell behinde the barne from
which itt was dytched by one Thomas Hilling about Forty yeeres
seince and now claymed by the Lord of the same Mannor.

Item one other close of Pasture ground adioyning to the highe waye
which leades to the Parsonadge house called by the name of Empase
contayning by estimacon three acres and a halfe, and one other close
of pasture ground adioyning to the Churchyard on the North and to
the Lords ground on the south called by the name of Hunts and
conteyning by estimacon two acres and a halfe and one other close of
Pasture ground called the Parsons Moore conteyninge by estimacon
one acre and a halfe butting uppon the Brooke on the one syde and
uppon the Lords ground on the other side, and one other close of pasture
ground att Brooke end conteyning one acre adioyning on the one syde
uppon a piece of ground called Brooke Furlonge and on the other
syde uppon the inclosures of Richard Babham Gent and one other
close of pasture ground att West end conteyning by estimacon halfe an
acre whereon is a tenement inhabited by one William More Laborer
and three yard meade in a Lott meade called South meade in a Hyde
called the Crosse and three yard meade in a Lott meade caled Stratford
meade in a Hyde called the Crosse.

The land as itt lyes in the Common Fieldes.

In the Cawsewaie Field in a Furlong caled Portwaie ij lands the land of Thomas Goodsone lyinge on the south and the land of Bartho: Baldwyn on the Northe, more in the same Furlong j land the land of Richard Browne on the south and Thomas Goodsons on the North.

j land more in Portwaie Thomas Goodsons land on the south William Ashes on the north.

j land more in Portwaie Thomas Goodsons land lyinge on the south, Thomas Graces North.

ij lands in the Spittles the land of Barth: Baldwyn on the south and the land of Thomas Worster on the north.

j land more in the spittles Barth: Baldwyns land on both sydes of itt.

In under Ridgewaie Furlong the land Thomas Goodsons land lying on the south and William Ashes on the North.

In the Cawsewaie Furlong j land, the land of John Sheppard lying on the south and Richard Brownes on the north, more in the same Furlong j land, the land of Sir John Paginton on the south William Ashes on the North.

ij lands more in the same Furlong Thomas Graces land on the south Barth: Baldwyns on the North.

j land on the Naule the land of Thomas Goodson on the south William Ashes on the North.

ij lands more on the Noule Thomas Goodsons land lying on the south Richard Brownes on the North.

In Colde meade Furlong j land Sir John Pagintons land lying on the south William Ashes on the North.

In a Furlong called greate Acre Furlong j land the land of Barth: Hill lying on the south and John Bakers on the north.

j land more in the same Furlong the land of John Baker on the south and John Sheppards on the North.

j land more in the same Furlong the land of Barth: Baldwyn on the south William Ashes North.

In Banlongs ij lands Thomas Leaches land lying on the south Barth: Baldwyn North.

j land more in the same Furlong Barth; Baldwyns land on the south Barth: Hill on the North.

ij landes in the Pathe over the land of Thomas Tuffin on the south and William Ashes on the North.

In little Goslong j whole yard acre the land of Thomas Grace on the south and Thomas Goodsons on the North.

j land in Long Goslong the land of Mr John Vintene on the south and the land of Mr Richard Balham on the North.

In Water Butts j yard of lea ground the land of John Baker on both sydes of itt.

j Butt of Lea ground in the same Furlong John Bakers land on the south Thomas Goodsons land on the North.

j Butt more of Lea ground in the same Furlong next the land of Sir John Pagginton.

j land in the Wane Richard Babhams land on the south John Illings on the North.

In the Midle Field in Stompelongs j land Thomas Goodsons land on the South Sir John Pagintons land on the North.

j land more in Stomplongs Richard Babhams land on the South William Ashes on the North.

j land more in stomplongs Richard Babhams land on the south John Illings on the North.

In a Furlong that shoutes Downe to Darle Ashe hedge j land the land of John Baker on the North and a land in the occupacon of Thomas Cooke on the south.

In Cache harme j land, the land of Thomas Goodson on the East Richard Browne on the West.

j land more in cache harme William Ashe on the West Bartho: Hill on the East.

more in cache harme j yard of lea ground John Illing East William Ashe West.

In Midle Norlongs.

j land John Bakers land lying on the East William Ashes on the west.

ij lands in little Norlongs Sir John Pagintons Land on the East Barth: Baldwyns on the West.

j land more in the same Furlong Barth: Baldwyn on the East John Illings on the West.

ij landes in Five acres Furlong Thomas Goodsons land on the east William Ashes on the west.

j land on White Dytche Furlong the land of Richard Balham on the North Thomas Goodsons on the south.

iij lands more in the same Furlong Sir John Pagintons land on the south William Ashes on the North.

In nether Myzings j land the land of Barth: Hill on the north Cobhams land on the south.

In upper Myzings j land, Thomas Goodsons land on the south Barth: Baldwyns on the North.

j land in little endlongs woodwaie William Ashes land on the West Thomas Grace East.

j yard of land lyinge nexte Wood waie on the west John Bakers land on the East.

In endlongs woodwaie j land Thomas Goodsons land on the West and a land in the occupacon of Thomas Cooke on the East.

In the Looes j Whole yard acre the land of Richard Babham on the North and John Bakers on the south.

j land more in the Looes John Bakers land on the North Thomas Graces on the south.

In Plache Leaes j Lea the land of Sir John Paginton on both sydes of itt.

In little Hill j land William Ashes land on the North Thomas Goodson south.

In nether Hill j land Thomas Goodson land on the south Barth: Hill on the North.

j land more in netherhill the land of Richard Babham on the North Richard Brownes south.

j land more in netherhill Richard Babham south and William Ashe on the North.

j land more in netherhill Richard Babhams land on the North and Bart: Baldwyns on the south.

In Midle hill j land Thomas Worsters land on the North John Bakers on the south.

j land more in Midle hill William Ashes land on the North Francis Cockmans on the south.

ij lands more in Midlehill John Illings land on the south Thomas Goodsons on the North.

In long hill j whole yard acre a Cottadge att one end of it Barth: Baldwyns land on the North William Mores on the South.

The Lower Field.

In the Brache ij landes Sir John Pagintons land on the South John Illings on the North.

In Robins pitt j land, the land of Richard Browne on the south and George Symcotts on the north.

j land more in the same Furlong George Symcotts land lying on the south and William Ashes on the North.

In a Furlong that shootes Downe to new close j land Richard Pawleys land on the West Thomas Goodson on the east.

j land more in the same Furlong William Ashes land on the West John Illings on the East.

In Wonham j land Sir John Pagintons land on the NorthWest Thomas Goodsons on the south east.

In Nether Marshe j land Sir John Pagintons land on the south William Ashes on the North.

more in the same Furlong j land Thomas Russell on the south Thomas Graces land on the North.

iiij lands more in the same Furlong Richard Babhams land on the south Barth: Baldwyns on the North.

In the upper Marshe j land John Bakers land on the south William Ashes on the North.

Att Ham j land of Lea ground John Bakers land on the south George Symcotts on the North.

In the Moore j land of lea ground Thomas Graces land on the east William Ashes on the west.

j land of lea ground in the Moore Thomas Goodsons land on both sydes.

In the claie ij lands William Ashes land on the west Thomas Graces on the East.

j land more in the claie Sir John Pagintons land on the West Thomas Graces on the East.

more in the upper Marshe j land Thomas Graces land on the North George Symcotts on the South.

j land more in the upper Marshe William Ashes land on the North Thomas Goodsons south.

In a little Furlong by Darle Waie ij land Thomas Worsters land on the East Thomas Goodsons West.

more in the same Furlong j land Thomas Goodsons land on both sides of itt.

In great stand hills ij lands Thomas Worsters land on the east George Symcotts on the West.

In little Standhills j land John Illings on the east William Ashe on the west.

j land in Meadelong Thomas Worsters on the North Thomas Goodsons on the South.

more in meadlong j land Richard Babhams on the North Thomas Russell south.

j land more in the same Furlong John Bakers land on the North Francis Cookmans on the south.

In the South Field.

j land Thomas Goodsons land on the North and John Bakers on the south beeing in a Furlong cald Bryer Furlong.

j land more in the same Furlong Thomas Goodsons land on the North Barth : Hills on the South.

j land in the homer south longs John Illings land on the West Thomas Goodsons on the east.

In the midle south longs j land William Ashes land on the West William Coopers on the East.

In litle pease Furlong j land William Ashes Land on the North Mr John Vinteners land on the south.

ij lands in the further syde of south Field j of them beeing a long land goeing through 2 Furlongs John Bakers land lying on the south and the other a Broade land next Thomas Goodsons land on the North.

In Hollam Waie iij land John Bakers land on the south Barth: Baldwyns on the North.

iij lands more in Hollam Waie Thomas Goodsons land on the south and that land on the North is a hedland hedding the Homer south longs.

In Bedgrove Field in the Cawsewaie Field and Cawsewaie Furlong j land Sir John Pagintons land lying on the south and John Hornes on the North.

In the midle Field j whole yard acre Thomas Keenes land on the South: John Hornes on the North.

In the same Field ij landes of lea ground cald the Parson Leaes Thomas Keene land lying on the south Sir John Pagintons on the North.

j land of lea ground in Brooke Furlong belonging to Weston Lower Field Thomas Leaches land on the South Thomas Worster on the North.

j picce of Meadow ground cald the Parsons mead adioyning to the lower Field on the West and in the ground of George Symcotts on the east conteyning ij acres and a di or therabouts.

The Whole number of Acres within menconed is lij acres i Roodes or yarde of Arable land iij Acres ij Butts and ij yardes of Lea ground vj yard meads in [...] Lott meade A peece of mead lying in Common conteyning by Estimacon ij acres and a di. cald the Parsons mead and x acres or there abouts of Pasture inclosed.

John Vintener   Rector

Edward Cutler
Richard Babham   Churchwardens
(D/A/Gt/9/14/1)

134. WEXHAM 1607

Primo die Octobris Anno Domini 1607 Annoque Regni Domini Regis Jacobi dei gratia Anglie etc Quinto et Scotie 41.

A survey or terror of all the possessions...

Inprimis the Homestall or Scite of the parsonage with divers Closes of land of arrable and pasture to the same adioyning bounding and lying betwene the landes of Edmund Arthur gent on the South west and North parts And the landes of All Soules College in Oxford on the Est parte within which boundes are conteyned One convenient dwelling howse built with tymber, halfe moted and tiled over consisting of three Baies, and disposed into these Roomes following *viz.* A hall A Kitchen a lowe Chamber all lofted over, and devided into Fower upper Chambers and two litle garrats over parte of them. A litle milke howse at the west side of the Kitchin tiled at the North ende and Est side of the Kytchen other litle oute letts thatched. A Barne of three bayes thatched, three outeletts annexed to the west side of the said Barne, And a Stable on the North ende, an other outelett and a porch fixed to the este side of the Barne. A litle Cowehowse of two Bayes Thatched. An orchard a garden and a yearde and two lanes, And syxe Cloases whereof one nowe is pasture conteyning by estimacon Fowre acres And the other fyve are arrable conteyning by estymacon Fiftene acres in the Whole xx acres *in toto* xxj acres.

Wood.

Item a parcele of coppis wood grounde parte of the possessions of the said Rectorie lying in a springe called west feild springe in Wexham aforesaid betwene the lands of Andrewe Windesor esquire called Callyans on the west and Southe partes And of Edward Woodward esquire on the North and butting uppon James Woldens spring or coppis on the est parte conteyning by estimacon one acre. i acre.

For Stockes implementes Tenementes or anie other thing inquirable by the Cannon and not herein before intimated and expressed there is nothing belonging to the said Rectorie as farr as we knowe or can learne.

Richard Radclyffe   Rector *ibidem*

William Carter   Churchwarden
James Wellden   mark
William Standishe   marke
John Knowlton   mark

(D/A/Gt/10/1/1)

135. WEXHAM 1639

Anno Domini 1639 Augusti 2 Annoque regni domini Regis Caroli primi Dei gratia etc decimo quinto.

A Survey or Terrier of all the possessions belonging to the Rectorie of Wexham made and taken by the viewe perambulacion and estimate of the minister churchwardens and other Inhabitants there whose names are subscribed the daye and yeare above written.

Inprimis the Homestall or Scite of the Parsonage scituate and lyinge betweene the landes late of Edward Woodward Esquire upon the south west and North and the landes of all Soules Colledge in Oxford upon the East.

Item within the said boundes are contained six closes of arable and pasture grounds as they are nowe divided *vizt.* one arable close called the spring close abutting upon a ground called little Quimbrookes upon the west and upon a ground called Stony Croft upon the North and upon a ground called Allmoth meade upon the East and the Parsonage ground upon the South conteyning by estimacon foure acres.

Item a pasture close nowe called the pound close abutting upon white pound and sometyme a meade upon the west and upon the parsonage land South conteyning by estimacon foure acres.

Item another litle close arable lying betweene the parsonage land of the North and a ground called shortfearne upon the South conteyning by estimacon tow acres.

Item another pitle divided from the said close nowe arable abutting East upon a ground called grove Parsons conteyning by estimacon one acre.

Item another arable close called the round close abutting East upon all Sowells college land and North upon Allmotts meade conteyning by estimacon foure acres.

Item another arable close called the barne close lying within the forenamed parsonage groundes conteyning by estimacon fower acres.

Item the tow lanes the barne yard and the house yard conteyning by estimacon halfe an acre.

Item within the said bounds are conteined one garden and one orchard well planted with fruite trees of divers sorts and well fensed with a water ditch and a hedge conteyning by estimacon halfe an acre.

Item the parsonage house consisting of six baies built with timber and covered with tyles hath in it a hawle a Kitchin and a lowe chamber all lofted over with bordes and divided into foure upper roomes and over the tow midle roomes towe garretts borded and att the west side of the Kitchin a litle milke house tyled and at North end and East side of the Kitchin other owtletts builded and thatched.

Item one barne consistinge of three baies and three owtletts annexed unto [...] west side of it, and a stable at the North end thereof and towe other owtlett [...] and a portch affixed unto the east side of the barne all built with timber and thatched.

Item there is in the barne yard one other litle howse consistinge of towe bayes and a Carthouse annexed unto it built with timber and postes in the ground and thatched, all which buildings mentioned are in good reparation.

Item there belongeth to the said Rectorie one parcell of coppis wood ground part of the possessions of the same lying in a springe or wood called westfeild springe in the parish of Wexham betwixt the lands late Andrewe Winsors Esquire called gallions upon the west and the south and the lands late Edward Woodwards Esquire upon the north, and abutteth upon George Bell his springe upon the east conteyning by estimacon one acre.

Lastlie there belongeth to the said Rectorie all the tithes of the parish of Wexham.

Ita attestantur

Richardus Radcliffe   *Rector ibidem*
Georgius Chapman   *Gardianus*
Willelmus French   *Inhabitantes*
Georgius Bell
Willelmus Knowlton senior
Thomas Grove

(D/A/Gt/10/1/2)

136. WHADDON 1639

Anno Domini 1639 June 20th.

A True Terrier of all the Glebe lande belonginge to the Vicar of Whaddon

In Stonbridge Feilde.

Inprimis Two roodes buttinge on John Danyells yarde next the bawke soe ij, the parson on both sides.

An Acre on the Middle furlonge the bawke north Jeffery Emmerton South.

An Acre on the same furlonge neare sugar lane the parson south.

A lande buttinge into Rushbrooke the bawke south.

A had acre on the upper breach William Whitchurch West.

iiij roodes on the same furlonge William Rose Est.

An Acre buttinge on Cookes Close William Rose est, John Chowne west.

An Acer on Stonbridge Peece the bawke and hedge south.

An Acer on the furlonge next the bawke soe one Acre the parson on both sides.

An Acer on longe Oathill Anthony Watts north the parson south.

An Acer on shorte Oatehill.

An Acer buttinge on bocrafte William Roes est Edward Hawkyns west.

The homermost Acre of meadow in Ladymeade, Edward Hawkyns west.

iiij shorte swathes of meade in Nash Feilde beyonde the brooke.

An Acre of leyes at vicars bush Betchampton hedge west.

An Acre in the myddle of Boicraft, William Lyne West.

Two Roodes shootinge into Rushbrooke hem hedge North.

In the Middell Feilde.

Inprimis a hadacre on Lancroft hill William Eddyns West.

A lande on the upper breach William Coles Est.

A lande on the neather breach Edward Hawkyns on both sides.

A lande on the same furlonge next the fallowe the parson north.

An Acre John Chowne North the Cunstables plot south.

A lande on the same furlonge Thomas Underwood North.

An Acre at scutbuts Thomas Underwood North.

An Acre on Whitelande John Chowne west.

ij yards at Cunstables plot the hye way goes over them Edward Hawkyns Est.

A lande on this side them soe one hadacer Thomas Underwood north the cartway goes over it.

A haveacre meade in bradimeade Robert Chappell north.

An Acer on playnleys John Chowne North.

An Acre shootinge into langmans slade William Whitchurch south.

Two yardes buttinge up to Priestes ponde hem hedge south.

In the March Feilde.

In Primis An Acre buttinge on priors Close corner, John Emmerton west.

Two lands shootinge into langmans slade with hades at both ends, John Cooke north.

iij Roods one of them is a hadroode at Jordans pit John Chowne Est.

A hadacer buttinge north into portwey John Cartwright west.

A lande buttinge on that hadacer John Emmerton North.

An Acre buttinge on Jacksbush William Elmer North.

The sixt roode on hollowey the parson south.

The third lande on this side the gutter on beanhill Richard Wodwart north.

An Acer of leyes on holloway Jeffery Emmerton south.

iiij Roods on the same furlonge John Chowne North.

An Acer in Smythmeade the parson South.

A vicaredge house with a parlor and kitchen both lofted and thatched over.

A little yarde and a little Close adioyninge severall from the xxvth day of March till harvest be home.

A barne and hay house.

John Allen   Vicar

Gyles Grome   his marke   Churchwardens
Henry Stevens   his marke
(D/A/Gt/10/2/1)

137. WHITCHURCH 1607

October 24 Anno Domini 1607 Annoque Regni Domini Regis Jacobi Dei gratia etc quinto Scotie quadragesimo primo.

A Survey or terrour of all the possessions...

Inprimis the home staule or scite of the vicaridg scitwate and lying betwene the grounds of Robart Nutting and John Water howse that is to saye Robart Nutting on the west syde and John Waterhowse on the east syde abbutting uppon the church lane Contayneth by estimation halfe an acre of ground.

Item within the which bounds is contayned the Vycaridge house consistinge of fowre bayes covered with tyle.

Item one plotte of meade grounde lying in buste meade abbutting uppon the brooke the grownde of John Duncombe gent on the south syde and the ground of Thomas Greene on the north syde and contayneth by estimation sixe acres.

Item a mortuarie due to the church by custom of the toune which mortuarye about 3 yeres sythens one of the parishioners [...] it to be a custom and denyed the payment so that the nowe incumbent stodde with him in lawe for it and hath Registred it to the church by lawe.

William Carenerie   Mynister

The marke of Thomas Copping   Churchwarden
Thomas Greene   Churchwarden
(D/A/Gt/10/3/1)

138. UPPER WINCHENDON 1607

Octobris 27 Anno Domini 1607 Annoque Regni Domini Regis Jacobi Dei gratia 5 et 41.

A Survey or Terrior of all the possessions...

Inprimis The Vicariage house consisting of 2 baies built partly of rough stone and partly of earthen matter, thatched with strawe, chambred over and boarded and the whole building disposed into 4 roomes.

Item one garden lying on the north side of the house, having the churchyard on the west, Sir Francis Goodwins sheepepens on the north the Vicariage orchard on the East, and the Vicariage house on the south.

Item one orchard having the churchyard on the west, the highe way on the south, the sheepe pens on the North.

Item a litle out house.

Item the churchyard.

For any other thing inquirable by the canon (and not here in before intimated and expressed) there is nothing belonging to this Vicariage as farre as we knowe or can learne.

Gabriel Wilkinson   Vicar

Anthony Addington   mark
Thomas Bull   mark
John Pollin   mark
Richard Young
(D/A/Gt/10/6/1)

139. WING 1607

Octobris 28 Anno Domini 1607 Annoque Regni Domini Regis Jacobi Dei gratia etc 5 et 41.

A Survey or terrour of all the possessions...

Inprimis The homestall or scite of the Vicarage adioyning unto the church yearde North and conteines by estimacion one acre and three Roods.

Item within the said bounds are conteined one gardyn and one orcharde inpayled and hedged by Estimacion di acre.

Item the vicarig house consisting of six bayes foure of them tyled and two thatched with loftes over Fyve of them.

Item one barne consystyng of fyve beyes one hey house of three beyes and one shepe house with a stable there adioyning of thre smal beyes and one cow house and a Wodhouse of ij beyes.

Item thre Closes adioyning conteyning by estimacion sixe Acres.

Item in the Arbour filde on the south side of the Arbor hill five acres in Woolande tenne acres and shotyng from the said hill to coppimore fyve acres shotin uppon coopers heads 2 Acres and buttyng uppon ligoes platt fowre Acres And on the north syde of the Arbor hill eight acres the whole some of the Arrable Lande in the Arbor felde is thirtie and foure acres.

Item in the prior or fyesin felde in the furlonge next the fyrsons thirtene acres and shooting from the same to shorne way nine acres and a halfe, and benearth the same waye shootyng to small brock foure acres and a halfe some of all in the prior felde is Twentie and seven acres.

Item in mole bank two acres, in the ham fyve acres, in the furlong shotyng on Wing grene hedge foure acres, in the lyttle furlong above that westwarde foure acres, in wheate close thre acres, at Courtendon in burcott felde eight acres, in crofton felde four acres.

Item further in the Arbor felde neare Kermsill Cotslow and the fyrson gate sixtene leyes of grasse grounde and one plott lying towards burcott Lane and in Woolande end ley and at the south ende of Woolande betwene Winggrene hedge and lygoes close nynetene heades.

Item in the forlong shootyng towards myddle hill tenne leyes and in the forlonge betwene that and the fyrson gate twentie and thre leyes and shootyng from shorve way to small brock foure leyes.

Item in ham meade and molebrokes the third parte of medow by measure besydes one hed Acre in the ham medow in Wyng meade two acres and two Roodes, and in Wyng meade one acre and a halfe.

Item the thirde parte of all dues and tythes belonging to the church of Wing and eightene pence by the yere out of the house of Thomas Jackman gent adioyning to the Vicarig orchard.

Memorandum that all the Arrable land is balked in the ridge at both endes and thereby known from all the lande in the felde.

William Bishoppe Clerke   Vicar of Winge

Benet Thede   Churchwardens   Edmund Shilburne
Richard Reeve   John Thede
Robart Mayne   Christofer Webb
Robert Russell   John Fowntayne
Alexander Newlande   William Grene   Cunstables
Sidemen
Richard Topping   Thomas Rackard

(D/A/Gt/10/7/1)

140. WINGRAVE 1607

Octobris 2 Anno Domini 1607 Annoque Regni Domini Regis Jacobi Dei gratia 5 et 41.

A Surveye or Terrier of all the possessions...

Homestall.

Imprimis The homestall or scite of the Vicaridge situate and lyeinge betwene the Parsonage hows and yearde West the Kinges high way East and southe and the close of Willyam Abram gent north.

Item within the saide boundes are conteyned one garden impailed by estimation 2 pooles square and aforesaid yeards of the [...] and a backe yearde by estimatyon one roode.

Edifices.

Item the Vicaridge Howse consisting of 4 small bayes builte of tymber and claye and covered with tyle all but Weste end which is covered with straw and ridged with turves, and the buildinge contryved parte in one storye and parte in towe storyes and disposed into 9 lytle roomes *viz.* the Hall, towe lytle chambers a small butrye a lytle drinke howse, 3 small lofts boarded and a lytle Kytchen.

Item one lytle barne and a small stable consistinge of 5 lytle bayes thatched.

Pasture.

There is none, but comen for 4 another and 10 sheepe in the fylds of the Parishe.

Meadowe.

Item one aker of Meadowe lyinge in Longe Meade Wherof one halfe aker lyethe upon Adston Willyam Abram gent Easte John Theede Weste and an other half aker lyethe upon Longe Hale, Wydowe Founteyne southe Roberte the Heire of Nicolas Goodspeede northe.

Arrable.

Item 4 akers and a half of arable grounde, in the 3 fylds *viz.* in the Easte fylde one half aker upon Ball Waye Mr Abram gent east and Weste an other half aker there the Mercers of London easte, John Brooke Weste: half an aker Upon Wycom Marye Delle easte, John Theede West half an aker betweene churche Wayes Mr Abram northe Sir Nicholas Hyde Knighte southe half an aker upon [...] Deane in Rowsam fylde, Thomas Steevens northe, John Brocke southe.

In the South Weste fylde, half an aker upon Rycrofte Mr Abram gent easte, George Chesshyre weste, half an aker upon Myddle Waye Sir Nicholas Hyde Knighte easte Salomon Brooke Weste half an aker upon Brodde lande Mr [...] East the Mercers of London Weste.

In the Northe fylde one half aker upon [...] furlonge Mr Abram east John Theede Weste.

Summa totalis prati et arabilis 5 akers and a half.

Oute tythes.

Item one Messuage [...] called Wydon Ferme, wherin Mr [...] nowe dwelleth situate in Wyngrave Paryshe but the Parson of Hardwycke receavethe the tythes thereof (except the emoluments of the churche) And payethe to the Vic[...] Wyngrave yearlye Fortye shillings and towe good loods of haye which the ancient composytion is, we knowe not.

For Stocks, implyments Tenements or anye other thinge inquirable by the canon (And not [...] there is noe thinge belonginge to this Vicaridge,[...] knowe or can learne.

[...] Norton   Wyngravie Minister

[...] Goodspeed   mark   Churchwardens
Thomas Theede
Rycharde Harley   Sydeman
Roger Gaffylde

(D/A/Gt/10/8/1)

141. WINGRAVE 1639

A Terrior of all the Glebe land medowes orchard gardens and houses within the parish of Wingrave and Rowsham.

Inprimis The viccaridge house of Foure bayes One barne of foure bayes with A close thereunto belonging lyeing next to the Land and house of William Abraham gent on the west and north side and the Kings high waie east.

East Feild.

Item one halfe acre of Ley ground lyeing on Balwaye furlonge the land of Thomas Cocke west and William Abraham gent east.

Item one halfe acre of arrable land on the same furlonge the land of William Brooks on the west and the Mercers of London east.

Item one halfe acre of arrable land lyeing on Wickcombe furlonge the land of Barnard Turney west and the land of William Abraham gent east.

Item one halfe acre of arrable land lyeing betweene Churchwaies the land of William Abraham gent north Mr Thomas Hide south.

South Feild.

Item one halfe acre of arrable land lyeing on hommer Midlewaye the land of Mr Thomas Hide east and Sollamon Brookes west.

Item one halfe acre of arrable land lyeing on Eccrofte furlonge the land of William Abraham gent east and the land late George Cheshires west.

Item one halfe acre of arrable land lyeing on Broadland furlonge the land of William Abraham gent east and the Mercers of London west.

North Feild.

Item one halfe acre of arrable land lyeing on Street furlonge William Abraham gent east and Barnard Turney wcst.

Item one halfe acre of arrable land lyeing on Rushdeane furlong the Mercers of London south and William Bate Junior North.

Medowe grounde.

Item one halfe acre Lyeing on Longe hale furlonge William Woodbridge North and [*blank*] Fountaine on the south.

Item one halfe acre on Adstone furlonge William Abraham gent east and Barnard Turney west.

Exhibited *Anno Domini* 1639.

(D/A/Gt/10/8/2)

142. WOLVERTON 1607

Octobris 27 Annoque Regni Domini Regis Jacobi Dei gratia 5 et 41.

A Surveye or Terroure of all the possessions...

Homstall.

*Inprimis*The Homstall of the Vicarage scituate and lyinge betwene the mansion or dwellinge howse of Sir Henrie Longeville towards the Northe and the highe Waye leading towards Stony stratford on the Southe and conteininge by estimation 1 acre.

Also the Churchward conteine about one Acre   1 acre.

Edifices.

Item the Vicaridge howse consisting of 4 baies builte of Stones and covered with thatche: 2 bayes beinge chambred over and borded etc. And the whole building contrived in 2 stories and disposed into sixe roomes *viz.* the halle, Parloure etc.

Item One Barne consistinge of 2 baies builte of Stones and covered with thatche etc.

For Stocks Implements, Tenements or any other thinge inquirable by the Canon (and not herin before intimated and expressed) there is nothing belonginge to this Vicaredge as farre as we knowe or can learne.

Robert Reighnolds   Minister

Edward Hensman   mark   Churchwardens
John Knight   mark
Thomas Marshe   mark   Sidman
Samuell Clerke   Assistants
Henry Mun
(D/A/Gt/10/9/1)

143. WOOBURN 1639

A Terrier of the Glebelands and other possession belonging to the Vicarage of Wooburne.

First an house with a Barne, backside garden orchard and Churchyard.

Item two closes one called Farthingcroft contayning two acres the other [...] contayning one Acre and six Acres lying in the common Feildes.

Item seven Cottages one is in the occupacon of Thomas Sergeant withe a backside and orchard, another is in the tenure of Richard Wiatt with a barne backside and orchard another in the occupation of Robert [...] orchard another in the occupacon of Jasper Heir wood the younger with a backside and Acre of ground another in the occupacon of Hugh Crane the younger with an orchard another in the occupacon of widow Rose with a backside and orchard another in the occupacon of John Westin with halfe an Acre of ground.

Item a Rent Charge of 20 li per annum issuing out of glory mills which Cottages lands rent were give by dede of Feoffment to the Vicar and his Successors for ever by Francis Goodwin Knight.

Gabriel Wilkinson   *Vicarius*

Thomas Heyward
John Harding   Churchwardens
(D/A/Gt/10/10/1)

144. GREAT WOOLSTONE 1607

Octobris Decimo sexto 1607 Anno Regni Regis Jacobi dei gratia Anglie 5 Scot' 41.

A Survey or terrier of all possession...

Homestall.

Imprimis The homestall or Scite of the parsonage scituate and lyinge between Rye furlong layes on the South, and Toms closse north and West the Kings highway on the East, and conteines by estimation i acre.

Item within the said Bowndes are conteined on litle orchard and garden.

Edifices.

Item the parsonage house consisting of 4 bayes built all of Timber, and covered with strawe, being all chambred over and boarded, and the wholl buildinge contrived in twoe stories, and disposed into 8 Roomes.

Item one Barne consistinge of fower bayes, buylt of Timber, 3 covered with strawe.

Item one other buylding of Timber and covered with tyles contrived into 3 Roomes *viz:* one litle parlour of 2 stories chambred and boarded with a litle chimney in the parlour with one hay howse and stables under the same roof combined.

Pasture Meadowe Arable.

For pasture, meddowe and Arable we finde none within this parish of Wolston magna, belonginge to the parsonage as farre as,yet, we either knowe or can learne.

Out tythes 2 Acres 1 Roode. One plott or peece of Meadow called tithe meadow lyeing within the parish of Litle Woolston, and belonginge to Woolston magna, conteininge by estimation twoe Acres and one roode plus minus bounded with William South feelde on the North, and litle Woolston Northen furlonge, on the South, the land of Richard Neate gent' on the West, and Smeni dole on the East.

Stocks Implements.

For Stocks, Implements, Tenements or anie other thing, inquierable by the Canon, (and not herein before intimate and expressed) there is nothing belonginge to this Rectorie, as farre as we yet knowe or can learne.

Thomas Dudley   his marke   *Eccle Gardiani*

John Mowlesoe   his marke
John Chevall   Inhabitants *ibidem*
Robert Dudley

per me Humphrey   Cleark *dict' Eccle' Rectorem*
(D/A/Gt/10/11/1)

145. WRAYSBURY 1607

Decimo die Octobris 1607 Annoque regni domini Jacobi dei gratia Anglie Francie et hibernie etc Regis fidei defensor etc quinto et Scotie quadragesimo primo.

A Survey or Terrour of all the possessions...

Imprimis the Homestall or vickaridge house scituate and lienge betwene the Messuage of Mathew Dyer on the Sowthe, and the landes of Jeames Haynes on the North, abuttinge upon the Common greene there on the east and upon Certen lande belonginge unto the said vickaredge Called Woodell on the west and Conteyneth by estimacon halfe an acre or theire aboutes dimid.acre.

Item within the same boundes is Conteyned a garden enclosed Conteyninge viij poole.

Item the Vickaridge howse Consistinge twoe bayes built of Tymber, Covered with tyle and Conteyninge iiijer roomes *viz.* twoe lowe roomes and twoe upper Chambers boarded.

Item one Barne adioyninge unto the said vickaredge howse consisting two bayes builte with Tymber Covered and thatched with strawe.

Item one Stable lickwise adioyninge unto the same Covered and thatched with strawe.

Item one Acre of meadowe lieinge in the Common feild Called Gaston betwene the landes of George Paltocke one the northe and the landes of Ambros Atkyns on the Southe.

Item xvij acres of arrable landes, whereof xij do lye in Oldefeilde *viz.* on of them there at Rye side abuttinge upon the Common Called Widmore, betweene the landes of Ambros Atkyns on the Sowthe and the Bridgeland on the Northe, twoe other acres thereof lienge together betwene the landes of William Peters gent' on the northe and the landes of Richard Holte gent on the Sowth twoe other acres thereof lieing therre together in Stayneshott, betwene the landes of George Paltocke on the Sowthe and the landes of Clement Ellys one the Northe, one other acre therof lieinge in Stayneshott aforesaid betwene the landes of Edward Bolstrode on the Sowthe and the landes late Hughe Griffins on the Northe, twoe other acres thereof lieinge together in midle shott, betwene the landes of Armenell Golde widowe on the northe and Sowthe, twoe other acres thereof lieing together at Scottes betwene the landes of Thomas Moore on the Sowthe and the landes of Jeames Heynes on the northe and twoe other acres thereof lienge together at Warbridge betwene the landes of George Paltocke on the east and the landes belonginge unto the Rectorie of wyrardisburie on the west And also twoe acres lienge together at Cambers betwene the landes of Clement Ellys on the west and the landes of Richard Holte on the east abuttinge one Canne meade on the northe and the residue three acres lienge together in a Certen feilde Called Woodell between the landes of Mathewe Dyer on the Sowthe and the landes of William Newe on the Northe, Soe all theise arrable landes doe amounte unto xvij acres.

As for Stockes implements tenements or any other thinge inquirable by the Canon and not herein intimated and expressed, there is nothinge belonginge unto this vickaridge as farre as we knowe or Can learne. In wittnes hereof we whose names are above written have to theise presentes sett our handes.

George Tyler

George Phillips   mark
John Paltocke   mark
William Balden   mark
Alexander Golde   mark
Thomas Mosse   mark
William Never   mark

(D/A/Gt/10/14/1)

146. WRAYSBURY 1639

Julij 20 1639.

A Terrier of the buildings and glebe Lands belonging to the Vicaridge of Wyrardisburie in the county of Bucks.

The Vicaridge house halfe tyled and halfe thatched containeth 5 lower roomes: *viz.* 1 the milke house 2 the Butterie 3 The Hall 4 the Parlour 5 the drink-house. All the building in good and suficient repaire.

Above the staires are 3 chambers the 1st over the hall with a closett 2d over the Parlour 3rd over the Butterie. windows all glazed.

A barne containing 2 baies of building with a stable and straw house adioining there-unto thatched with strawe.

About the house, a greene grasse plott, with a garden and back-side.

3 Acres of arable ground neere the house enclosed called Wood hills.

1 Acre of meddowe lying in a Common meade called Gassons.

3 Acres of arable lying in a common feild, called Old feild, in a shott called Stanshott.

2 Acres of arable in the old feild aforesaid, Lying in a shott, called the church way.

2 Acres of arable in the said Old-feild, lying in a shott, called the Bottome.

1 Acre of arable in the said old-feild lying in a shott called Rye side.

2 Acres of arable in the old-feild aforesaid, butting upon the Bridge land commonly called and knowne by the name of Greenes.

2 Acres of arable in the said Old-feild, lying in a shott called Warbridge.

2 Acres of arable lying neere the Kings high way leading to Stanes, commonly knowne and called Camberse.

In toto 18 acres.

John Scrimshaw   Vicar

Richard Moore   Churchwardens
John Marshall
(D/A/Gt/10/14/2)

INDEX OF PERSONS

References are to the numbers of entries. Names have generally been left in their original spelling.
Where a name has been indexed in an altered form, the original form or variant is given
in brackets.

Abbott (Abbot), William, 47, 80
Abraham, John, 109; Robert, 109;
    William, 141
Abram, William, 140
Abridge, Nicholas, 48
Adams (Addams), John, 115; Robert,
    114
Addington, Anthony, 138
Alday, William, 100
Aldridge, Peter, 72
Allen, John, 136; Thomas, 86; William,
    74
Allibond, Peter, 30
Andrews (Andrew, Andrewes),
    Nicholas, 24; Thomas, 1;
    William, 11
Anstey, Benjamin, 115
Archer, widow, 102
Aris, John, 89; Thomas, 125
Armitage, John, 128
Arnett (Arniat, Arnott), [-], 104;
    Jeffery, 108; Richard, 42;
    Thomas, 42, 104
Arthur. Edmund, 134
Ash(e), William, 133
Ashton, George, 17
Askew, Thomas, 115
Aston, John, 104
Atkins (Atkyns), Ambrose, 145; Doctor,
    92; Henry, 93; John, 70
Atlee, John, 122
Atwood, Richard, 47, 83
Avery, John, 115
Ayre, Robert, 35
Ayres, widow, 104

Babham (Babame), Mr, 127;
    Richard, 6, 133
Bachelor (Bachelar, Batchiler), Robert, 3;
    Thomas, 35, 56

Badham, Richard, 133
Baguley, Hugh, 55
Bainns, Anthony, 22; Richard, 22
Baker, Aaron, 3; Edward, 80; John,
    133
Balden, William, 145
Baldwin (Baldwyn(e), Bauldwin),
    Bartholomew, 133; Edmund, 27;
    John, 106; Richard, 127; Silvester, 6;
    Thomas, 127; William, 3
Balham, Richard, 133
Balstrood, [-], 26
Bampton, Thomas, 6; William, 73
Bankes, Thomas, 92
Barefoot (Barfite), John, 30
Barker, Roger, 9
Barley, John, 43
Barlow (Berlowe), [-], 104
Barnard, John, 60
Barne, Jeffery, 88
Barnes, Thomas, 92
Barrett (Baret), Thomas, 120, 121
Bartlett, George, 122
Barton, George, 119; John, 94;
    Thomas, 26; William, 44, 108
Basen, Henry, 58
Batchiler, *see* Bachelor
Bate, George, 83; Robert, 42;
    William, 141
Bauldwin, *see* Baldwin
Baylie, Adrian, 108; Thomas, 48
Beake, Mr, 7, 128
Beale, Bartholomew, 124
Beckley, Edmund, 114
Bedford(e), Earl of, 3, 30; John, 119
Bell, George, 135; William, 69
Bennet, Thomas, 96, 106; widow, 3
Benning, Henry, 128; Thomas, 128
Benson, Richard, 106
Bett(s), Thomas, 18
Biddell, Robert, 67

Carter, Christopher, 108; John, 55; Nicholas, 7; Robert, 115; Samuel, 44; William, 134; widow, 108
Cartwright, John, 136
Cave, Mr, 109
Chaloner, Robert, 3
Chamberlayne, Henry, 108
Chambers, John, 129
Chapline, Edmund, 16
Chapman, George, 135; John, 7; William, 124
Chappell, Robert, 1, 136
Chard, Edward, 52
Charden, the lordship of, 47
Charlett, Mr, 18
Cheney (Chenie, Cheny, Chenye), Francis, 3; John, 36; widow, 112
Cherry, Robert, 5
Cheshire (Chesshyre), George, 140, 141
Chester, Anthony, 92, 93
Chevall, Jo:, 16; John, 144; Mr, 17; Thomas, 17; William, 16, 17
Chibnall (Chybnal), Godfrey, 8; James, 9; Thomas, 9
Chilburie (Chilbey), John, 116
Child(e), John, 90
Chinhold, John, 1
Chowne, John, 136
Church, John, 22; Richard, 28
Chybnal, see Chibnall
Clark (Clarke, Clearke, Clerke), Christopher, 3; Francis, 72, 128; George, 63; Henry, 42; Humphrey, 144; John, 65; Nicholas, 70; Richard, 116, 119; Samuel, 142; Thomas, 2, 47, 79; William, 63, 64, 85
Cleeve, [-], 104
Clements, Fabian, 128
Clemson, [-], 83
Clerke, see Clark
Clethero, Thomas, 92
Clifton, Hugh, 94; rector of, 94
Clinton, John, 51
Clutterbuck, Mr, 44
Coate, Henry, 8
Cobham, [-], 133
Cocke, Thomas, 141; William, 6
Cockman (Cookman), Francis, 133; William, 95

Cogram, widow, 122
Coleman (Colman), Mr, 18; William, 18
Coles, Richard, 96; William, 17, 136
Coller, John, 127
Collett, John, 128
Collins, John, 126; Richard, 125
Colls, Richard, 115
Colman, see Coleman
Combes, Mr, 29
Come, Richard, 93
Coo, John, 68
Cooke (Cook), Edward, 17; Henry, 48; Hugh, 16; J., 17; Jeffery, 96; John, 136; Nicholas, 16, 17; Richard, 43; Septimus, 96; Thomas, 6, 16, 17, 43, 133; William, 6, 16, 17, 96
Cookman, see Cockman
Cooper, Edward, 49; William, 133
Coosley, John, 103
Copping, Thomas, 137
Corby, William, 2
Coryes, widow, 106
Cost, John, 6
Cotterill, [-], 84
Cowden, John, 6
Cowley, George, 119; Henry, 77; Jasper, 130; Thomas, 53; William, 119
Cox (Coxe), James, 28; John, 101, 102; Richard, 101; Robert, 56
Coxen, Thomas, 19, 97
Crane (Crayne), Hugh, 143; John, 80; William, 63
Cranwell, Daniel, 39; Mr, 126; Tristram, 111
Crawley, Robert, 43
Crayne, see Crane
Crips, Thomas, 51
Crocket, Richard, 129
Crooke, Henry, 48
Crosely, Richard, 17
Crosse, Ruth, 69
Crowley, Robert, 43
Croxton, John, 1
Curle, Ambrose, 115; Thomas, 115
Cutler, Edward, 133

Dancer, John, 6; Thomas, 6
Dane, Thomas, 130

INDEX OF PLACES

References are to the numbers of entries. Parishes are indexed under their modern form. Field and minor names have generally been left in their original spelling. Where a name has been indexed in an altered form, the original form or variant is given in brackets.

275

Ware hedge, 95
Warren, 89, 106, 111
Warren field, 63, 64
Washpoole, 115
Wasp Hill (furlong), 109
Waste ford, 18
Water Butts, 133
Water Farrowes, 1
Water furlong, 44
Water furrowe(s), 18, 36, 47, 101, 126
Water plaish Close, 116
Water slade, Waterslade Furlong,
    20, 21, 83, 86, 120, 121
Water Stratford, 125
Watery hadland, Watrie fere,
    16, 17, 122
Wavendon, Wavendon way, 126
Waytinge tree bush, 83
Wayting Hill, 104
Weald gate, Weald Leas furlong, 36
Weaving hedge furlong,
    Weaving Hedges, 102
Webbed, Webbed furlong, 47
Webes Bush, 18
Weedbed, Wede bed meadow,
    102, 110
Weed(e) furlong, 18, 29
Weedehooke, 42
Weedon (Wedon) field and hill, 58
Weekes furlong, 93
Weere, 29
Welhead pond furlong and peece,
    Welheade, 106, 126
Welland, 115
Well furlong, 109, 119
Wellmatch hedge, 44
Wellmore (Well moor), 83
Welly, 67
Wendover, 40, 127, 128
Wendover Dean(e), 128
Westall furlong, 101
Westbury (Westburi), 107, 120,
    129, 130
Westcroftes, 86
West End, 133
West Field, Westfeild spring, 6, 28, 29,
    44, 47, 58, 59, 85, 87, 88, 96, 100,
    102, 104, 110, 114, 115, 119, 125,
    134, 135
West Half, 49
Westhill, West hill furlong, 29, 77, 78
West Layes (furlong), 44

Westlonge furlong, Westlongs, 6, 126
Westmarsh, 112
West Meade (meadow), 7, 29, 49, 92,
    93, 102, 114
Weston path, 78
Weston Turville (Tyrvell), 126, 133
Westowne field, 63, 64
West Slade, 108
Wexham, 134, 135
Whaddon, 136
Whaddon field, Whadden Furlong,
    56, 60
Whatland way furlong, 125
Whaw furlong, 125
Wheat close, 139
Wheat Creast, 18
Wheat field, 58
Wheat hill, Wheatehill furlong, 126
Wheatley hill, 85
Wheele, 42
Whipple Deane, 128
Whitbury (Whitberie), Great and Little,
    14, 15
Whitchurch, 137
Whiteclay, White cleye, 129, 130
Whitecroft, 49
White Ditch Furlong, 133
Whiteland(e), Great and Little, 80, 94,
    95, 136
White leyes furlong, 101
Whitemore, 109
White peece, 106
White pound, 135
Whiteway, 6
Whitfeild, 108
Whithard (field), 89
Whitson path, 77
Whittage (Whytage) lane, 63, 64
Whwhople Deane, 127
Whorrage, Long and Short, 86
Wickens, 6
Wickhammon, see Wycombe
Wickhils way, 43
Widmore, 145
Williams Cross, 120
Willmatch hedge, Willmatch furlong,
    44
Willow Close furlong, 124
Willow Coppice, 15
Willow(e) bedd, 80
Willow (Wilowe) bridge meadow, 110
[...] Willowes, 102

BUCKINGHAMSHIRE RECORD SOCIETY

The Society was founded in 1937 to publish transcripts, calendars and lists of the primary sources for the history of Buckinghamshire, and generally to stimulate interest in archives relating to the county. The annual subscription for individual members is £10, which entitles a member to receive one free copy of each volume published during the year. Members also have the privilege of purchasing previous volumes still in print at special prices.

Recent and forthcoming volumes include:

20. *The Letters of Thomas Hayton, Vicar of Long Crendon, Buckinghamshire, 1821–1887,*
    edited by Joyce Donald (1979) £8 (£6)

21. *Buckinghamshire Contributions for Ireland, 1642, and Richard Grenville's Military Accounts, 1642–1645,*
    edited by John Wilson with an introduction by John Morrill (1983) £15 (£10)

22. *The Buckinghamshire Posse Comitatus, 1798,*
    edited by Ian F. W. Beckett (1985) £18 (£15)

23. *The Autobiography of Joseph Mayett of Quainton, 1783–1839,*
    edited by Ann Kussmaul (1986) £10 (£7.50), paperback edition £4.50

24. *Buckinghamshire Probate Inventories, 1661–1714,*
    edited by Michael Reed (1988) £18 (£15)

25. *A Calendar of the Feet of Fines for Buckinghamshire, 1259–1307,*
    edited by Anita Travers (1989) £14 (£9)

26. *Descriptions of Lord Cobham's Gardens at Stowe, 1700–1750,*
    edited by G. B. Clarke (1990) £12 (£9), paperback edition £5.50

27. *Buckinghamshire Returns of the Census of Religious Worship, 1851,*
    edited by Edward Legg (1991) £14 (£10)

28. *Buckinghamshire Dissent and Parish Life, 1669–1712,*
    edited by John Broad (1993) £20 (£16)

29. *Inquests and Indictments from Late Fourteenth Century Buckinghamshire*
    edited by Lesley Boatwright (1994) £25 (£20)

    Descriptions of Earl Temple's Gardens at Stowe, 1750–1779,
    edited by G. B. Clarke *(in preparation)*

Prices quoted do not include postage. Special rates for members are given in parentheses. Publications and details of membership may be obtained from the Honorary Secretary of the Society, County Record Office, County Hall, Aylesbury, Buckinghamshire HP20 1UA.